Wrestling

FOR

DUMMIES®

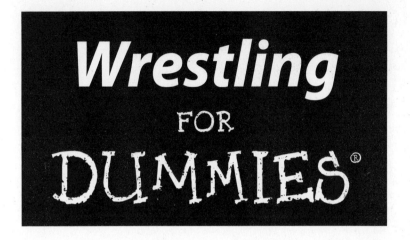

by Henry Cejudo
Olympic Gold Medalist

with Phil Willenbrock, Ed.D.

WILEY

John Wiley & Sons, Inc.

Wrestling For Dummies®

Published by
John Wiley & Sons, Inc.
111 River St.
Hoboken, NJ 07030-5774
www.wiley.com

About the Authors

Henry Cejudo, the youngest of seven children, was born on February 9, 1987, in South Central Los Angeles. He attended the resident freestyle wrestling program at the Olympic Training Center in Colorado Springs, Colorado, during his high school years. After graduating from high school, Henry began training full time for the 2008 Olympic games and represented the United States in the Beijing Olympics, where he became the youngest American to ever win an Olympic gold medal.

In January 2010, Henry authored the book *American Victory,* an autobiography about his remarkable and inspirational journey to the 2008 Olympics. As a bilingual spokesperson for the Latino community, as well as a number of programs for underprivileged children, Henry also mentors kids across the country and works with numerous outreach, charity, and nonprofit organizations.

Phil J. Willenbrock, Ed.D., alumnus of Gettysburg College, served as a high school and college wrestling coach for twenty years including positions at San Francisco State University, The University of South Dakota, Allegheny College, and The University of Puget Sound.

He is the author of *Complete Wing-T Offensive Line Play: Coaching the Skilled Athlete in the Wing-T,* which can be found at wingtoffensiveline.com. Currently an athletic director in Seattle, Washington, he is also author of a team captain leadership development curriculum and serves as a leadership consultant. The leadership curriculum can be found at sharedteamleadership.com. Phil currently resides in Gig Harbor, Washington.

Dedication

Henry: This work is dedicated to Nelly Rico, my mother, my number one fan, and my inspiration. Thank you to my wonderful family who continues to provide motivation and support.

Phil: This work is dedicated to Karen, Kelsea, Jacob, Kendal, and the entire Willenbrock team. I could not ask for more.

Authors' Acknowledgments

Henry: I am grateful to Novuss Media, Inc., CEO Bill McFarlane, Phil Willenbrock, and John Wiley & Sons for the opportunity to author this book. The efforts of Coach Bobby Douglas and photographer Larry Slater merit my thanks as well.

The John Wiley & Sons staff, including acquisitions editor Erin Calligan Mooney, project editor Chad Sievers, copy editor Amanda Langferman, and technical editor Brian Anderson, provided timely and efficient guidance during this journey.

Phil: I am grateful to Bret Draven and Novuss Media Inc. CEO Bill McFarlane for their trust and the opportunity to be involved in this project. The efforts of Bill's team including coach Bobby Douglas and Olympic Gold Medalist Henry Cejudo merit my thanks as well. To business partner Gerry Woodruff, thank you.

The John Wiley & Sons, Inc. staff, including acquisitions editor Erin Calligan Mooney, project editor Chad Sievers, copy editor Amanda Langferman, and technical editor Brian Anderson, provided timely and efficient guidance during the journey.

Finally, thank you to my parents Dr. Jack H. Willenbrock and Marsha F. Willenbrock for instilling faith and a lifelong passion for the pursuit of knowledge.

Publisher's Acknowledgments

We're proud of this book; please send us your comments at http://dummies.custhelp.com. For other comments, please contact our Customer Care Department within the U.S. at 877-762-2974, outside the U.S. at 317-572-3993, or fax 317-572-4002.

Some of the people who helped bring this book to market include the following:

Acquisitions, Editorial, and Vertical Websites

Project Editor: Chad R. Sievers

Acquisitions Editor: Erin Calligan Mooney

Copy Editor: Amanda Langferman

Assistant Editor: David Lutton

Editorial Program Coordinator: Joe Niesen

Technical Editor: Brian Anderson

Editorial Manager: Carmen Krikorian

Editorial Assistant: Rachelle Amick

Art Coordinator: Alicia B. South

Cover Photos: Novus Media

Cartoons: Rich Tennant (www.the5thwave.com)

Composition Services

Project Coordinator: Nikki Gee

Layout and Graphics: Melanee Habig, Joyce Haughey, Christin Swinford

Proofreaders: Lauren Mandelbaum, Penny L. Stuart

Indexer: Steve Rath

Photographer: Lawrence Slater

Publishing and Editorial for Consumer Dummies

  Kathleen Nebenhaus, Vice President and Executive Publisher

  Kristin Ferguson-Wagstaffe, Product Development Director

  Ensley Eikenburg, Associate Publisher, Travel

  Kelly Regan, Editorial Director, Travel

Publishing for Technology Dummies

  Andy Cummings, Vice President and Publisher

Composition Services

  Debbie Stailey, Director of Composition Services

Contents at a Glance

Table of Contents

Introduction

Wrestling is perhaps the purest form of athletic competition because you don't have any bats or balls, sticks or pucks, or teammates out there with you on the mat. It's only you and your opponent of equal size and weight and very little time to pause, strategize, or even catch your breath during a match. Experience, preparation, knowledge, technique, skill, and the will to succeed determine the victor.

The only aspect of wrestling this book can't help you with is experience. The good news: I show you how to gain an edge on your opponent mentally and physically. I also break down the technical aspects of wrestling and show you the escapes, reversals, takedowns, pinning combinations, and drills that have helped me become an Olympic champion.

Wrestling takes all that you have to give, but you won't find another sport that gives you the satisfaction and pleasure of knowing you've given your all against your opponent and defeated him one on one. Wrestling is a gentleman's (and also gentlewoman's) game. It's about playing fair, respecting the sport, and appreciating the effort of both you and your opponent.

About This Book

Congratulations! You've selected a one-of-a-kind resource designed to guide you in understanding everything you need to know about wrestling, whether you're an athlete, a parent, a coach, or an interested observer. One of the many unique aspects of *Wrestling For Dummies* is its format. Not only is it a broad introductory how-to guide for the wrestling novice, but it's also an in-depth step-by-step resource for the most advanced wrestler.

Where you start doesn't matter in the least because each chapter is essentially a reference of its own, intended to allow you to move from one chapter to the next according to your preference. In this book, you find all the information you'd ever want to know about wrestling. I start by leading you through a basic understanding of the sport and then dive into the bread and butter of scoring, strategy, and training for every wrestling level from elementary to Olympic.

One of the book's greatest highlights includes the numerous chapters on wrestling-specific offensive and defensive techniques as performed by yours truly. Under the tutelage of master wrestling technician and Olympic wrestling coach Bobby Douglas, I take you through all my favorite moves and show you in a step-by-step format how to do them successfully. The level of detail in the technique sections makes them easy to follow whether you're a beginner or a state champ.

Conventions Used in This Book

As you read this book, keep in mind the following conventions that I use to help make your journey through the text as quick and painless as possible:

- ✔ As I walk you through the different wrestling moves in this book, I describe the steps based on my position in the photos that accompany the steps. In some cases, I use the terms *near* and *far* to help you better understand which body part I'm talking about. In other cases, I use the terms *right* and *left.* As a rule, *near* refers to the body part (arm, wrist, knee, and so on) that's closest to you, and *far* refers to the limb that's farthest from you.

- ✔ Throughout the text, I use both masculine and feminine genders (him/her and he/she), but I stick with masculine gender when referring to step lists and figures because most of the figures are of me. Please understand that wrestling is for both males and females; in fact, women's wrestling continues to gain popularity across the country.

- ✔ I use *italics* to point out new terms, but don't worry about not knowing what they mean because I provide basic definitions close by.

- ✔ I use **boldface** to highlight the action part of numbered steps. Any extra explanatory information that follows is in roman.

- ✔ I use `monofont` to highlight websites. If you want to check out any of the web addresses from this book, just type exactly what you see. I didn't insert any extra characters (like hyphens) when an address goes onto a second line.

What You're Not to Read

You're busy. If you're in school, you're studying for quizzes and tests and trying to fit in your extracurricular activities. If you're a coach, you're planning your season to ensure your wrestlers improve and become better individuals on and off the mat. If you're a parent, you're working, running errands, and trying to find a little time for yourself. Not to worry. Throughout this book, I make sure to give you just the essential, need-to-know information.

Although the following information is interesting, feel free to skip it if you need to:

- ✔ **Text preceded by the Technical Stuff icon:** The purpose of this text is to provide extra information that may be helpful for some readers who want to go deeper into a few of the finer points, but everything you need to know is in the main body of the text.

- ✔ **Sidebars:** This material appears in gray shaded boxes. It's usually anecdotal information that isn't critical to your understanding of the main text.

Foolish Assumptions

I wrote this book to help you understand the ins and outs of wrestling, get a firmer grasp on the different techniques and moves, and develop your skills to defeat your opponent. As I wrote, I made the following assumptions about you:

- ✔ If you're an athlete, you want to master several foolproof techniques that will help you defeat your opponent, and you want to understand the finer points involved in mental and physical conditioning.

- ✔ If you're a coach, you want to discover how to be a better motivator, organizer, and technician so that you can help all your wrestlers reach their full level of potential on and off the mat.

- ✔ If you're a parent, you want to understand the sport in more detail and find out how to best support your wrestler, the coach, and the entire wrestling program.

- ✔ If you're a fan of wrestling, you want to gain insight into what makes an average wrestler good, what makes a good wrestler great, and what you can do to become a true fan of the sport.

No matter what your motivations are, this book is just the right resource for you. Keep reading to find out which parts of the book you may want to read first.

How This Book Is Organized

Although each chapter in this book stands alone as an independent resource, the overall organization flows in a purposeful pattern that's easy to follow. The book is made up of five parts that cover everything from foundational material that every wrestler needs to know to technique-specific step lists to basic how-to information for parents and coaches. The following sections provide a brief overview of these parts.

Part I: Wrestling 101: Understanding the Ins and Outs of the Sport

Here, you find a general overview of what wrestling is, including the different styles of wrestling, the level of physical and mental training you need to prepare for before becoming a wrestler, and the equipment you need to buy before you take to the mat.

Part II: Creating a Solid Wrestling Foundation before Your First Match

Part II looks closely at what happens during a typical wrestling match, including the rules of the sport, the role of referee, and the ways in which you can score points. It also outlines the physical and mental preparation you need to be a successful wrestler. The part ends with a quick introduction to wrestling fundamentals and basic movements.

Part III: Hitting the Mat and Using Your Moves

In this part, I share my secrets and show you the proper way to execute moves that will be critical to your success on the mat. Specifically, I show you how to get into the different starting positions and how to do escapes, reversals, takedowns, and pinning combinations. To help you understand the technical aspects of all these moves, I include step-by-step photographs and plenty of explanatory text to go with the steps themselves.

Part IV: The Adults behind You: Coaches and Parents

Most successful wrestlers don't find success by mistake. They work hard, and they rely on a handful of people to help them be the best wrestlers they can be. This part is committed to the coaches and parents who play an important role in every wrestler's development both on and off the mat. This part is an invaluable reference for adults who want to positively affect not only their own children but also the other kids around them.

Part V: The Part of Tens

This classic trademark section of *For Dummies* books breaks down my top ten tips for success in wrestling and provides information on the top wrestling camps and clinics in the United States.

Icons Used in This Book

I use the following icons throughout this book to highlight different types of wrestling information:

This icon highlights information that can help you improve your wrestling skills, so be sure not to skip anything marked with it.

This icon alerts you to information that you need to know as you begin your wrestling career or as you continue to develop your already-strong skills.

Pay attention to any text marked with this icon because it covers important information related to health and safety issues to help you prevent injury and heighten your risk awareness.

Because *Wrestling For Dummies* appeals to a wide audience, some readers may want to know everything they can about wrestling, while others may not be interested in too much detail. This icon points out those instances when I provide a little more detail for those who want the full scoop. Feel free to skip text marked with this icon if you're in a hurry or if you just want to focus on the need-to-know stuff in the rest of the book.

Where to Go from Here

As a final note before you get started, remember that I didn't write this book in a linear fashion. In other words, you can start anywhere you wish. If you get to a concept you need more information about, follow the cross-references in the text (or the table of contents), which point you to other places in the book where I cover that concept in depth.

For those of you who don't know where to begin, I offer a few suggested starting points based on your specific situation:

- ✔ **If you're a fan who's new to wrestling**: Start with Chapter 1 to establish a good fundamental understanding of the sport.

- ✔ **If you're a parent:** Start with Chapter 15 to find out how to be a supportive parent. Then turn to Chapter 4 to see what a typical wrestling match looks like.

- ✔ **If you're a beginning coach:** Start with Chapters 13 and 14 for the fundamentals of coaching, and then start back at the beginning of the book and read it all the way through.

- ✔ **If you're an advanced wrestler:** Go straight to Chapters 8 through 12 to find out how I execute the critical wrestling moves and techniques.

- ✔ **If you're a beginner:** Start with Chapter 16, which covers the top ten tips for success. Then head to Part I to figure out what wrestling is all about and what equipment you need to get started.

- ✔ **If you're looking for new drills:** Start with Chapter 14 to see some of the drills I use to prepare for the Olympics.

No matter which situation describes you, don't be afraid to dive into this book. Its easy-to-follow format makes it the perfect guide to becoming a better wrestler whether you're just starting out or you've been in the sport for years.

Part I

Wrestling 101: Understanding the Ins and Outs of the Sport

The 5th Wave   By Rich Tennant

"I know you're nervous, but take a deep breath, remember your technique, and next time wear your cup on the inside of your shorts."

In this part . . .

The chapters in this part serve to give you some fundamental information on what the sport of wrestling is all about. In it, you can find some of the variations of the sport and discover how to get started regardless of your current experience level or age.

I also tell you the importance of getting a doctor's physical before you start competing and the types of equipment you need to buy so you can show up for your first practice well prepared.

Chapter 1

Getting Familiar with Wrestling Before You Sign Up for the Sport

In This Chapter

▶ Uncovering the ins and outs of wrestling

▶ Surveying the moves you'll use in practice and competition

▶ Knowing how to be a successful coach and a supportive parent

▶ Deciding whether wrestling is the right sport for you

▶ Highlighting six points that can help you reach your wrestling potential

*T*his chapter gives you a quick overview of what you're in for when you sign up to wrestle. But it doesn't just cover the fluff around the sport. It dives into specific details of technique and provides notable tips for how to become a better wrestler. In addition to expert technique instruction, it also provides some helpful information on coaching, parenting, following the rules, and training. In essence, this chapter serves as a jumping-off point to the rest of this book and the world of wrestling.

Knowing What You're Getting into When You Become a Wrestler

Wrestling is a fun sport that allows you to face your opponent one on one. Whoever can use the right combination of tactics, strategy, and strength to outmaneuver his opponent can score a victory or even a pin. But before you even take to the mat, you absolutely must have a basic understanding of what wrestling is and what you need to do before your first match. The following sections give a brief overview. Chapters 2 and 3 provide more thorough insight into wrestling, covering everything from the different styles of wrestling to the equipment you need to get started.

Identifying what wrestling looks like for your club or school team

Depending on your age, experience, and location, you have a plethora of options for how to get started in wrestling. But all those options essentially fall into two categories:

- **Club teams:** Some communities have *club teams*, or organizations that are affiliated with a regional governing body. Club teams offer limited consistency across the country, so search your area to find out what teams your community offers and how much joining such a team costs. Club teams require a team member fee that can be as high as $2,500 per year, so be sure to do some investigating before you sign up for anything.

- **School teams:** Many schools offer wrestling as a sport for both boys and girls as early as fourth grade, but some schools may not offer it until the seventh grade or high school. The benefit of school programs is that participation is usually free or a very low cost. Furthermore, the coaches are approved individuals who have met state fingerprinting and security requirements and who have a good level of wrestling knowledge.

  You may have to wait until high school to wrestle if your school doesn't offer a middle school or youth program. In that case, make sure to talk to your school's athletic director or visit your state's athletic association website to find out exactly what opportunities exist in your area or school district.

If club teams and school programs aren't accessible in your area, visit the local recreational facility to see if you can take some wrestling classes to get you started before the school or club programs begin. Chapter 2 shares more helpful information on how to get started in the sport and addresses the differences between Greco-Roman, freestyle, and folkstyle wrestling.

Preparing for the season to start

Before the season begins, you need to get a sports physical from your doctor and acquire the equipment you need for practice and competition. The good news: Wrestling doesn't require a lot of expensive equipment to participate, but it does require a few important items that you must have to compete. Chapter 3 is where you find everything you need to know about doctors' physicals and wrestling equipment.

Being Ready before You Step on the Mat

Before you can hit the mat and start wrestling, you need to do three things:

- ✔ Condition your body for the physical act of wrestling.
- ✔ Understand the rules and basic moves of the sport.
- ✔ Prepare your mind for the mental aspect of wrestling.

Chapters 4 through 7 are great resources to help you establish a strong foundation before you start getting into the specific moves and drills involved in wrestling.

Knowing the rules of competition

To be successful as an athlete, you must have a solid understanding of the rules of play before you enter into your sport. Reaching your full potential as a wrestler is impossible if you don't know what the referee is looking for during your match. Specifically, you absolutely must know the rules, procedures, and policies involved in wrestling before you start competing.

Chapter 4 shows you what happens during a match and helps you understand the different weight classes and categories as well as the role of the official in the match. It also explains how scoring works so you'll know how to win when you get out on the mat.

Staying healthy and getting in shape

Enduring an intense six-minute wrestling match without getting tired takes hard work. Hence, wrestlers go through countless grueling practices during which they prepare their bodies for competition. If you're ready to get started, turn to Chapter 5, which provides a game plan for your physical development as a wrestler. There, I show you how to set up a training program to build your muscles, become more flexible, and develop your cardiovascular fitness level.

Getting the right fuel into your body is just as important as physically working out, so I dedicate a chunk of Chapter 5 to that topic, as well. Many wrestlers, and athletes in general, ignore the nutritional aspect of preparation, so you'll be ahead of your competitors if you focus on fueling your body the right way before, during, and after your practices and matches. I provide some guidelines for hydration and a suggested eating schedule for you to use as a reference so that you can make sure you're giving your body the nutrients it needs.

Maintaining a healthy lifestyle is another important aspect of being successful as a wrestler. I provide some examples of exactly what that entails in Chapter 5.

Focusing your mind

Because every wrestling competition is a one-on-one matchup, you need to take some time to focus on the mental aspect of the sport, not just the physical. I discuss mental preparation as it relates to wrestling, provide techniques for mental training, and explain how to develop a positive approach to your match in Chapter 6.

In addition to being mentally prepared for your matches, you need to know how to be a good teammate and a good wrestling student, how to develop a strategy that leads to success on the mat, and how to be a good sport whether you win or lose. I explain all this and more in Chapter 6.

Understanding the basics

Before you can start practicing the more difficult moves in wrestling, you need to know how to do the basic movements and techniques. Lucky for you, I dedicate all of Chapter 7 to helping you master the fundamentals so that you can eventually move on to the more exciting moves that I cover in Part III. The basic fundamentals that I share with you include general principles of movement on the mat, the all-important issue of changing levels, and the penetration step.

Hitting the Mat for Practice and Competition

When you're on the mat ready to face your opponent, you want to be well versed in many moves so that you can keep your opponent on his toes and win the match. Chapters 8 through 12 cover a plethora of moves to help you do just that. These chapters make this book a resource truly second to none. In them, I walk you step by step through many major moves from the neutral, top, and bottom positions. Coach Bobby Douglas coaches me through each move, and I accompany each one with sequential photos to ensure your understanding. I break down even the most complex moves in an effort to help you understand what you need to know to start working on them in practice.

In addition, Chapter 14 includes drills you can use to practice and develop universal wrestling skills that can help take your mat skills to the next level. The following sections give you a brief overview of what you can find in Chapters 8 through 12.

Starting positions

Chapter 8 shows you the three possible wrestling starting positions: neutral position, top of the referee's starting position, and bottom of the referee's starting position. Each one requires different skills and moves to score points and win the match:

- ✔ The *neutral starting position* is where every match starts. Your main objective from this position is to take your opponent to the mat. Chapter 11 shows you how to perform takedowns.

- ✔ The *top starting position* is all about maintaining control of (or *riding*) your opponent. Your objective from this position is to use a pinning combination to end the match (see Chapter 12 for details).

- ✔ In the *bottom starting position,* your objective is to earn points by using an escape or reversal to get away from your opponent and take control. (See Chapter 9 for details on escapes and Chapter 10 for more on reversals.)

Mastering moves for muscle memory

Because wrestling is a very tiring sport, you're going to experience times in a match when you feel as though you just want to give up. At times like these, you need to be able to rely on your favorite takedowns to help you take down your opponent in the last minute to achieve victory. How can a few favorite moves help you when you're feeling helpless? As with all sports, wrestling requires practice, practice, and more practice on the basic moves so you can do them with speed and efficiency. By practicing only one or two takedowns every day, you create muscle memory that will help pull you through when you feel like you're too tired to continue. Bottom line: To be a successful wrestler, focus on becoming excellent at one or two takedown moves instead of being average at five or more.

Takedowns

Every great wrestler has a favorite way to get his opponent to the mat. For instance, my favorite is the single-leg takedown. Chapter 11 walks you through low-, mid-, and high-level takedowns, or *attacks* (including my favorite), and shows you how to do them successfully. You don't have to be an expert at all of them, so after you read through all the moves I include in Chapter 11, pick one or two of them to master based on your personal style.

As an added bonus, I dedicate a section of Chapter 11 to showing you how to avoid a takedown from the defensive perspective with counterattack moves like the duck-under and the shrug.

Breakdowns

When you start in the top of the referee's position, you have to use special moves called *breakdowns* to keep control of your opponent and take him to the mat. After all, the last thing you want to do when you start on top is to lose control and let your opponent get away. If he does, he scores points in his favor. Chapter 9 shows you how to execute different moves, such as the cross face, far ankle, and many other breakdown techniques.

Escapes and reversals

Escapes and reversals are two fundamental moves that you must become familiar with because every wrestler likely has to start in the bottom position at some point during the match.

- ✔ You use *escapes* when you're in trouble to get away from your opponent and stand up in the neutral position. Experts at the sit-out and other escape moves are exciting to watch. Plus, you earn one point for every escape you perform. See Chapter 9 for details on escapes.

- ✔ You use *reversals* to go from the bottom position to the top position and gain control over your opponent. These crafty moves may take a while to master, but they're worth two points, so they make good additions to your wrestling arsenal. I show you how to do a couple of reversals in Chapter 10. For instance, I explain how to do the roll series for those of you who are beginning and intermediate wrestlers, and I explain how to do the Granby series for advanced wrestlers.

As with takedowns, you don't have to be an expert at every escape and reversal, so pick a couple of them that you can rely on and do better than your competitors.

Pinning combinations

The main objective in any competition is to defeat your opponent. In wrestling, you do so either by outscoring your opponent or by pinning him. A *pin*, or *fall,* is when you hold any part of both of your opponent's shoulders in contact with the mat for two seconds. The techniques involved in pinning your opponent are the most important of all to master because by the time you're ready to use a pinning combination, you already have your opponent on the mat and you just need to finish him off.

Chapter 12 shows you how to finish off your opponent. In it, I explain how to do three main pinning series, including the half nelson, the arm bar, and the cradle. After you understand how to do each of these moves, try them all in practice and decide which one is your favorite. Then practice, practice, practice until you become an expert at your favorite move.

For Coaches: Leading Your Team to Success

Not only is this book a great resource for beginning wrestlers who want to grasp the basics of wrestling and more advanced wrestlers who want to perfect their techniques and master new moves, it's also a great tool for coaches at all levels who want to improve how they coach and work with their teams.

Chapters 13 and 14 offer special guidance for coaches. They give you everything you need to know as you accept one of the greatest responsibilities imaginable — working with kids. Specifically, they provide tips for creating a year-round plan of attack for competition, training, and conditioning, and they walk you through numerous drills to use at your practices. The following sections give you a quick snapshot of what you, the coach, can find in this book.

Being a leader and a teacher

Being a wrestling coach is an extremely complex job because of the many people you have to communicate with on a daily basis and the many decisions you have to make that relate to both your athletes and the entire program. I dedicate Chapter 13 to helping you work through the complexities of the job. There I provide an outline for how to manage your team, how to develop credibility as a coach, and how to establish team guidelines. I also explain why those guidelines are important and provide a handy checklist for you to evaluate whether or not your team is operating effectively.

Because you have to juggle so many responsibilities as a coach, you need to be aware of exactly what your roles are and whom those roles affect. In Chapter 13, I walk you through your five main roles as a wrestling coach — modeling, inspiring, innovating, encouraging, and evaluating — and explain how to effectively communicate with your three main constituents — players, parents, and officials.

Handling all the other stuff

As a head coach, your attention gets pulled in so many directions that you may feel like your main role is to put out multiple fires all at once. In fact, many head coaches find that true coaching is easier to do as an assistant because they don't have to worry as much about the many administrative functions head coaches have to deal with.

To help you prepare for the many duties you have to perform as a coach, I provide some tips on managing issues like fundraising, team logistics, parents, booster clubs, and volunteers in Chapter 13. After reading that chapter, you'll have the tools you need to be a well-organized, effective coach.

For Parents: Being Supportive

The words *supportive* and *parent* likely stir up different emotions depending on perspective. To athletes, a supportive parent is one who shows up for every match, gets them to practice, and provides the financial commitment they need to compete. To coaches, supportive parents are those who don't question playing time, complain about their kids' experience, or draw attention to themselves during matches.

On the other hand, to you, the parent, support may mean that you advocate for your child, cheer him on, and intervene whenever things aren't going so well. Before you set out to be your own version of a supportive parent, I strongly suggest that you head over to Chapter 15, where I explain everything you need to know about being the best, most supportive parent you can be for both your kid and his coach. The following sections outline what I cover in Chapter 15.

Understanding your role

I outline the major differences between the roles of players, coaches, officials, and parents, and I explain how these differences play out during the wrestling season. If you're a parent who wants to be a coach, go coach. If you want to be an official, get a referee's license. If you want to be a wrestler, join an adult league. Bottom line: You're a parent, not a coach, player, or official, and you must understand exactly what your role is.

Parents can be both a great help and a tremendous hindrance to their athletes. You have a direct effect on their enjoyment of the sport they play. So make sure you actively show your support (and set a good example) by what you do and say in those key times before, during, and after a match.

Adding value to your kid's experience

Wrestling parents help their kids the most by understanding the rules of the sport and by being knowledgeable, well-educated spectators. After you're familiar with the ins and outs of wrestling, you can better help your child deal with the many issues he'll face as a wrestler, including nutrition, rest, and positive encouragement. Chapter 15 breaks down what your child needs from you into three areas: before the match, after the match, and during the match.

Supportive parents can help their wrestlers by making sure they stay healthy; skip to Chapter 15 for a quick overview of nutrition, injury treatment, and injury prevention. That chapter also provides tips for how to deal with conflicts that arise between your child and his teammates and coaches.

Figuring Out Whether Wrestling Is Right for You

One of the great tragedies in life is not having the courage to give something new a try, and wrestling is no different. Keep in mind, though, that everyone's body matures and develops differently, so just because things aren't going well for you early doesn't mean the tide won't turn in a few years when your body fully develops. In case you're wondering whether or not wrestling is right for you, I provide the following list of questions that you can ask yourself to help you determine the answer:

- ✔ **Am I a hard worker who's inspired by wrestling?** Do I have the internal drive to work hard? Do I want to wrestle for myself and not for my parents or coaches? If you're not a hard-working self-starter who truly enjoys wrestling, you may need to find another sport.

- ✔ **Do I have a positive attitude?** Sure, everyone is critical of himself once in a while, but do you have an overall positive outlook? If you're a negative person who's always looking at the down side, this sport may be too mentally demanding on you, and you probably won't find success as a wrestler.

✔ **Am I a disciplined person who can live with the monotony of doing the same drills and exercises day in and day out?** You need a lot of discipline to drill and drill until you master the basic fundamentals of wrestling. If you're a one-time Charlie who thinks practice is for the birds, you need to move on to a different, less challenging activity. Wrestling will definitely test your level of discipline.

✔ **Am I a confident person?** You're going to be out on the mat in the spotlight for six minutes with an opponent who's main goal is to take you to the ground. You need to be okay with being the center of attention and letting everyone in the gym watch you either succeed or fail. Only a confident person can handle that type of public scrutiny. If you're not comfortable being in the spotlight, you may be better suited for a more team-oriented sport in which you can easily get lost in the action.

✔ **Do I hate losing?** I'm not saying you have to lose in an unsportsmanlike manner, but you do need to really enjoy winning and really hate losing. If you're competitive in school and in recreational activities and you have a hard time toning it down in a simple game of checkers, you're in the right sport. Good wrestlers love competing.

✔ **Do I have fun in the wrestling environment?** This question is pretty simple, but you're the only one who can answer it accurately. If you have fun on the mat, try to stick with wrestling regardless of how successful you are. But on the flip side, if you aren't having fun, regardless of how successful you are, move along to another interest.

Identifying Six Keys to Reaching Your Wrestling Potential

To reach your potential when wrestling, remember the following six important pointers:

✔ **Be inspired.** You must have an internal drive to be a great wrestler. You have to wrestle because you want to succeed, not because your parents, coaches, or friends want you to do so. The way I see it, motivation lasts only so long; to be truly successful, you must be inspired.

✔ **Maintain a positive attitude.** Great wrestlers have a positive, no-nonsense mindset; in other words, they take a championship approach to practices and matches every day. Sure, everyone has bad days, but the best wrestlers keep them to a minimum.

✔ **Master the basics first.** You can't find a substitute for working hard and drilling the basic fundamentals and skills every day. Expect to spend an entire practice working on just one drill or one move until you get it right; then do it 100 more times to make sure you've got it. Most great wrestlers are great because they love doing drills over and over and over again. Repetition creates *muscle memory*, or your body's ability to automatically react in a certain way based on mass repetition.

✔ **Love your style.** If you're new to wrestling, don't expect to know right away what your style is. After a year or two, you'll begin to develop an understanding of how you wrestle and what types of moves work for you. Everyone's body is different, so don't feel like you have to fit into a certain mold to be a great wrestler. Wrestle according to the way your body functions and be confident with your individuality.

✔ **Compete.** Don't wait for your first match to get the competitive juices flowing. Take any and every opportunity to pit yourself against someone in a one-on-one matchup to learn more about yourself and to develop a competitive spirit. Great wrestlers welcome competition of any type, and of course, they prefer to finish first.

✔ **Have fun.** When you feel as though wrestling is more of a job than it is fun, find a new activity. Only you know whether you truly enjoy the sport, so be your best advocate. Just remember that everyone has days when things don't seem fun or when practices are tough, but if you're consistently not looking forward to wrestling practices or matches, you may need to step away from the sport and find your passion elsewhere.

These six points have helped me a lot in my career, and I'm confident that they can help you. So incorporate them into your wrestling and revisit them often.

Chapter 2

Identifying What Wrestling Is

In This Chapter

▶ Understanding the sport of wrestling

▶ Surveying three different wrestling styles

▶ Answering a few basic questions about how to get started in wrestling

When many people think of wrestling today, they think of "professional" wrestling with visions of dramatic characters and entertaining dramas played out in a boxing ring. Or they think of mixed martial arts (like karate and kung fu), which have gained more attention and respect in the past few years.

However, authentic wrestling or *amateur wrestling* — which is what this book is all about — is much different from what you see on television in a so-called professional wrestling match. The athletes in amateur wrestling aren't acting their way through their matches or using their fists to pummel their opponents; they're strategizing and putting forth an effort, both physically and mentally, to take control of their opponents on the wrestling mat.

Amateur wrestling is one of the oldest organized sports in the world, and it's practiced on every continent in various styles. In this chapter, I define the sport of wrestling, identify the three most common styles, and discuss how you can get started in wrestling (and why you may want to do so).

Defining the Sport of Wrestling

Amateur wrestling is an ancient, physically competitive sport that consists of two opponents who wrestle (or *grapple*) with each other in an attempt to gain physical control of the other and ultimately win the game (known as a *match*) by holding the other wrestler on her back for a set amount of time (called a *pin*). Wrestlers use hundreds of moves, including breakdowns, takedowns, escapes, reversals, and countermoves, to that end. I show you how to perform many of these moves in Part III of this book.

The history of wrestling: Origins all over the world

Amateur wrestling is an international sport, prevalent in almost every country's culture and history. In fact, wrestling is recognized as the oldest competitive sport. Egyptian wall paintings and Greek architecture from more than 5,000 years ago show wrestling as a popular sport in both cultures.

Wrestling was also a major part of the Olympics when they began in 776 B.C., and it became a main event when the modern Olympic games were instituted centuries later. In the modern Olympics, wrestlers compete in the Greco-Roman style, because historians believe that the ancient Greeks and Romans used that style. (See the section "Identifying the Different Styles of Wrestling" for details on this and other styles.)

Wrestling has enjoyed many years of popularity in the United States, drawing record crowds in places like Madison Square Garden in the 1920s. At that time, wrestling attracted a larger audience than any other sport. Around the same time, promoters invented "professional wrestling" with the goal of attracting an even larger crowd. They thought they could do so by adding a wrestling ring, characters, and drama.

Although wrestling does have a unique team element to it because wrestlers wrestle on a team, it's still considered an individual sport for two reasons:

- ✔ **Teams only win through collective points that their individual wrestlers score during matches.** Basically, one wrestler competes against another wrestler in a match with the ultimate goal of pinning her opponent. The winning wrestler earns points for her team.

- ✔ **A wrestler must rely completely on her individual physical and mental abilities and strengths.** Wrestling requires split-second thinking to implement a maneuver against your opponent before your opponent can employ a move against you. Your teammates can't help you when you're in the middle of a tough match with a fierce opponent (other than by cheering for you).

Wrestling requires personal physical and mental training to combat and defeat opponents. However, it doesn't involve physically harming your opponent. Wrestling is a sport of control, not violence.

The rest of this chapter discusses the different types of wrestling out there and zeroes in on folkstyle wrestling, which is the main focus of this book.

Identifying the Different Styles of Wrestling

In the United States, the most popular styles of wrestling are folkstyle, Greco-Roman, and freestyle. Folkstyle is the most common and is what's practiced in junior high, high school, and college wrestling programs. Greco-Roman and freestyle are the official Olympic styles of wrestling.

The differences between these three styles can be confusing to an observer or a novice wrestler. But you need to understand the distinctions because they affect strategy, objectives, rules, and scoring. The following sections take a closer look at these types. Throughout the rest of this book, I focus on folkstyle wrestling.

Folkstyle wrestling

Folkstyle wrestling, also known as *scholastic wrestling*, is the style of amateur wrestling practiced in the United States at the junior high, high school, and college levels. You find a few differences from the junior high and high school levels to the college level, but the overall style is essentially the same. As a beginning wrestler, you'll likely compete in folkstyle wrestling on your school team or on a local club. Hence, I focus the majority of this book's discussion on this style of wrestling.

Here's a quick overview of folkstyle wrestling (see Parts II and III for a whole lot more detail):

- ✔ **The main objective of folkstyle wrestling is to control and pin your opponent.** To *pin* your opponent, you have to hold both of her shoulder blades on the mat simultaneously for at least two seconds. A pin is also known as a *fall.*

- ✔ **You can also win a folkstyle match by scoring more points than your opponent.** You earn points through a variety of moves. Different moves have different point values. The main categories of moves are takedowns, escapes, reversals, and back points, also known as *near falls.* If you develop a lead of more than 14 points at any time during a match, you win. Otherwise, whoever has the most points at the end of the third period wins the match. Turn to Chapter 4 for more on scoring.

✔ **A folkstyle wrestling match consists of three periods.** Depending on the age of the participants, periods last from one to three minutes. In folkstyle wrestling, wrestlers start each period in one of two positions: the neutral position or the referee's starting position. Check out Chapter 4 for a lowdown on what happens during a match and Chapter 8 for more information on the starting positions.

Freestyle and Greco-Roman wrestling

Freestyle and *Greco-Roman wrestling* are the two main styles of international competitive wrestling. Although these styles share the same overall objectives as folkstyle wrestling — to either pin your opponent or score as many points as possible — they differ in how points are awarded. As a result of this key difference, the moves and strategies wrestlers use in these styles are also different from those used in folkstyle.

The International Federation of Associated Wrestling Styles (FILA) establishes the international rules of freestyle and Greco-Roman wrestling and supervises their application at the Olympics and other international games. The two styles share many of the same rules, but they differ in which parts of the body they allow wrestlers to use and attack:

✔ In Greco-Roman wrestling, participants can use only their arms and upper bodies to try to pin their opponents. They can't use their legs or attack their opponent's legs.

✔ Freestyle wrestling allows wrestlers to use their upper and lower bodies, including their arms and legs. They can hold their opponents above or below the waist.

Note: Even though freestyle wrestling bears a resemblance to the folkstyle practiced in U.S. scholastic and collegiate programs, enough differences exist to warrant two different styles.

A quick snapshot of wrestling in U.S. schools

The style of wrestling used at the junior high, high school, and college levels in the United States is folkstyle. Folkstyle originated in the United States in the early 1900s and isn't practiced anywhere else.

Here are a few interesting facts about folkstyle wrestling from the National High School Federation of Associations:

✔ Folkstyle wrestling ranks sixth of all boys' sports in terms of participation at the high school level with more than 273,000 participants nationwide.

✔ Since 2003, the number of high school wrestlers has grown by more than 30,000.

✔ More than 10,400 schools sponsor wrestling; that's the highest number ever.

Although these differences cause variations in stance, technique, and some rules, requirements for scoring, winning, losing, and advancing are the same for both freestyle and Greco-Roman styles. Here are the main points you need to know about these two styles:

✔ Matches are one or two periods long, depending on the age group and FILA guidelines. Check out `www.fila-wrestling.com` for details.

✔ Wrestlers begin each period in the neutral position (see Chapter 8 for details on this position).

✔ Referees can stop a match before the time limit if either wrestler scores a pin or achieves *technical superiority* (a lead of ten or more points).

✔ After a takedown, the top wrestler has 15 seconds to expose her opponent's back to the mat; otherwise, the referee may give a stalling warning and the wrestlers may have to restart in the neutral position.

✔ A wrestler can earn points by turning her opponent's back within 90 degrees of the mat.

✔ From the standing position, a wrestler can lift her opponent off the mat and onto her back and gain five points. This move is known as the *grand amplitude hold.*

✔ Two or three officials have to referee each match.

✔ Headgear is permitted but not required.

Getting Started in Wrestling

If you're new to wrestling (I assume you are since you picked up this book), you need to get acquainted with the sport before you jump in with both feet. The best way to do so is to sign up for the wrestling team at your school (or local club) and start attending practices.

Before committing to any sports program, you have to consider whether you're ready for the time and training. After all, wrestling requires a lot of physical and mental effort. Sure, the payoffs can be health, fitness, and a strong sense of accomplishment that can last a lifetime, but you have to put in tons of time and hard work before you can experience any of these results.

In this section, I discuss some of the questions you may be wondering, such as who can wrestle, what you can do to start wrestling, where and when wrestling matches generally take place, and why you might want to wrestle in the first place.

Who?

In the sport of wrestling, every wrestler has to start somewhere. The good news: Wrestling is a sport for everyone. You can be male or female, rich or poor, overweight or thin, fast or slow. Whatever abilities and characteristics you have, your school or local club team probably has someone of the same size and ability who can compete against you and help you develop your skills.

Physically speaking, wrestling has weight classes from 106 pounds to 285 pounds, so guys and girls of all sizes can compete. (Chapter 4 highlights the different weight classes so you can see where you fit in.)

But wrestling isn't just physical. It's also mental. In fact, I'd say that most of my success has been due to my mental decision to win. As I developed as a wrestler, I didn't like to lose, but I didn't let losing stop me. I still don't like to lose, but with each loss, I learn how to be a better wrestler. This mental aspect is why wrestling is one of the few sports that provides opportunities for the blind and physically handicapped. (Chapter 6 discusses the mental aspect of wrestling and shows you what you can do to strengthen your fortitude.)

The bottom line is that if you want to wrestle, you can. Consider the following:

- ✔ According to the National High School Federation of Associations, the number of women who wrestle in high school has grown from 804 to more than 7,000 since 1994.
- ✔ Anthony Robles, an Arizona State University wrestler, won the 2011 NCAA Championship. He was born without a leg.
- ✔ I won a gold medal at the 2008 Olympics even though I grew up in extreme poverty and without much guidance.

To find out if you have what it takes to become a wrestler, ask yourself the following questions and then contact your school's team or your local club team for more details:

- ✔ Are you looking for an individual sport?
- ✔ Do you want to get into great physical shape?
- ✔ Do you have or want to have strong mental discipline?
- ✔ Are you okay with the highs and lows of individual competition — meaning that sometimes you will win and sometimes you will lose?

What?

Getting involved with your school's wrestling program is a great way to get started in wrestling. But don't worry if your school doesn't have a team (especially if you're in elementary school). You can get involved with local wrestling clubs instead. Many local independent wrestling clubs have programs for kids ages 4 and older.

USA Wrestling is the national governing body for the sport of wrestling in the United States; it charters wrestling clubs in each state. You can find local clubs near you by going to www.themat.com/usawrestling.org.

Additionally, you can attend wrestling camps; they offer a great way to learn the sport from some of the best wrestlers out there. Turn to Chapter 17 to find out more about wrestling camps.

When?

Just like any other sport, wrestling has a season, but you can wrestle almost year round if you want to. Basically, you can wrestle for your school and/or an individual club during the folkstyle wrestling season and then wrestle for that same club or a different one for the freestyle and Greco-Roman wrestling season.

In general, the folkstyle wrestling season begins in November and runs until early March. If you wrestle in a school program, you usually have to attend after-school practice sessions and weekly meets and tournaments. Independent clubs may have only two or three practices a week with tournaments on the weekends. The season may vary from program to program and state to state, but this setup is typical for most folkstyle wrestling programs.

The freestyle and Greco-Roman wrestling season begins in March and ends in July. Wrestlers who want to be competitive on the international level often wrestle in their school's folkstyle program during the season and then in a freestyle or Greco-Roman program in the spring and summer.

The who, what, when, where, and why of wrestling for Henry Cejudo

I was born on February 9, 1987, in Los Angeles, California. My mom, a hard-working, undocumented immigrant from Mexico moved me and my five older brothers and sisters from place to place while looking for work. She often worked two jobs to support us. I spent my early years living in fear of my criminal father and immigration officials. We were incredibly poor and lived in some of the worst neighborhoods in Los Angeles and Phoenix.

My older brother, Angel Cejudo, was an amazing wrestler. He introduced me to the sport when I was about 11 years old, and I started wrestling soon after I watched Michael Johnson, the famous American sprinter, break records and win a gold medal at the 1996 Olympics. I knew that I, too, wanted to be an Olympic champion. I was also determined to prove myself to the world and to the father I never really knew. Although I focused on winning in the Olympics from an early age, I didn't really start competing in wrestling until junior high.

Angel and I dominated the competition while attending Maryvale High School in Phoenix. He graduated in 2004 with four state championships and a record of 150-0. I was a sophomore when he graduated, but I had already won two of my own state championships (see the first photo). The national developmental freestyle coach for USA Wrestling invited both Angel and me to Colorado Springs, Colorado, to attend the resident freestyle program at the Olympic Training Center. Leaving high school and skipping a college wrestling program to begin training for the Olympics was an unusual move to make, but this invitation was the biggest and best thing that had ever happened to me. I had to go.

While training, I finished high school at Coronado High School in Colorado. I wrestled in the school program and trained at the Olympic Training Center; I lived and breathed wrestling. I added two more state championships to my record and graduated with a combined record of 120-3.

I participated in two Junior World Championships, placing fifth in 2005 and second in 2006. Also in 2006, I received the ASICS High School Wrestler of the Year award and became the first high school student to win the U.S. Nationals since the formation of USA Wrestling in 1983.

After graduating from high school, I began training full time at the Olympic Training Center to prepare for the 2008 Olympic games. I represented the United States in the Beijing Olympics and brought home a gold medal (see the following photo). I not only achieved my dream of becoming an Olympic champion but also made history by becoming the youngest American wrestler to ever win an Olympic gold medal.

Where?

Your school wrestling program may have a wrestling room set up for practices, or you may practice in the school gym. Wrestling *meets* usually take place in school gymnasiums and involve only two schools. Wrestling *tournaments* take place in gyms or larger multipurpose arenas and involve multiple schools.

Many individual clubs use space in high schools or colleges for their practices, but some have their own gyms. Clubs usually use schools or multipurpose arenas for their weekend tournaments. At these club tournaments, the kids who wrestle at the same club wrestle against kids from other clubs.

Why?

You may want to wrestle because you want to be involved with a sports program that fosters your physical and mental health. Like all sports, wrestling can prepare you for life's challenges by teaching self-reliance, self-respect, responsibility, confidence, humility, and teamwork. It can also help you mature. In this section, I discuss the physical and mental reasons why you may want to be a wrestler, and I explain how wrestling can be a gratifying experience that will influence you for the rest of your life.

Physical reasons

Wrestling offers many physical benefits. Some you can take advantage of now, and others you won't fully appreciate until later. Here are just a few of those benefits:

- **Wrestling puts a strong focus on health and wellness.** You must eat healthy and work out properly to be consistently successful in wrestling. Learning how important exercise and nutrition are to the performance of your mind and body early in life is something that will serve you beyond your years on the wrestling mat.

  Although wrestling requires you to achieve and maintain a weight at which you can wrestle at your best, it requires you to do so in a healthy way. Unfortunately, in the past, wrestlers have used unhealthy methods to "make weight" before a wrestling match; such methods include starving themselves, sitting in a sauna for hours at a time, exercising in sweat suits that have no ventilation, and taking pills that force urination and water loss. Today, wrestling programs enforce strict weight-related guidelines and an overall positive focus on health and wellness. Chapter 5 gives you more information on hydration, weight management, and other health and safety issues.

- **Wrestling engages your entire body (and mind) for the duration of the competition.** You can't rely on a bat, ball, club, or glove to get you through the match; you are your only resource.

- **The skills you learn in wrestling can help you succeed in other sports; not to mention, they're invaluable for self-defense.** Wrestling helps develop flexibility, quickness, grip strength, muscle endurance, and balance, all of which can help you in other sports like football, baseball, softball, lacrosse, and basketball.

Mental aspects

Wrestling is as mentally grueling as it is physically challenging. To that end, you can experience numerous mental benefits just by taking to the mat. Here are just a few of them:

- **Wrestling improves your mental sharpness.** Wrestling is a game of strategy and control. To be a successful wrestler, you must learn dozens to hundreds of complex moves to use against your opponent. In addition, you have to know when to employ each move and how to counter your opponent's moves in order to end up on top. Quick and disciplined thought is an invaluable skill that can help you achieve success in many other areas of life.

- **Wrestling helps you improve your mental attitude.** In a wrestling match, you can never give up because the next move you decide to use may be the one that tips the match in your favor. To be successful, you have to stay mentally strong. If you give into thoughts of losing or feelings of fear, you'll waste precious time that you could spend on deciding what to do next. The ability to think positive thoughts in the midst of difficulty is key to achieving any goal.

- **Wrestling helps you develop self-reliance, self-respect, and responsibility.** When you're wrestling your opponent on the mat, you have no one but yourself to rely on or turn to for help. You can't blame a lost match on a bad pass or a botched catch. You're responsible for your own performance, including both your wins and your losses. When you lose, you have to examine your weaknesses and respect the strengths of your opponent. Only then can you figure out how to improve your skills and your situation.

- **Wrestling competitively opens the door to countless opportunities for your future.** For example, as a successful wrestler, you may receive a scholarship to wrestle in college or an opportunity to wrestle internationally or even in the Olympics. Hey, it happened to me!

As a wrestler, you'll be in good company. Some of the famous wrestlers throughout history include George Washington, Abraham Lincoln, Benjamin Franklin, Robin Williams, Tom Cruise, Tony Danza, and almost every successful mixed martial arts fighter.

Taking your wrestling to the next level

Are you wondering where the sport of wrestling can take you or how you can take your wrestling to the next level? Perhaps you've been wrestling for a few years on your school team, have really enjoyed it, and have excelled so far. You're reading this book because you want to perfect some of the moves in your repertoire and have thought about wrestling after you graduate.

Your two main post–high school options are wrestling for your college's team or competing internationally. Wrestling in college (and earning a scholarship to do so) and wrestling for the U.S. National or World Teams require commitment, focus, training, and sacrifice. If you love the sport and know you want to dedicate yourself to being a world-class wrestler, you first have to set goals that will help you do so. Then you have to put everything you have into achieving those goals. (I went straight from high school to training for the 2008 Olympics, but that's an unusual scenario. I'm currently training for the 2012 Olympics.)

Today, wrestlers don't have the option of going "pro" because no authentic professional wrestling league exists. *Professional wrestling,* as you know it, is a staged performance.

The closest thing to authentic professional wrestling is mixed martial arts (MMA). Almost every successful MMA fighter has an impressive wrestling background, and most people involved in the sport insist that having a good "ground" game (in other words, wrestling) is imperative to MMA. However, the two sports are extremely different. Wrestling isn't a violent sport; it's about controlling your opponent. Although MMA is more regulated than it used to be, it's still violent in that opponents hit and kick each other during competition; serious injuries do occur.

Making the move to the next level isn't easy, but you can do it. After all, I did! I started out with just the desire to beat any opponent I faced. I was tired of being poor and being looked down on by others, and I was angry and had something to prove. But what fueled my success won't be the same as what fuels yours. Motivation is intensely personal and can't be bottled or framed. So before you take wrestling to the next level, figure out what goals you want to achieve in your life. If wrestling is a part of them, get ready to work hard and don't give up until you reach your goals.

Chapter 3

Being Equipped to Wrestle

In This Chapter

▶ Passing a medical physical

▶ Gathering the right wrestling equipment

*O*bviously, you're ready to get on the mat and wrestle (after all, you're reading this book!). But before you can jump in and start battling, you need to first make sure you're healthy enough to compete and then gather up the right equipment.

The key to having a long wrestling career is staying healthy and safe. A good place to start is by getting a physical. You may not think much about health and safety, but if you're interested in wrestling, you're going to have to start thinking about both because most athletic programs require that you get a physical before you can participate.

Furthermore, being properly equipped is important in any sport, and wrestling is no different. Although equipment doesn't make the athlete, having headgear that fits correctly, shoes that help you grip the mat, and a comfortable outfit helps you wrestle better and keeps you safe.

In this chapter, I explain why getting a physical is important, and I go over what you can expect when you see your doctor. I also provide you with some information about the equipment you need to participate in wrestling, such as headgear, wrestling shoes, and singlets. I go into more detail about staying healthy, safe, and in shape in Chapter 5.

Seeing Your Doctor: Getting a Physical Before You Hit the Mat

A *sports physical,* or in other words, a thorough medical exam performed by a physician, generally happens a month before practice begins. The goal and hope of requiring students to participate in a thorough exam before the season starts is to identify any potential health problems that could be triggered through strenuous activity. An athlete with an illness or condition may have to restrict his participation in order to stay safe and healthy.

During the last several years, reports of injuries (and even a few deaths) related to school and league sports programs have increased. These reports have driven a majority of schools and leagues to require each athlete to get a physical before the athlete can participate in any sports program. For example, many state athletic associations now require all student athletes to turn in a signed physical form before they can participate in practices.

Many school and league programs bring in a doctor of their choice to perform physical exams for their athletes. Although this service is great, the best way to make sure you're healthy enough for wrestling is to undergo a physical exam with your family doctor who is familiar with your health and family history. Make sure to have regular doctor's checkups and to report any unusual symptoms as they arise. The American Academy of Pediatrics encourages parents to have their children undergo a thorough Preparticipation Physical Evaluation (PPE) before participating in any sport. Such an exam can help keep you safe and healthy and ensure that you have a long career in sports. Find details about the PPE at `www.ppesports evaluation.org`.

If you haven't had a physical in the past, you may wonder what to expect. Generally, your doctor will start by having you and your parent or legal guardian fill out a health history questionnaire that asks about the following:

- ✔ Emergency contact information
- ✔ Family history of illness or conditions
- ✔ Personal history of illness, conditions, or injuries and the way in which you're managing them
- ✔ Diagnosed medical conditions
- ✔ History of heart problems
- ✔ Medications
- ✔ Allergies

- History of head injury
- Hospitalizations
- Immunizations
- Menstrual cycle irregularities (for female athletes)

After you complete the questionnaire, the doctor performs the physical exam. During the exam, the doctor considers any injuries, conditions, illnesses, or symptoms that you reported as he checks for the following:

- Heart rate and rhythm
- Joint pain or tenderness
- Curvature of the spine
- Elevated blood pressure
- Wheezing
- Muscle imbalance
- Urinalysis
- Vision loss
- Hearing problems
- Problems with reflexes

If the doctor suspects any problems, he may conduct one or more of the following tests:

- Blood tests
- EKG or echocardiograms
- X-ray, MRI, CT, or bone scan
- Muscle strength testing

Gearing Up: Selecting the Right Equipment

Unlike other sports, wrestling doesn't require massive amounts of equipment and gear. So you don't have to carry an enormous duffle bag filled with gloves, pads, uniforms, helmets, bats, balls, and shoes. In wrestling, you're the main piece of equipment. Although you do need a few pieces of equipment, you can rest easy, knowing that your gym bag won't weigh 50 pounds.

The only equipment you need are headgear, shoes, and a few uniforms. Finding these items at a sports store can sometimes be difficult, but you can find dozens, if not hundreds, of websites that sell a wide variety of wrestling equipment.

In this section, I talk about headgear, wrestling shoes, singlets, and a few optional pieces of equipment so that you know what to buy when you start shopping.

Headgear

Headgear is the most important piece of equipment you need as a wrestler. You wear *headgear* to protect your ears — not your head, as the name implies. Most stores and online sites label the equipment as *headgear,* but some brands call it *ear protectors* or *ear guards.* (I refer to it as *headgear* in this chapter.)

This section identifies why most sports programs require wrestlers to wear headgear during competition and what you should look for when shopping for headgear.

Why you must wear headgear

Whether you have to wear headgear to compete depends on the type of wrestling program you're in, but I recommend that you always wear headgear to protect yourself. Here's a breakdown of how different programs treat headgear:

- ✔ High school and college wrestling programs require all wrestlers to wear protective headgear during competition.

- ✔ Headgear isn't mandatory in freestyle or Greco-Roman wrestling, but many wrestlers choose to wear it to avoid ear injuries.

- ✔ Youth wrestling doesn't require headgear, but many coaches recommend that kids wear it so they can become accustomed to wearing headgear while wrestling.

As the competition becomes more physical — this can happen as early as middle or junior high school — wearing headgear becomes more important in protecting your ears from injuries.

The most common ear injury wrestlers sustain is *cauliflower ear.* Cauliflower ear is a painful condition that occurs when the ear suffers multiple blows and is pushed and turned on the mat. A collection of fluid forms under the external portion of the ear, separating the cartilage from the overlying *perichondrium* (a dense layer of connective tissue), causing it to die and form fibrous tissue in the overlying skin. The ear resembles a cauliflower as it becomes permanently swollen and deformed.

Treatment for cauliflower ear is painful and requires a doctor to drain the blood and fluid from the ear with a needle. However, even after this treatment, the ear still resembles a cauliflower. In many cases, the only way to get rid of the cauliflower look is plastic surgery.

What to look for when selecting headgear

The good news: Which headgear to buy isn't a difficult decision to make. Most headgear comes in one size and adjusts to fit your head. However, you may want to purchase a youth size depending on your age.

Most headgear consists of a single piece of equipment with a soft inner pad covered with a layer of durable protective plastic to protect the ears, two straps that run behind the head, two straps that go over the front and top part of the head, and one strap that goes under or on the chin. You have many design styles of headgear to choose from, and all are made from materials such as plastic, polymer, and neoprene. The traditional style is the most common because it's comfortable and offers plenty of room around the ear. Check out Figure 3-1 for two examples of traditional headgear.

Figure 3-1: Two examples of traditional headgear.

a

b

Many wrestlers don't like the plastic style of headgear because it's often less comfortable than the softer materials and can actually contribute to cauliflower ear.

Choosing headgear is a personal decision because the best style and design for you depends on which one fits well on your head and over your ears. Whatever headgear you choose, make sure that it fits snug to your head. Ask your coach to help you adjust your headgear so that it fits you right.

I recommend trying on different styles and asking your teammates what brands and styles they recommend. Depending on which brand and style you choose, you can expect to spend between $15 and $45 on headgear.

Shoes

Wrestlers wear special shoes to protect their feet and to gain better traction on the mat. Wrestling shoes are lightweight and have a soft sole, allowing you to be quick on your feet and protecting you and your opponent from injuries.

Wrestling shoes come in a variety of sizes and colors (see Figure 3-2 for an example of wrestling shoes). Children who wear a size five or smaller shoe may have a difficult time finding wrestling shoes in sporting goods stores. My signature Brute-Adidas wrestling shoes are the best-selling shoes in the country, and if you can't find them at a local store, visit www.adidas.com, where you can order them.

Figure 3-2:
Wrestling shoes allow you quick movement on the mat.

Your wrestling shoes should be a half to a full size larger than your normal shoe size, especially if your feet are still growing. A high-quality wrestling shoe usually lasts one to two years, so allowing a little room for your feet to grow is a good idea.

Wrestling shoe manufacturers, such as Adidas, Asics, Matman, and Nike (just to name a few), offer a wide range of colors. The less expensive shoes generally offer fewer choices, such as black, blue, and red. The more expensive brands often have additional colors, such as white, silver, orange, pink, and a variety of pastels, although those colors are usually only available in women's sizes.

Wrestling shoes are made of leather, nylon, or a combination of both. The higher-end shoes are made primarily of leather, are lighter in weight, and have lace guard mechanisms. A *lace guard mechanism* is a piece of leather or nylon that fastens over the laces with Velcro to keep the laces from coming undone. Lace guard mechanisms also keep fingers from getting stuck in the laces and are required of all wrestling shoes in the United States.

Prices for wrestling shoes range anywhere from $35 to $115, depending on the brand, model, and features. You can find them at most sporting goods stores, but you'll find a larger selection of brands, sizes, and colors online. Sometimes ordering online is the easiest way to go, especially if you know your size. But don't worry if you don't know your size. Some websites have sizing charts and guarantee their method of sizing. High school wrestling teams usually prefer you to purchase shoes that are in the team's colors, and they sometimes provide an option to buy them at a discount through the school.

The right clothes: Singlets or doublets

When you hit the mat, you want to be garbed in the right clothes. You have a couple of different options, although your team may supply you with your uniform. If your school or club doesn't, you have to purchase either a singlet or a doublet.

- ✔ **Singlets:** A wrestling *singlet* is a one-piece, tight-fitting uniform worn by amateur wrestlers during wrestling matches. Singlets are designed for comfort and durability, they fit close to the body, and they should cover all the appropriate body parts. In general, the garment covers the torso and has straps that are much like a tight-fitting tank top.

  The traditional singlet has three different styles:

  - • **Low cut:** The low-cut wrestling singlet is rarely used in the United States anymore, and it's illegal in Olympic and high school wrestling. The style is cut to the abdomen in the front, cut to the hips on the sides, and has a single strap that runs up the back of the wrestler.

  - • **High cut:** The high-cut wrestling singlet covers the chest and comes up to just beneath the under arms, as you can see in Figure 3-3a.

  - • **Fila cut:** The fila cut is similar to the high cut, except that it doesn't rise up as high beneath the arms (see Figure 3-3b for an example).

- ✔ **Doublets:** *Doublets* are two-piece singlets that have sleeves. The style is becoming popular in collegiate wrestling for men and women and in mixed martial arts. Many high school athletes also wear doublets in practice.

Figure 3-3:
The high-
cut singlet
(a) and fila
cut singlet
(b) are both
popular
among
wrestlers.

Figure 3-3: The high-cut singlet (a) and fila cut singlet (b) are both popular among wrestlers.

Both singlets and doublets are made of materials such as nylon, Lycra, and spandex. They're all tight fitting so that your opponent can't grasp your clothes during competition (doing so is illegal in amateur wrestling). The tight-fitting garments also allow the referee to clearly see when awarding points or declaring a pin.

You may choose to wear any of the following underneath your singlet or doublet, or you can wear just the singlet or doublet:

✔ Boxers

✔ Compression shorts

✔ Jockstrap

✔ Regular underwear

✔ Sports bra

✔ Tights

You can wear a T-shirt under your singlet if you gain special permission. The most common reasons for wearing a T-shirt are sanitary reasons, such as excessive acne on your back or chest.

The National Collegiate Athletic Association (NCAA) banned the singlet for years and didn't sanction its use until the late 1960s. Instead, wrestlers wore shorts and tights and no shirts. Today, however, singlets or doublets are mandatory in all NCAA competitions, and shirtless wrestling is illegal. As more women participate in wrestling, the sport may need to move to a more universal uniform.

High school, college, and some middle school wrestling teams require their wrestlers to wear singlets or doublets in their school colors and usually provide them. League wrestling and international-style wrestling often require wrestlers to have one red and one blue uniform for a match. They find out which color to wear before the match.

Depending on the style and brand of uniform you purchase, you can expect to pay between $25 and $115 per singlet or doublet, although some doublets are even more expensive.

Make sure that you find out the specific uniform requirements of your school wrestling program and your league so that you don't spend money on something you may not need.

Other optional equipment

At some point in your wrestling career, you may want to invest in two additional but optional pieces of equipment. The first one is a mouth guard. A mouth guard is optional unless you have braces; if you have braces, you must wear one.

The other optional piece of equipment is a face mask. If you've had a broken nose or you have stitches on your face, you may want to wear a face mask, but you must have a note from your doctor that states that the face mask is required.

Part II

Creating a Solid Wrestling Foundation before Your First Match

The 5th Wave   By Rich Tennant

THE BLOWFISH ESCAPE

In this part . . .

The chapters in this part serve to take your knowledge of wrestling to the next level. Here I break down the details of what happens in a wrestling match, outline the ins and outs of the rulebook, and explain how scoring works.

I also include a good deal of information on taking care of your body, from what to eat to how to maintain an overall healthy lifestyle. I share everything you need to know about strength training, endurance training, mental training, flexibility, and hydration, and I tell you how to be a good teammate and make others around you better wrestlers.

Finally, I go over the fundamentals of the sport, including the basics of movement, footwork, and stance, to get you ready for the different wrestling moves that I discuss in Part III.

Chapter 4

Knowing What Happens during a Wrestling Match

*L*ike any other sport, wrestling involves a long list of rules that you have to follow whenever you compete. Long before you participate in your first match, you need to take the time to understand the rules of competition, including what happens during a match, what the referee does before, during, and after a match, and how you score points for you and your team. This chapter gives you the information you need to be a successful, rule-abiding, point-scoring wrestler every time you enter the gym and take to the mat.

College rules, high school rules, middle school rules, and elementary rules have many similarities, but they also have some differences. In this chapter, I focus on rules at the high school level, but I provide some information on higher and lower levels, too.

Note: Many of the rules in this chapter come from the National Federation of High Schools 2011-2012 Wrestling Rules Book. To stay up to date on national rule changes, go to www.nfhs.org. Even though these rules are for the high school level, for the most part, they're consistent with the rules at the middle school and college levels.

Weighing In on Weight

In wrestling, to make sure no one wrestler has an advantage, you compete against someone who is nearly the same weight as you are according to your pre-match weigh-in. Thus, your weight essentially determines your opponent on match day.

Weights are broken down into classifications, so someone who is, for example, 145 pounds wrestles against other wrestlers who are near 145 pounds and not wrestlers who weigh 180 pounds. The following sections spell out the different weight categories and explain what happens during the weigh-in process before the match.

Understanding weight classifications

Weight classifications are an important part of all wrestling programs because they help ensure the safety of all wrestlers by promoting safe, healthy weight gain and loss during the season and by making sure you don't compete against wrestlers who are twice your size. To take wrestler safety one step further, the National Federation of High Schools (NFHS) requires each state to use a weight-control program to guard against excessive weight gain or loss because either one may be harmful to you as an athlete.

Before the season starts, each high school wrestler must be approved by a state-certified assessor. The assessor tests the wrestler's urine and checks the wrestler's body weight, body fat percentage, and hydration level. When the assessor confirms that the wrestler's body fat percentage and hydration percentage are within approved standards for her weight, the assessor certifies a weight for that wrestler. Some wrestlers fail the test the first time, usually because their hydration levels are too low for their weight. The state weight assessor's job is to make sure kids are healthy and are wrestling at a weight that's safe for them. Chapter 5 discusses health and safety issues in detail.

Table 4-1 shows the different weight classes in folkstyle wrestling by age group. To determine your weight class, simply take your weight and round up to the next class. So if you weigh 112 pounds and you're competing at the high school level, you'd be in the 113-pound weight class.

Table 4-1	Weight Classes by Age Group (in Pounds)		
Middle School	*High School*	*College Men*	*College Women*
78	106	125	105
86	113	133	112
93	120	141	121
103	126	149	130
110	132	157	139
117	138	165	148
124	145	174	159
134	152	184	200
142	160	197	
152	170	285	
165	182		
185	195		
275	220		
	285		

You can wrestle either in your weight class or in the weight class one above your actual weight class. For example, if you're a high school wrestler who, at weigh-in, tips the scale at 119 pounds, you can wrestle at either the 120-pound weight class or the 126-pound weight class. But you're too heavy for the 113 weight class, and you can't wrestle at 132 because that's two classes above your own.

Weighing in before the match

In order to qualify for a certain weight class, you must weigh in on the official scale a maximum of one hour before the meet begins. (After your weigh-in, you may have to wait two to three hours until your match takes place, or you may be one of the first to compete. Your match time depends on the random draw that determines the competition order of weight classes; see the next section for details.)

At the weigh-in, all wrestlers must report to and stay in a designated weigh-in area. The referee supervises the weigh-ins, which start with the lowest weight class and move up to the highest. After all the wrestlers for a particular weight class have had a chance to weigh in, the referee closes that weight class and calls the next weight class to get weighed in.

For the weigh-in, male wrestlers must wear an undergarment that completely covers the buttocks and groin area, and females must wear a uniform that covers their chest. If you fail to *make weight* (weigh in at your class) during the weigh-in period, you can't compete in that weight class. Instead, you have to wrestle in one of the next two weight classes, but you don't have to repeat your weigh-in.

Because a large part of your body weight consists of water, wrestlers used to use techniques such as hot showers, whirlpool tubs, rubber or plastic suits, other heating devices, pills that make you urinate more, and other unsafe methods for quick water weight loss. Today the rules clearly prohibit the use of these and other unsafe weight loss tactics, and you'll be disqualified immediately if you choose to use them.

Walking through Match Day: What Happens during Competition

One of the best ways to get familiar with what happens on match day is to go to a local high school or college wrestling meet and observe the event. In the following sections, I outline the different types of matches you may see, and I walk you through a typical competition to get you mentally ready for your first match.

Identifying the types of matches

Wrestling competitions come in two primary formats:

- **Dual meet:** In a *dual meet,* your team competes against one other team in a head-to-head competition. In a *double dual meet,* your team competes against two other teams in each of the weight classes (see the preceding section for details). A random draw of weight classes determines the order of competition in a dual meet.

  Random draw is the random selection of weight classes to determine the order of matches for the meet. The draw takes place following the weigh-ins, and the referee supervises it. The first weight class drawn gets to begin the meet; the other classes follow in the order in which they're drawn.

- **Tournament:** A *tournament* is a series of matches in each weight class that takes place between two or more teams. (Each series of matches is called a *bracket.*) If you win, you continue to move through the bracket from one round to the next based on the results of your matches. To understand how tournaments are set up, check out the nearby sidebar.

Setting up a wrestling tournament

The advantage of competing in a tournament is that you can compete in several matches in a day (and the more you wrestle, the better you'll get). Tournaments are a great way to test your skills against a variety of competitors. Usually the director of the tournament sets the matches in a bracket format before the day of the competition with winners advancing to face other winners and losers advancing to face other losers. The specific breakdown of matches depends on the number of wrestlers who have entered into the tournament.

Without a doubt, you'll get to attend at least one tournament in your first year of wrestling. Many tournaments are well attended with as many as eight matches going on in the gym at one time, each with its own mat, referee, and scorer.

Ready, set, go! Match time

Regular folkstyle wrestling matches consist of three two-minute periods for a total time of six minutes per match. The only rest you get between the periods is the time the referee takes to position you for the next period.

The only people allowed on the mat during a match are the two contestants, the referee, and the assistant referee (if one is present). Strict mat rules are in place to ensure the safety of both contestants and to make it easier for the match officials to do their job.

Here is what happens during a match:

1. **You and your opponent report to the scorer's table as soon as the referee calls you over to start the match.**

   Any delay in getting to the scorer's table may result in your forfeiture or disqualification.

2. **Shake hands with your opponent as soon as you take the mat.**

3. **The referee starts the match; the first period always starts with you and your opponent facing each other in the neutral position.**

   You begin wrestling at the sound of the referee's whistle. If no pin occurs during the first period, you move into the second period (see the later section "Pin" for details).

4. **At the start of the second period, the wrestler who won the toss gets to select one of the following three starting positions, or he can choose to defer his choice to the third period.**

   In a dual meet, the referee tosses a disk into the air at the beginning of the meet to determine which team gets to decide the starting position for the second period; in a tournament, the referee tosses the ring after the first period of every match to determine which wrestler gets to select the starting position in the second period.

- Neutral position

- Bottom of the referee's starting position

- Top of the referee's starting position

Check out Chapter 8 for details on these three starting positions.

5. **At the start of the third period, the other wrestler gets to select his preferred starting position, unless, of course, the first wrestler chose to defer at the start of the second period.**

Keep in mind that if a pin occurs, the match is over immediately.

6. **If the referee's whistle sounds to end the match's six minutes and no one has won the match by a pin, the referee will direct you back to your starting spot in the middle of the mat, where you and your opponent will shake hands again.**

The referee verifies the score with the scorer (see the later section "Identifying the other officials" for details) and declares a winner by lifting that wrestler's hand high in the air. (Refer to the later section "Scoring: What's the Point?" for the lowdown on how to score points during a match.)

If the third period ends in a tie, a one-minute sudden-victory period occurs. Both wrestlers start in the neutral position and the first wrestler to score a point wins. If neither wrestler scores a point in the sudden-victory period, two 30-second tiebreaker periods occur. The wrestlers start in the referee's starting position; the wrestler who scored the first points of the match gets to choose the top or bottom position. Whoever scores the most points during these two 30-second periods wins the match. If the score is still tied, a 30-second ultimate tiebreaker occurs, and the first wrestler to score wins the match. If no scoring occurs in the ultimate tiebreaker, the referee declares the offensive wrestler the winner.

Before you head back to the team area and your coach, be sure to be a good sport and shake the hand of your opponent and your opponent's coach after the referee has recognized the winner.

Stopping the match

Sometimes the referee needs to temporarily stop a match in the middle. The following list presents some of the most common reasons that the referee may have to stop a match:

- Two of your supporting parts (arms, feet, or knees) and those of your opponent are out of bounds.

- You and your opponent are in a *stalemate,* a position in which neither of you can improve your position.

- You or your opponent becomes injured, including bleeding, due to legal or illegal action.

- The required ear guard comes loose.

  Note: Each wrestler must wear an ear guard for protection. If it comes loose, the referee will stop the match to have the wrestler replace it. Chapter 3 discusses ear guards in more detail.

As soon as the referee solves the issue, he returns both wrestlers to the center of the mat. If neither wrestler had control when the match stopped, both wrestlers begin in the neutral position. If one wrestler was in control of the other, the wrestler in control starts on top in the referee's position, and the wrestler being controlled starts on the bottom.

Ruling the Mat by Knowing the Rules

The sport of wrestling has many rules. Some are more important to you, the wrestler, and some are more important to your coach. The following sections highlight some of the significant rules that you and your coach need to know before you head to your first match.

Weight class rules

Because your weight as a wrestler is so important to your competition (namely, who your opponent is), many of the rules of wrestling have to do with weight class and weight management. Here are the important weight-related rules you need to know. (Check out the earlier section, "Weighing in on Weight" for more information on weight.)

- ✔ Each team can enter only one wrestler in each of the weight classes, and your coach can't make any substitutions after the weigh-ins.

- ✔ No wrestler can be in more than one weight class during a wrestling meet or tournament, and you can't wrestle in more than five matches in any one day.

- ✔ If you make weight in one class, you may wrestle in either that class or one class higher.

- ✔ The home team must provide a scale for weigh-ins that's certified for accuracy every year. Your coach is responsible for making sure a local scale verification professional has checked and certified the scale before match day.

The mat and mat area

The *mat*, or wrestling surface, must meet certain criteria to be used for an official match. The mat itself must have a marked-off circular wrestling area (conveniently called the *wrestling area*) that's no fewer than 28 feet in diameter surrounded by a safety area that's at least 5 feet wide on all sides (see Figure 4-1). Most mats also have a 10-foot starting circle in the middle.

Figure 4-1:
The wrestling mat.

The *mat area* includes the mat and its surrounding safety area, which must be a free space of at least 10 feet on all four sides of the wrestling mat to insure a safe perimeter. Immediately outside the mat area are the team benches and the scorer's table, which you can see in Figure 4-2.

During a match, all your teammates and coaches must stay at least 10 feet away from the mat. However, in some situations, one or two coaches can sit in chairs that are at least 5 feet away from the edge of the wrestling mat.

Infractions

Infractions are illegal acts that can cause you to lose points or to lose the match. Table 4-2 offers a snapshot of some of the most common infractions, along with their penalties. A *yes* in the Warning column means that the referee will warn you for that particular infraction before taking away a point. A *no* in the Warning column means that the referee immediately takes a point from your score.

Figure 4-2:
The mat area.

Table 4-2	Common Infractions and Their Penalties	
Violation	*Warning*	*Penalty*
Illegal holds and technical violations	No	Your opponent earns a point.
Stalling	Yes	You receive 1 warning; then your opponent earns 1 point for each successive stalling violation. On the fifth stalling infraction, you're disqualified from the match.
Unsportsmanlike conduct	No	Your opponent earns a point.
Unnecessary roughness	No	Your opponent earns a point.
False start	Yes	You receive 2 warnings; then your opponent earns 1 point for each subsequent infraction.
Flagrant misconduct	No	You get disqualified.
Illegal equipment or uniform (see Chapter 3 for details)	Yes	You have 1 minute and 30 seconds to change or you get disqualified.
Greasy substance on body	Yes	You have 1 minute and 30 seconds to remove the substance, or you get disqualified
Improper grooming (such as sideburns below the earlobe or hair below the collar)	Yes	You have 1 minute and 30 seconds to correct the grooming issue, or you get disqualified.

In the following sections, I discuss these common infractions in more detail so that you can avoid them during competition.

Illegal holds and maneuvers

Any hold or maneuver that could endanger the health and safety of your opponent is illegal. The following list provides some common examples of illegal holds and moves that you need to avoid when you wrestle. The first and second time you do one of these holds or moves, your opponent immediately earns a point without warning. The third time you do one of these moves, your opponent earns two points, and the fourth illegal hold or maneuver gets you disqualified.

- Lifting and returning your opponent to the mat with unnecessary force (called a *slam*)

- Pulling back on the thumbs or fingers of your opponent rather than just grabbing them for control

- Locking your arms or hands around your opponent's head without also encircling an arm or leg

- Applying pressure over your opponent's mouth, nose, throat, or neck and restricting your opponent's breathing or circulation

- Bending or twisting your opponent's head or any other body part, forcing it beyond its normal limit of movement

- Putting your hands in or near your opponent's eyes

Technical violations

Like any other sport, wrestling has some basic rules that guide competition. If you fail to follow one of these rules, you'll get a technical violation, which results in your opponent earning one point for the first two violations, two points for the third violation, and your disqualification for the fourth violation. Here are some common technical violations that you need to be aware of:

- Moving out of bounds, or outside the 28-foot wrestling circle, in order to avoid wrestling and force the referee to temporarily stop the match (also called *fleeing the mat*)

- Grasping the uniform, the mat, or your opponent's ear guards to gain or prevent an escape, reversal, takedown, or near fall

- Interlocking or overlapping your hands, fingers, or arms around the opponent's body or both legs when in the top position

- Reporting to the scorer's table unprepared to wrestle or leaving the mat area without the referee's permission

Conduct

Without rules that promote fair play and safety, wrestling could become a pretty brutal sport. Referees, coaches, and players must pay close attention to the rules of conduct that keep wrestling safe and fun. The following list gives you an idea of some of the conduct violations that result in points for your opponent or your disqualification:

- **Unnecessary roughness:** The referee calls you for this conduct violation when you act in a way that exceeds normal aggressiveness, including when you use excessive force with your arms, hands, or legs. The referee may also declare unnecessary roughness if you seem to use a hold for the sole purpose of punishment alone.

✔ **Unsportsmanlike conduct:** This infraction includes failing to listen to the referee, pushing, shoving, swearing, taunting, intimidating, spitting, throwing equipment, and failing to comply with end-of-match procedures (see the earlier section "Ready, set, go! Match time" for details on these end-of-match procedures). Unsportsmanlike conduct also includes any action that's intended to embarrass, ridicule, or put other people or your opponent down.

✔ **Flagrant misconduct:** Flagrant misconduct is any physical or nonphysical act that the referee considers to be serious enough to disqualify a contestant from the match; flagrant misconduct actions may occur before, during, or after a match and include using or possessing a banned substance and striking, butting, elbowing, kicking, or biting an opponent.

All flagrant misconduct violations result in immediate disqualification, deduction of three team points, and removal from the premises. The wrestler is eliminated from further competition for the remainder of the event.

Stalling

By rule, each wrestler must make an honest attempt to stay within the 10-foot starting circle on the mat and wrestle aggressively. If you give the impression that you're no longer interested in continuing the match or if you're ahead and you stop taking risks, the referee may call you for stalling. You get one stalling warning. After the warning, your opponent earns one point for the next two violations, your opponent earns two points for the fourth violation, and you get disqualified after the fifth violation.

Here are some examples of when you may be called for stalling:

✔ You continually avoid contact with your opponent.

✔ You stay on or near the edge of the wrestling circle.

✔ You prevent your opponent from returning to or remaining inbounds.

✔ You're not attempting to secure a takedown.

✔ You make no attempt to aggressively try an escape or reversal move.

✔ You repeatedly grasp one of your opponent's legs to prevent her from scoring.

✔ You try to delay the match in any way.

Other infractions you need to know

Here are a few other infractions you need to be aware of:

✔ **False start:** This common infraction happens when you start before the official's signal or when you assume an incorrect starting position. After two warnings, your opponent earns one point for each subsequent infraction.

✔ **Illegal equipment or uniform:** The referee disqualifies any wrestler who reports to the scorer's table wearing illegal equipment or uniform if she doesn't correct the problem within the one-and-a-half-minute injury timeout (see the next section for details). Equipment or uniform guidelines include the following (see Chapter 3 for more details on equipment):

- **Uniform:** The male wrestler's uniform must consist of a one-piece singlet with or without full-length tights underneath. The cut in the front or back must be no lower than the armpits. The female wrestler's uniform must completely cover cleavage.

- **Footwear:** All wrestlers must wear light, heelless wrestling shoes that reach above the ankle and secure tightly.

- **Ear protection:** All wrestlers must wear a protective ear guard.

Check with your local association (elementary, high school, or collegiate) to make sure that your apparel complies with the rules.

✔ **Greasy substance on body:** Wrestlers can't apply any foreign substances to their skin. The referee will disqualify any wrestler who reports to the scorer's table in violation of this rule if she doesn't correct it within the one-and-a-half-minute injury timeout (see the next section for details).

✔ **Improper grooming:** All wrestlers must be clean shaven, their sideburns must not extend below the earlobe, and their hair must not extend below the collar in its natural down state. Both male and female wrestlers can wear a permissible hairnet or cover to satisfy this rule. Wrestlers also can't wear any jewelry. The referee disqualifies any wrestler who reports to the scorer's table in violation of this rule if she doesn't correct it within the one-and-a-half-minute injury timeout (see the next section for details).

Injuries

If you suffer an injury during a match, you can stop wrestling and take an *injury timeout* (a temporary stoppage of the match because of injury). Each wrestler gets a maximum of one-and-a-half-minute injury timeout that accumulate throughout the match. You can take two injury timeouts as long as you don't use all one and a half minutes during your first timeout. A third injury timeout ends the match.

If you're injured as a result of an illegal hold, you get an additional two minutes that don't count as part of your original one and a half injury timeout minutes. If the referee determines that an injury to Wrestler A was not the result of a violation or illegal hold or maneuver by Wrestler B, Wrestler A loses points or loses the match according to the following guidelines:

- When Wrestler B legally executes a pinning combination and a near fall is imminent but Wrestler A suffers an injury, indicates an injury, or has excessive bleeding before the referee can declare a near fall, the referee temporarily stops the match and awards Wrestler B a two-point near fall (see the section "Near fall" for details).

- When Wrestler B meets the criteria for a two-point near fall but Wrestler A suffers an injury, indicates an injury, or has excessive bleeding, the referee stops the match and awards Wrestler B a three-point near fall.

- When Wrestler B meets the criteria for a three-point near fall but Wrestler A suffers an injury, indicates an injury, or has excessive bleeding, the referee stops the match and awards Wrestler B a fourth point in addition to the three-point near fall.

- The referee declares a *default* when one of the wrestlers is unable to continue for any reason. The wrestler who defaults gets to add a loss to her individual season record, while the wrestler who could've continued the match earns a win.

Any time either wrestler bleeds, the referee has to stop the match so that someone can clean the blood off the mat and uniform and treat the wrestler's wound to make the bleeding stop. The wrestler who's bleeding is charged with *blood time*. The referee determines the amount of blood time the wrestler gets, but if the bleeding goes uncontrolled for five minutes, the match ends.

Understanding the Role of the Referee

As you may have guessed, the referee is in charge of the match. The referee makes the judgment calls that determine scoring and penalties. He has full control of the match and bases all his decisions on the rules of the sport. He also uses signals to let the wrestlers and the scorer know who has scored points. All the referee's decisions are final; using any type of video replay or TV monitor to assist in the calls that are made during a match is illegal.

But the referee isn't just in charge of individual matches; his jurisdiction begins as soon as he arrives at the wrestling site and concludes only after he has signed the official scorebook at the end of all the matches. The host school or organization hires the referee, who is licensed by the local wrestling organization or the state. For example, high school officials attend year-round training and attend classes to become certified as officials.

You can recognize the referee as soon as you walk into the gym because all referees wear similar uniforms that consist of the following elements (see Figure 4-3 for an example):

✔ A short-sleeved, black-and-white-striped or solid gray shirt

✔ Black pants, black belt, black socks, and black shoes

✔ A red armband on the left wrist and a green one on the right

✔ A lanyard, a whistle, and a colored disc for the toss

Figure 4-3:
The referee.

The referee not only makes decisions on scoring but also acts as the final authority on the legality of all equipment, mats, mat markings, uniforms, pads, and taping on a wrestler's body. A referee can call a timeout to correct any equipment issues that come up while a match is taking place.

The following sections explain what the referee does before, during, and after the match. These sections also identify the other people who have official duties during a match.

Make sure you're respectful to all the officials you come into contact with as a wrestler. These professionals work hard to be experts at what they do, and they deserve your respect. Officiating isn't an easy job, and when you cooperate with the referees, they're very appreciative.

Before the match

When the referee arrives at the match site, he has to follow a specific procedure before any matches can start. Here's a quick look at the standard procedure high school referees have to follow. (Other wrestling levels may do things a little differently, but the basic process is the same.)

- The referee inspects all wrestlers for the presence of oils or greasy substances on the body or uniform, illegal pads, improper clothing, jewelry, or other health and safety issues.
- The referee answers any questions the wrestlers or coaches may have about the rules.
- The referee has each head coach verify that every member of the team is well groomed, properly equipped, and ready to wrestle.
- The referee meets with the scorers and timekeepers to review the signals and procedures that he'll use during the match.
- The referee meets with the team captains and head coaches of both teams to explain that he expects them to make sure everyone shows good sportsmanship throughout the match.
- The referee manages the weigh-in process. See the section "Weighing In on Weight" for details on this process.

During and after the match

After the referee calls two wrestlers to the scorer's table and then to the center of the mat, he blows the whistle to start the match. He then follows this procedure during and after the match:

- The referee enforces the rules, consistently penalizing infractions and awarding points. He also has to rule on any situation not covered by the rules.
- The referee stops the match to penalize either wrestler and to deal with injuries and bleeding (see the section "Injuries" for details). When stopping the match for penalties, he uses appropriate signals and announces the penalty so that coaches, wrestlers, spectators, and scorers are aware of what's going on.
- The referee stops potentially dangerous or illegal holds and maneuvers (see the section "Illegal holds and maneuvers" for details).
- At the end of each match, the referee signs the official scorebook to certify the time, day, and results.

Identifying the other officials

In addition to the head referee, each match also has two other people who have official duties: the scorer and the timekeeper. The following sections outline what they do.

Scorer

Each team has an official *scorer,* who sits at the scorer's table and keeps score of the match (go figure!). The official scorer is responsible for

- Recording the points that each wrestler scores, as signaled by the referee

- Circling the first points scored in the match

- Keeping track of which wrestler chooses the starting position at the beginning of the second and third periods and which positions the wrestlers choose

- Communicating with the timekeeper when a correction needs to be made on the scoreboard regarding the time or the score

- Recording the completion time for matches and presenting the scorebook to the referee at the end of the meet to verify team scores with his signature

Timekeeper

The *timekeeper* is responsible for keeping time during the match. She has to keep time on both the large scoreboard clock and a manual clock in case the scoreboard loses function.

In addition, the timekeeper fills the following important roles during a wrestling match:

- Records the accumulated timeouts for injury and blood time

- Monitors recovery time

- Notifies the referee of any situation that comes up when the match is stopped or when a disagreement arises between the scorer and the timekeeper

- Assists the referee in determining whether a situation occurred before or after the end of a period

- Calls the minutes to the referee in the last minute of a period in 15-second intervals or taps the referee on the shoulder at the end of a period (if a visual clock is unavailable)

The referee's right-hand man: The assistant referee

In some matches, the referee may have an assistant referee who's there to minimize human error in the application of rules and judgment calls. An assistant referee isn't a requirement, but at high level or championship matches, chances are good that a second referee will be there to help out. The head referee still makes all the calls, but if the assistant sees something illegal, he informs the referee. In the case of a near fall (which I define in the section "Near fall"), the head referee goes down to the mat to determine near fall points or to declare a pin.

Scoring: What's the Point?

When you're wrestling, the objective is to score as many points as you can and pin your opponent. At the end of each individual match during a wrestling meet, the referee declares the wrestler with the most points the winner (unless, of course, either you or your opponent earns a pin, in which case whoever earned the pin is the winner). If the score is tied, the match goes into overtime as I describe in the earlier section "Ready, set, go! Match time." The following sections detail how you can score points in a match and how your individual points impact your team's points.

If you don't pin your opponent but you do beat her by 1 to 7 points, you earn a *regular decision*. If you beat your opponent by 8 to 14 points, you earn a *major decision*, and if the margin of victory is greater than 15, you earn a *technical fall*. Flip to the section on team scoring at the end of this chapter to find out why these distinctions matter.

Takedown

A *takedown* occurs when you and your opponent are in the neutral position and you gain control by taking your opponent down to the mat while keeping your opponent's head, hands, arms, feet, and legs inbounds. You earn two points for a successful takedown.

Two other ways to think about a takedown are

- ✔ When one or both of your opponent's knees are touching the mat
- ✔ When you have control of your opponent's torso or legs and the majority of her weight is supported by her hands

Check out Chapter 11 for how to execute different takedown moves.

Escape

An *escape* is when your opponent has you controlled on the mat and you get away and return to a neutral position. You earn one point for a successful escape. Chapter 9 has all you need to know about escapes.

Reversal

A *reversal* occurs when your opponent has you controlled either on the mat or in front of her and you come from underneath or behind her to gain control. The difference between an escape and a reversal is that in a reversal, you not only get away from but also take control of your opponent. You score two points for a successful reversal. See Chapter 10 for the lowdown on the different types of reversals you can use.

Near fall

A *near fall* happens when you have control of your opponent in a pinning situation but you can't quite get his shoulders on the mat. If you hold your opponent in a near fall position for two seconds, you earn two points. If you hold your opponent down for five seconds or more, you earn three points. For the referee to begin counting seconds for a near fall, you must hold some part of one of your opponent's shoulders (or his head) on the mat while holding the other shoulder at a 45-degree (or less) angle to the mat (or within four inches of the mat). The wrestler with control is the only one who can score a near fall, as shown in Figure 4-4.

Figure 4-4:
A near fall happens when you have control of your opponent but can't get his shoulders on the mat.

Pin

A *pin,* also called a *fall,* happens when any part of both of your opponent's shoulders are in contact with the mat for two seconds. For a pin to be successful, you must hold your opponent's shoulders inbounds in continuous contact with the mat (see Figure 4-5). When a pin occurs, the match is over.

Figure 4-5:
A pin happens when both of your opponent's shoulders are in contact with the mat.

Note: The referee's two-second count begins when he determines that a pin is going to happen, and his count goes like this: "One-thousand-one, one-thousand-two."

Technical fall

A *technical fall* occurs when you have a 15-point advantage over your opponent but you haven't been able to get the pin. The only way you can lose a match when you're leading by 15 points is if the referee charges you with flagrant misconduct.

Flagrant misconduct includes acts that the referee considers serious enough to remove a wrestler from the competition. A few examples of flagrant misconduct are striking an opponent, biting, elbowing, kicking, or using or possessing a banned substance. (See the earlier section "Infractions" for more on this and other wrestling infractions.)

Team scoring

In a wrestling meet, team scoring is based on the results of each individual match. Hence, your match is just as important as your teammates' matches in determining the team score. Here's a quick look at how many points your team earns for each individual match based on the results of that match:

- ✔ **6 points:** A win by default, disqualification, pin, or forfeit
- ✔ **5 points:** A win by technical fall
- ✔ **4 points:** A win by major decision
- ✔ **3 points:** A win by regular decision
- ✔ **0 points:** Double forfeit (the result of having no wrestlers enter in a weight class)

Chapter 5

Staying Healthy, Safe, and in Shape

*T*o be the best wrestler you can be, you need to have a lot of self-discipline. After all, few athletes train as hard and as long as wrestlers do. In addition to being disciplined, you need to be in tiptop shape. When you show up for practice or at a match to face your opponent, two factors go a long way in determining your chances for success. One is your technical skill, and the other is your level of physical well-being, nutrition, and fitness. In this chapter, I tell you what you need to know to show up at your next practice or match ready to wrestle healthy and physically well prepared.

Many of the other chapters in this book address the technical aspects of wrestling (like when and how to use certain moves), but this chapter focuses solely on *you* — and what *you* can do to be as well-prepared as possible for your next match. Here, I tell you how to manage your overall health, how to train your muscles and heart the safe way, how to make good lifestyle choices, and what (and what not) to eat or drink to fuel your body. All these aspects play a role in determining your short- and long-term success as a wrestler.

Focusing on Your Health

Your health is a key factor in your success as a wrestler (and as a person in general). Although the general term *health* refers to your emotional, physical, mental, and spiritual well-being, I focus on the physical aspect in this section, particularly on how it relates to keeping your body and its systems in optimal operating condition. I discuss safe ways to manage your weight, whether you're trying to drop, gain, or maintain. I also discuss the importance of preventing skin diseases, being aware of concussions, getting enough sleep and rest, and taking care of your body so that it can take care of you.

Managing your weight

Wrestling is one of the only sports that puts you in a category or class based on your weight. In other words, your weight determines which opponents you face. Because weight management is such a big deal for most wrestlers, you need to be aware of the pitfalls and processes involved with managing your weight.

At the high school level, each state has a weight-control program whose main job is to make sure all high school wrestlers lose and gain weight in a healthy way. The weight-control program requires you to establish a certified minimum weight and prevents you from recertifying at a lower weight during the season. Work with your parents, coaches, and doctor to determine your minimum healthy weight — and then make sure you stay above it.

 Your doctor may want to do a body-fat assessment to figure out what percentage of your body mass is fat. This assessment can tell you whether your weight is within a healthy range (and if it isn't, what it should be). As a rule, your minimum body fat should never be lower than 7 percent for males and 12 percent for females.

During your wrestling career, you may find yourself in a situation where you need to add a little weight, drop a little weight, or carefully maintain your current weight. In the following sections, I give you some suggestions and general guidelines to help you manage your weight the healthy way.

Losing weight

Basically, the only safe way to lose weight is by exercising more and eating a little less every day. *Safe weight loss* for a typical person means losing 2 or 3 pounds per week. If you need to lose a little bit to be able to wrestle in the next weight class, follow these suggestions to drop a couple of pounds:

✔ Eat small meals often — perhaps five to seven small meals per day. Don't skip any meals!

✔ Avoid fried foods, white bread, bagels, and foods high in fat.

✔ Eat most of your daily carbohydrates in the morning and during the daytime; eat more protein, vegetables, and fruits for dinner and late-night meals.

✔ Eat quality, healthy foods that combine carbohydrates, protein, and healthy fat at each meal. (See the later section "Reviewing general nutrition" for details.)

✔ Drink lots of water.

Gaining weight

The equation for gaining weight the healthy way is very similar to the one I discuss in the preceding section for losing weight. The idea is to put more calories into your body than you lose while exercising, training, and simply going through your daily routines. However, when you're training and you want to put on a little weight, you need to make sure you fuel your body with good calories and not junk and fast food. Try these tips to help increase your weight in a healthy way:

✔ Add two scoops of peanut butter to your oatmeal or other warm cereal.

✔ Add lowfat granola to your cereal, oatmeal, or yogurt.

✔ Add nuts to most of what you eat, including salads, tuna, and cereal.

✔ Add peanut or almond butter and honey to waffles, pancakes, toast, and bagels.

✔ Mix high-calorie protein powder with chocolate pudding.

✔ Eat carbohydrate-heavy meals closer to bedtime and add a peanut butter and jelly sandwich to your nighttime routine.

Maintaining your weight

Understand that your body goes through major changes between the ages of 12 and 18 and beyond, and your growth depends on a lot of factors, including some that you can't control, like your genes and your individual rate of maturity. Regardless of what you may try to do, you may weigh in at 105 pounds as a freshman in high school and weigh in at 185 pounds four years later. That being said, if you weigh in at a certain weight class at the beginning of your season and you want to maintain the same weight throughout the year, you can follow these tips to help you maintain your weight:

✔ Record how many calories you typically consume in an average day and then shoot to consume that amount each day.

✔ Stay away from extremes. Avoid late-night overeating (after 7 p.m.) and always eat breakfast, lunch, and dinner.

✔ Try to get most of your calories from fruits, vegetables, whole grains, and other healthy foods (see the later section "Eating Healthy Before and After You Exercise" for details).

Getting enough rest and sleep

Two aspects of your overall health that you may be tempted to overlook when you're in the heat of the wrestling season are rest (between workouts) and sleep. I'm here to tell you that you need both to be a successful wrestler.

Rest days with little or no exercise are an important part of your training program. (I know. You may not want to take a day off, but trust me. You need to.) So focus on *quality* training rather than *quantity* training and give your body the time it needs to recover between workouts. Remember these points when you're tempted to skip your much-needed day of rest:

- ✔ Rest helps your body recover and prepare for the next workout.

- ✔ Rest reduces the risk of injury to joints, bones, and muscles.

- ✔ Rest helps you keep a bright and energized outlook on training and prevents burnout.

Furthermore, you need to fuel your body with sleep. A restful night's sleep provides the energy and alertness you need to maintain a balanced lifestyle and perform at your best. Not to mention, inadequate sleep can increase your risk of obesity, hypertension, impaired immunity to colds and sickness, and in some cases, depression. Follow these tips to get a good night's sleep every night:

- ✔ **Stick to a sleep schedule.** Set a regular time for sleeping and waking to help your body develop a healthy internal rhythm.

- ✔ **Avoid caffeine.** This stimulant can keep you awake and decrease the quality of your sleep.

- ✔ **Relax before going to bed.** Settle down mentally and physically before you go to bed so that you don't lie there awake for too long. Only lie down when you're ready to call it a night.

- ✔ **Limit naps.** Taking naps during the day can negatively affect the quality of your sleep later at night. If you need a nap, try to sleep for less than 45 minutes. If you find that you need one or more naps during the day because you're too tired, you may need to see your doctor to make sure your body is functioning normally.

Preventing skin diseases

Communicable skin diseases are a big concern in wrestling because you're constantly coming into contact with other wrestlers' skin and with surfaces that other wrestlers touch (namely, the mat). For this reason, all referees perform skin checks before matches. If they identify any signs of a skin disease, you have to get a doctor's clearance before you can compete.

But you need to monitor the health of your own skin, too. The best way to do so is to check your skin every day and look for anything that looks or feels different, especially on and near cuts or scratches. Look for areas that become reddened, irritable, sensitive, or swollen; if you find anything, contact your doctor or athletic trainer immediately.

Here are some of the most common skin ailments wrestlers face:

- ✔ **Impetigo:** This bacterial skin infection is highly contagious and is easily spread via skin-to-skin contact. Impetigo presents as red sores that break open, leaving oozing sores that eventually form a yellow crust. These lesions appear most commonly on the head, face, and neck. You can treat impetigo with both oral and topical antibiotics, but you can't wrestle until you've been treated for at least 48 hours and all lesions have healed.

- ✔ **Herpes:** This viral infection causes a rash made up of a cluster of blisters that may or may not be painful to the touch. Herpes commonly appears on the face, neck, shoulders, or arms. You can treat it with prescription drugs from your doctor, but the rash usually lasts from seven to ten days. You can't have any skin contact with any uninfected person while the herpes rash is present; in other words, no wrestling until the rash is gone.

- ✔ **Ringworm:** This fungal rash is usually round, slightly raised, itchy, and scaly with occasional small pus-filled bumps. It appears on the skin, feet (athlete's foot), scalp, and groin (jock itch). Over time, the rash can spread from one area to the next if you don't treat it with an antifungal cream. Occasionally, a doctor may prescribe oral medication for treatment. Keep treating the infected areas even after the rash disappears, or it may show up again.

As a wrestler, you need to take a proactive approach to prevent these and other skin diseases. You can do so by following these guidelines:

- ✔ Wrestle only on mats that are cleaned daily with a cleanser specially designed to clean wrestling mats.

- ✔ Wrestle only in rooms that have good ventilation and air flow.

- ✔ Clean all your workout gear, including towels, clothes, headgear, knee-pads, and any other items that come in contact with your skin and the mat, after every practice and match.

- ✔ Shower with an antibacterial soap after each practice and never share soap bars. In fact, use a dispenser whenever possible.

- ✔ Don't share T-shirts, shorts, headgear, towels, or other clothing with teammates unless it has been washed thoroughly.

- ✔ Check your skin every day and report anything that doesn't seem normal.

Understanding concussions

You may be at a perfect weight and in great physical condition, but if you don't understand the signs and symptoms of head injuries, you're not ready to start wrestling just yet.

Concussions are very serious conditions that you need to be aware of before you head to the mat. A *concussion* is a traumatic brain injury that interferes with normal brain function and occurs when your brain is rocked back and forth inside your skull. What may appear to be only a mild jolt to the head or body can result in a concussion, and a concussion can lead to short- and long-term changes in brain function. So even if you think you've suffered nothing more than a stinger or a ding to the head, talk to your coach *and* your doctor about it before you start wrestling again.

 Every head injury is a brain injury and should be immediately treated with care. Only qualified healthcare professionals can evaluate an athlete after a head injury and give him permission to continue wrestling. Neither referees nor coaches can diagnose a concussion.

If you, as a wrestler, experience any of the following symptoms during a meet or practice, immediately let your coach, referee, or parents know so they can observe you and make the necessary decision to have you seen by a medical professional:

- Dazed or stunned appearance
- Inability to recall events before or after the hit or fall
- Little memory of the match, score, or opponent
- Slow response time to questions
- Headache or pressure in your head
- Blurry vision, dizziness, or loss of balance
- Sensitivity to light or noise
- Feelings of sluggishness, fogginess, grogginess, or confusion

 Never try to tough out a suspected concussion. If you return to action before fully recovering from a concussion, you run the risk of having another one and doing more damage to your brain. Don't let your teammates, coaches, or parents encourage you to continue the match. Wrestling too soon after a concussion can lead to permanent brain damage or even death.

 If you or your coach suspects that you have a concussion, you can expect to go through the following process before you start wrestling again:

1. **Your coach or the referee will immediately remove you from the match or practice.**

2. **A doctor will immediately evaluate you for symptoms of a concussion.**

3. **A doctor will inform your parents or guardians about the possible concussion and give them a fact sheet on concussions.**

4. **A doctor will give you permission to start wrestling again.**

Maintaining a healthy general appearance

Part of being a competitive wrestler is having a healthy (and safe) appearance. In wrestling, having a healthy appearance means keeping up with your personal hygiene to reduce the likelihood of infection. Because of the close skin-on-skin contact inherent in wrestling, you need to make personal hygiene one of your top priorities.

Furthermore, strict rules apply to your appearance and physical health when you wrestle for a school or club. If you violate one of these rules, you may not be able to compete. Here are a few of the common appearance-related rules you have to follow:

✔ You must be clean shaven, and your hair can't be below your eyebrows in the front or below your shoulders in the back. If your hair is longer, you may need to wear a hair cover (hairnet); just make sure you wear it to the weigh-in (see Chapter 4).

✔ Wrestlers who wear braces must wear a tooth and mouth protector at all times during the match. (See Chapter 3 for details on mouth guards and other wrestling equipment.)

Training to Prepare for the Season

For many of you reading this book, the wrestling season lasts only a few months during your school's wrestling season. If you compete at the club level, you may extend your season by a couple more months. As a result, your coach only has so much time to teach you and improve your wrestling skills. He doesn't have the time to get you into wrestling shape. Thus, you need to be aware of a few basic training principles so that you can get ready on your own for the grueling season ahead.

This section deals with some general concepts related to training. Specifically, it covers endurance training, strength training, and flexibility, the three main training elements that lead to a healthy and prepared body. With proper training, not only can you become physically stronger, but you can also reduce your risk of injuries and muscle soreness so you can practice every day without missing a beat.

Note: This section doesn't include a specific training program because one size doesn't fit all. After you understand the basic principles of training that I cover in this section, ask for help from a coach, a physical education teacher, your family doctor, or a certified athletic trainer. Whomever you talk to should be able to either help you design a personal training plan that fits your unique situation or direct you to a trusted professional who can.

Boosting endurance

In wrestling, two aspects of *endurance* determine your ability to stay strong and continue competing at a maximum level from the start of the match to the end. You have to train for both to be successful on the mat:

- *Muscular endurance* refers to your ability to perform prolonged activities (like wrestling matches) that use your body's large muscles.

- *Cardiovascular endurance* refers to the efficiency with which your heart and lungs work together to allow you to be as effective in the sixth minute as you were in the first minute of a match.

Exercise improves both types of endurance by increasing the activity of your body and its systems beyond what they normally experience. The longer you train, the more your body adapts to the stresses related to physical activity and the higher your fitness level becomes. Endurance is an important part of your wrestling training routine for two main reasons:

- Better endurance increases your overall level of fitness, allowing you to finish both normal tasks (such as walking up the stairs) and more challenging activities (such as running one mile) with less stress on your body.

- Endurance training burns a large number of calories and, in doing so, helps you maintain an appropriate weight.

Endurance training can include doing any aerobic exercise, such as jogging, jumping rope for more than ten minutes in a row, running, cycling, swimming, and playing team sports, such as basketball. No matter which activities you do to build endurance, every endurance workout needs to consist of a warm-up, a conditioning phase, and a cool-down. I describe what each of these phases entails in the following sections.

Warming up

Start every endurance workout with five to ten minutes of light activity to increase blood flow throughout your body and gradually increase your heart rate. You can try many different activities, but I suggest doing a few of the following:

✔ **Light calisthenics:** These total body movements require only 50 percent total effort. You don't want to do anything at full speed until you've stretched and warmed up your body first. Examples include doing jumping jacks, jogging with a lateral shuffle, jogging backward, and doing arm circles.

✔ **Dynamic stretches:** These movements focus on *stretching,* or warming up, a certain muscle group (hamstrings or quadriceps, for example). Examples include walking as you do toe touches, doing forward single-leg lunges, and running with high knees.

Which specific exercises you decide to do doesn't matter. You just need to get your blood flowing before you dive into full-speed conditioning.

Conditioning

The conditioning phase of your endurance workout is based on the *FITT principle,* which stands for frequency, intensity, time, and type. The following list breaks down the details of each to give you a better understanding of what your conditioning program needs to include. Running or jogging is a great way to increase your endurance for wrestling, so keep that in mind as you read through this list.

✔ **Frequency:** *Frequency* refers to the number of days per week you set aside for endurance training. To see improvement, you need to do your endurance workout three to five days per week. I recommend doing your endurance training five days a week as you prepare for your season to get in great shape. Then you can go down to three days during the season. Your coach can help you determine exactly how much endurance training you need to meet your wrestling goals.

✔ **Intensity:** *Intensity* is how close you are to your maximum, full-speed exertion during your workout. As your level of conditioning increases, your level of intensity also increases. Generally, you should exercise at a *moderate level* of exercise, meaning that you should be able to carry on a conversation (albeit a labored one) with your workout partner. The more conditioned your cardiovascular system becomes in maintaining an increased heart rate in training, the slower your rate of breathing will be at rest and the more efficient your heart will be overall. Besides being a part of good health, an efficient heart also allows you to complete six minutes of wrestling and still be ready for overtime.

When you're in the conditioning phase of exercise, your heart rate should be high enough that carrying on a conversation with someone is difficult but still possible. If you can talk easily, pick up the pace, but if you can barely get a word out, slow down.

✔ **Time:** *Time* represents the length of your exercise. Your initial fitness level determines how long your workouts are at the start, but you need to work toward being able to jog at a moderate-intensity level for

40 minutes straight. Maybe that means starting with a 10-minute jog and 30 minutes of walking for the first week. Then you can gradually build up to the steady 40-minute jogging pace.

✔ **Type:** *Type* simply refers to the specific activity you do for your endurance training and the level of technical skill involved. The great part about wrestling endurance training is that you can get a lot of what you need from running and jogging. Although if you're wrestling in the heavier classes (see Chapter 4), you may want to mix in some cycling or swimming to help keep some pressure off your knee joints. Some wrestling workouts even count for endurance training. For example, if your coach designs a few workouts that require constant motion for 30 to 40 minutes with limited or no breaks, you can count them as part of your endurance training.

If you build up to a 35- to 45-minute jog or run at a moderate-intensity level that you can do four days per week before your season starts, you'll be in great shape to begin working on wrestling-specific techniques. You'll also have plenty of endurance to get through a six-minute match.

Cooling down

The cool-down is the bookend to your workout. After the initial warm-up and the conditioning portion of your workout, finish with a five- to ten-minute cool-down to allow your heart rate to return to normal. I suggest that you repeat the warm-up exercises, especially the stretches, that I describe earlier in this section for your cool-down. Notice how much easier stretching is after your workout than it was before your workout because of the increased blood flow to your muscles. A good cool-down can help reduce muscle soreness if you stretch all the major muscle groups in the body (hamstrings, quadriceps, lower back, abdomen, calves, and shoulders, for example).

Building strength

In addition to building cardiovascular endurance, which I discuss in the preceding section, you also need to develop muscular strength as part of your preseason training. *Muscular strength* is basically the maximum amount of force that a muscle can exert against some form of resistance in a single effort. As a wrestler, you have to exert a tremendous amount of force on your opponent, so the stronger you are, the more likely you are to be an effective wrestler, especially when doing lifts and breakdowns that require a good deal of muscular strength.

To develop muscular fitness, you need to add *strength training* (also called *resistance training*) to your weekly workout routine. Strength training is the process of straining or stressing your muscles through their normal range of motion by using some type of resistance. You can try many different forms of resistance; they all accomplish the same goal of placing stress on your muscles. Here are just a few examples:

- Free weights (barbells and dumbbells)
- Weight machines (various types)
- Medicine balls
- Elastic tubing

You don't need an expensive gym membership or a set of fancy weights to develop an effective strength-training routine. A five-pound bag of sand weighs just as much as a five-pound barbell. Your muscles don't know the difference, so be creative if you don't have access to a gym or a set of weights.

The ability to lift more weight with less effort isn't the only benefit you can get from developing a strength-training program. Here are just a few of the many other benefits you get from building muscle:

- Favorable changes in body composition
- An increase in lean muscle mass and a reduction of body fat percentage
- An increase in bone strength and a decrease in blood pressure
- An increase in your body's resistance to disease (thanks to the fact that strength training helps your body use sugar more efficiently)

In the following sections, I outline three major aspects of a good strength-training program — progressive overload, specificity, and regularity — and give you some tips for how to use each principle as you train for wrestling. (Check out the nearby sidebar for a sample strength-training workout.)

Progressive overload

If you remember only one thing about building muscle through strength training, remember this: To gain strength, you must exercise your muscles at a level beyond the point of strain that they're used to. In other words, you must provide your muscles with a more challenging routine than what they're used to. This concept is called *progressive overload*. By increasing the following, you can incorporate progressive overload into your strength-building workout:

- **Repetitions:** One *repetition* (sometimes referred to as a *rep*) is a single movement. Generally speaking, doing 12 to 15 repetitions develops muscular endurance, and doing 8 to 12 repetitions develops muscular strength.
- **Sets:** A *set* is more than one repetition done without a break. So you may do ten reps three different times (each group of ten reps is a set).

✔ **Resistance:** *Resistance* is the weight being moved. In a push-up, your body weight is the resistance. If you're lifting a 20-pound dumbbell over your head, the dumbbell is the resistance. As you increase the resistance, your muscles force themselves to become stronger over time to handle the extra load.

For details on how to incorporate progressive overload into your strength-training routine, see the sidebar "A walk-through: A sample strength-training workout."

Specificity

Specificity is a fancy word that means two things in wrestling:

✔ **You need to give special attention in your workouts to each of the major muscle groups of the body.** A squat exercise, for example, primarily develops the lower body, so after you do a few squat exercises, you need to perform specific exercises focused on the upper body, such as push-ups and pull-ups.

✔ **You need to design your strength-training workout specially for you.** For example, your workout as a wrestler will be different from the workout of a baseball player, because each sport requires different strength needs. (A baseball player will never have to lift another person off the ground, but you will.)

Regularity

Regularity refers to the number of days per week that you train a group of muscles with resistance. Always give your muscle groups a 48-hour break between workouts so they have enough time to recover and prepare for the next resistance session. On some occasions, you may train on two consecutive days as long as you use different muscle groups each day. To get the most out of your strength-training program, you should do your resistance workout three days per week (Monday, Wednesday, and Friday works well). A three-day-per-week regimen guarantees that you get 48 hours of rest between workouts and prevents you from doing too much, or *overtraining*. If you make efficient use of your time, you should be able to get all the strength training you need in 45 minutes or less for each workout.

Increasing flexibility

Your flexibility is perhaps the most important aspect of becoming a good wrestler, so don't ignore this key component of fitness. When I talk about *flexibility,* I'm referring to the ability of your joints and muscles to move through their full range of motion.

A walk-through: A sample strength-training workout

If you need help getting started with a strength-training workout for wrestling, take a look at the sample three-month-long workout I outline in this sidebar. This workout is ideal for high school wrestlers between the ages of 14 and 17. (If you're beginning strength training at a younger age, talk to your coach and family doctor for safe but effective workout ideas.) Notice that I mix the three strength-training principles of progressive overload, specificity, and regularity into this workout (see the section "Building strength").

✔ **Do exercises that work on different muscle groups.** Select 12 strength-training exercises to include in your workout — seven for the upper body (with one being the bench press) and five for the lower body (with one being the squat). Effective upper-body exercises include bench press, incline press, military press, upright rows, shoulder shrugs, triceps extensions, and arm curls. Good lower-body exercises include leg press, leg curls, leg extensions, lunges, squats, and explosive plyometric jumps. Talk to your coach for advice on how to properly do these exercises.

When you're ready to begin your workout, start with the bench press, followed by the squat, and then alternate between upper- and lower-body exercises until you finish all 12.

✔ **Incorporate progressive overload into your workout.** Perform three sets of 16 repetitions (reps) for each exercise during the first month, three sets of 12 reps during the second month, and three sets of 10 reps during the third month. Start with an amount of resistance with which you can finish all sets and reps. Then increase the weight gradually so that by the third week of training, you can't complete all the reps of the third set on your own. At that point, ask a partner to help you. Eventually (two or three workouts later), you should be able to do all the sets and reps on your own. After you do so, increase the resistance again.

✔ **Practice (and track) your reps regularly.** Follow this plan consistently three days a week for three months. Be sure to record your sets and reps on paper so that you can track your progress. Throughout the three months, you should see progressive strength gains as long as you also pay attention to nutrition and rest (see the section "Focusing on Your Health" for details).

The best way to improve and maintain your flexibility is through a consistent stretching program. In fact, you need to stretch out all the major muscle groups of the body every time you do a workout, whether you're doing a strength-training workout or an endurance workout.

Because muscles are elastic, stretching a warm muscle (one with blood flow) is more beneficial than stretching one that you haven't loosened up yet. So be sure to do your stretching exercises after you do a five- to ten-minute warm-up. You can try two different types of stretching:

- ✔ **Static stretching:** Slowly moving a joint until you feel tension and then holding that position for 15 to 30 seconds is static stretching. Some examples include standing toe touches, standing quadriceps stretches, and seated toe touches (sitting with the legs out and reaching to each toe and then down the middle, all while keeping the back of the knees on the ground).

- ✔ **Dynamic stretching:** Slowly moving through a full range of motion while gradually increasing the reach and speed of the movement in a controlled manner. Some examples include walking as you do toe touches, doing forward single-leg lunges, and running with high knees.

I recommend that you also do a stretching routine after every workout. Take five to ten minutes at the end of your workout to repeat the stretches you used before the workout. Doing so helps reduce soreness and allows your heart rate to return to a normal resting level. Plus, stretching both before and after exercise helps increase flexibility in general.

Making Important Lifestyle Choices

Your *lifestyle* includes all the decisions you make that affect the way you want to live your life. For example, Olympic-class wrestlers maintain a different lifestyle than high school athletes based on their level of commitment, personal goals, and expectations. The choices you make as a wrestler today will determine your success, not only as an athlete, but also as a student and positive member of your community. In fact, the choices you make now (particularly those related to health and fitness) can develop into positive patterns of health for the rest of your life. The sections that follow discuss just a few of the lifestyle choices you may have to make as a wrestler in high school or college (or beyond). Make the right choices now, and your chance for success on the mat increases greatly.

Managing stress

Stress refers to the psychological (mental) and physiological (physical) responses that you have to the people around you and the events that happen to you. Stress can be good and bad. Stress is good when it causes you to focus and release natural pre-match *endorphins* that stimulate your muscles, but it's bad when you let stress prevent you from focusing on the task at hand and reaching your full potential. If you hang out with positive people, avoid disciplinary trouble, and maintain an overall enthusiastic perspective toward people and events, you can avoid the negative results of stress.

Keep these tips in mind for managing stress:

✔ **Plan your schedule every day.** Being aware of the things you know you need to do and the important dates related to those things can help you deal with sudden situations in a more positive way.

✔ **Stay active.** As a wrestler, you'll be plenty busy during the season, but staying active and exercising out of season is equally important. Maintaining an active lifestyle all year long allows you to spread out your training so that you don't have to try to cram everything into one short season.

✔ **Maintain a good diet to stay healthy at all times.** Obesity is a major problem in the United States and is related to high blood pressure and stress, so you must always watch what you put in your body. Check out the section "Eating Healthy Before and After You Exercise" later in this chapter for specific details.

✔ **Develop positive friendships.** The people you hang out with can make a world of difference in the amount of stress you experience on a day-to-day basis. Discuss stressful situations with friends and other people you can trust. Doing so can help you keep a positive outlook on life.

Saying no to drugs

Drugs are nonfood substances that change the body's normal function. Although some drugs, such as prescription and over-the-counter drugs, are legal, you should avoid taking any drug that your doctor hasn't directly prescribed or recommended to you. Illegal drugs, such as marijuana, cocaine, heroin, and anabolic steroids, are especially dangerous because they change the way your brain and body work. For instance, some drugs cause addictions, which force your body to feel as if it needs the drugs.

The following sections describe three drugs that you may be offered at some point in your career as an athlete. All three can have negative consequences in your life. The bottom line: Just say no.

Relying on training, not anabolic steroids, to get stronger

At some point, a friend or teammate may tempt you to take *anabolic steroids* (illegal substances that cause an increased production of *testosterone,* a naturally occurring male hormone in the human body). No matter what your friend or teammate says to get you to take anabolic steroids, say no and walk away. Maintaining a healthy lifestyle is a whole lot more important than winning a game or match.

Steroids are bad news. They're taken orally or injected through a needle into the body to increase muscle growth from the added testosterone. Here are just a few of the major side effects that anabolic steroids can cause:

- Liver tumors and cancer
- High blood pressure
- Uncontrollable trembling
- Severe acne
- Shrinking of the testicles and development of breasts (in men)
- Deepened voice and facial hair growth (in females)
- Hair loss (in men and women)

If you feel the pressure to get bigger, faster, or stronger, make sure you do so with a healthy training program and healthy nutrition because the short-term gain in strength you may get from anabolic steroids is no trade-off for the harm you do to your body and the consequences you'll face when you get caught using these illegal substances.

Keeping your lungs happy by avoiding tobacco

Using and smoking tobacco are poor lifestyle choices. *Tobacco* is a plant whose leaves are dried and used to make cigarettes, cigars, and chewing tobacco, all of which contain a drug called *nicotine*. As soon as nicotine gets into your system, it enters your bloodstream and causes your brain to release harmful chemicals that can cause an addiction that's hard to overcome. Nicotine is highly addictive, which is why people have such a difficult time stopping tobacco use after they start.

Tobacco contains benzene and tar, which cause cancer and greatly reduce your lung capacity. Lung capacity is especially important to wrestlers because poor lung capacity greatly reduces your level of cardiovascular endurance. Some statistics to further show you the detrimental effects of smoking include the following:

- Smoking harms nearly every organ in the body and accounts for one out of every five deaths in the United States.
- Smoking increases your risk of developing heart disease by up to four times. Coronary heart disease is the leading cause of death in the United States.

Reaching your full athletic potential by avoiding alcohol

Drinking alcohol is a poor lifestyle choice that can have countless negative effects on your athletic performance — not to mention consuming alcohol in the United States is illegal until you're 21, and most schools and athletic programs have very strict penalties if you're caught drinking. Is having to sit out half or all of your season worth having a couple of drinks? I didn't think so.

Take a look at these facts on how alcohol use negatively affects athletic performance:

✔ Alcohol causes dehydration, which puts you at risk for muscle cramps, muscle pulls, and muscle strains. Dehydration causes a loss of muscle mass, which results in a lower level of strength and performance. (See the later section "Drinking Water and Staying Hydrated" for more on dehydration.)

✔ Alcohol slows down your reaction time and mental activity for several days after its consumption. It also decreases your hand-eye coordination, which is extremely important in wrestling.

✔ Alcohol increases fat storage and the overall amount of fat in your body at the same time that it decreases muscle recovery and energy levels.

Eating Healthy Before and After You Exercise

What you put in your body determines what your body can do for you. Your body is like a diesel truck. If you put regular gas into its engine, the truck won't work and will eventually shut down completely. Likewise, if you don't put the right type of fuel into your body, it won't do what you want it to do. Giving your body healthy foods for energy and fuel is essential when you play any sport, but it's especially important when you play something as physical as wrestling, which demands repeated bursts of energy over a short amount of time.

In the following sections, I show you how to make good nutrition choices and fuel your body with the right stuff so that you can reach your maximum potential. I start with general nutrition, and then I lay out some specific directions on what to put in your body before, during, and after your practice or match to help you perform well.

Reviewing general nutrition

The food and drinks that you put in your body give it the energy it needs to perform on the mat. Just like lights need electricity, your body needs healthy fuel to function properly. Proper nutrition is especially important for you when you're still growing because of the natural needs your body has even when you're not exercising. But it's important when you exercise, too. During a wrestling workout, you can expect to burn more than 1,000 calories easily, so you definitely have to pay attention to nutrition if you want to be a successful wrestler.

Proper nutrition improves your performance as you compete in matches and practices and as you train off the mat. Specifically, nutrition can help change your body composition (through weight gain or loss) and provide the energy you need to be active and to recover after exercise.

Foods are made up of three main categories: carbohydrates, protein, and fat. I discuss these three nutrients in the following sections. (Water is just as important as food, so I devote a whole section to the topic of hydration later in this chapter.)

Stay away from drinks that advertise instant energy. Most of them have high levels of caffeine and can be dangerous to your body's system because caffeine is a diuretic that puts stress on your kidneys. Other items to keep out of your body include chips, sugared breakfast bars, soda, candy bars, and creamy sauces like Alfredo sauce. Your body processes these high-fat, high-sugar foods at suboptimal rates.

Carbohydrates

Carbohydrates provide your body with the main fuel it needs for your brain and body to function correctly. Your body absorbs all the carbohydrates you eat and breaks them down into *glucose*, or energy as sugar. *Glycogen* is stored carbohydrates or energy in your muscles and liver that your body can use later during practice and exercise.

Some carbohydrates are better for you than others. For example, whole grains are rich in vitamins and give you lots of energy, but white bread is a complex carbohydrate that takes a while for the body to break down. The following good carbohydrates need to be part of your diet every day:

- ✔ Whole grains and wheat products (such as wheat bread, bagels, and oat bread)
- ✔ Fruits and vegetables
- ✔ Lowfat dairy products
- ✔ Multigrain cereals and pastas (such as oatmeal, brown rice, and whole-wheat pasta)

Try to avoid the following not-so-good carbohydrates:

- ✔ White rice
- ✔ Doughnuts or cake
- ✔ White pasta

Protein

Protein is an important part of every wrestler's well-balanced diet. After all, protein builds and repairs muscles, boosts your ability to fight off colds and disease, stimulates the growth of your skeletal system, and helps your blood carry oxygen throughout your body during exercise. As an athlete, you need protein in your body because it serves as a recovery food to help heal muscle tears and encourage muscle growth after exercise.

The following foods are good sources of protein and must be part of your daily diet:

- Lean meats (such as turkey, ham, fish, and tuna)
- Eggs
- Lowfat dairy products (such as milk, cheese, yogurt, and cottage cheese)
- Smoothies and shakes made with whey protein

Fat

Fat is an important energy source in your body. When you're at rest (in other words, when you're sleeping, studying, or just hanging out), your body relies on fat for fuel. Fat also helps cushion your body's organs against damage and helps regulate your body temperature, so you definitely need to get some fat in your diet.

Fats come in two varieties: healthy and unhealthy. Unhealthy fats include saturated fat and trans fat. Healthy fats include monounsaturated fat, polyunsaturated fat, and omega-3 fatty acids, which have been found to decrease the risk of heart disease. Obviously, you want to focus on eating more of the healthier fats, such as the ones found in the following foods:

- Almond butter
- Nuts and seeds
- Avocado and flaxseed
- Salmon and other coldwater fish like tuna and halibut

Stay away from these foods, which consist mostly of unhealthy fats:

- Pasteurized, high-fat dairy products
- Vegetable oils and butter (found in fried foods)
- Red meat and pork

In long-duration *(aerobic)* exercises, such as a 30-minute jog or a long wrestling practice with a steady level of exertion, your body uses both fat and carbohydrates for energy. In short, high-intensity *(anaerobic)* exercises, such as 20 seconds of weight training or a 40-yard sprint, your body's primary source of energy is carbohydrates, not fat.

Eating well before practices and matches

As a wrestler, you need to be aware of when and how much you eat before a practice or match. After all, the last thing you want is to get a major food cramp or bloated feeling while taking an opponent to the mat.

In general, follow these rules for when and how much to eat before each practice or match:

✔ Allow three to five hours for a large meal (650 calories) to digest.

✔ Allow two to three hours for a smaller meal (450 to 500 calories) to digest.

✔ Allow one to two hours for a blended snack, like a smoothie or protein drink (250 to 400 calories), to digest.

What you eat is just as important as how much time you give your body to digest your food before practice or a meet. Keep these tips in mind for what you should eat before practice or a meet. (I provide a sample meal plan for meet days in the nearby sidebar, "A model match-day menu.")

✔ Eat a carbohydrate-rich snack, such as a piece of fruit (about 80 to 120 calories) 60 minutes before you exercise for a sudden energy burst to help improve your performance.

✔ Stay away from fat and fiber because these foods take a long time to digest.

✔ Drink plenty of fluids (namely, water), but stay away from milk.

✔ For your pre-competition meals that you eat more than three hours before the meet, combine carbohydrates and protein, but don't overdo it with the protein. In general, your meal should include 400 to 800 calories, of which 250 to 500 are carbohydrates. For example, you may want to eat a whole-grain bagel with tomato slices and lowfat cheese and one cup of banana slices in vanilla yogurt to get the right combination of carbohydrates and protein.

Use these guidelines to help you decide what to eat for a pre-practice or pre-match meal:

✔ 50 percent: Carbohydrates, such as whole-grain pasta, rice, bread, oatmeal, bagels, potatoes, or corn

✔ 20 percent: Salad and other vegetables

✔ 30 percent: Chicken, fish, or turkey

Nourishing your body during exercise

A wrestling tournament can last an entire day. You probably don't have the time or the appetite to eat full meals during a long day at the gym, so you need to replenish your body through snacks. Follow these guidelines to nourish your body during exercise or between your matches:

- Fill up on carbohydrates and stay away from fats, protein, and fiber.

- Replenish your calories. As a rule, eat 100 to 300 calories for every hour after the first hour of a day at the gym. For example, if your practice lasts three hours, you need to get 200 to 600 calories in your post-practice meals to make up for the calories you lost during practice.

- Drink 12 ounces of water every 15 minutes. (See the later section on hydration for more details.)

- Eat easy-to-digest foods that you know won't have any negative side effects. For example, eat energy bars, fruits, and crackers; avoid foods like breads, pastas, beans, and candy bars.

 If you go out to eat in between matches, head to the local grocery store or sandwich shop and grab a healthy sandwich made on whole-wheat bread. Whether you like turkey, ham, chicken, or salami, a sandwich is a great option when you're looking for a quick bite away from home.

Replenishing nutrients after practice

Your body has a specific time period after an extended workout (whether it's a match or practice) when you need to replenish the nutrients that you lost during the exercise. To replenish and refuel your body, consume plenty of carbohydrates and 16 to 32 ounces of water within the first 45 minutes after the workout because that's when your muscles have the greatest ability to absorb nutrients (see the section on hydration for more specifics on replenishing water). Here are some good options for what you should eat immediately after your workout, or within the first 45 minutes:

- Lowfat chocolate milk (one of nature's best recovery drinks)

- Lowfat yogurt and fruit

- Trail mix with nuts, raisins, and dried fruit (no chocolate)

- Low- or no-sugar cereal (like bran flakes or oat cereal) with milk

A model match-day menu

What you put in your body 48 hours before a match is critical to your success during the six-minute competition. Assume you have a wrestling match at 7:00 p.m. on a school night. Follow this eating schedule to make sure your body is ready to go when the ref blows the whistle:

- **6:15 a.m.:** Wake up after eight to ten hours of sleep.

- **7:00 a.m.:** Eat a healthy breakfast. (Example: 2 eggs, 2 slices of whole-wheat toast, 2 tablespoons of peanut butter, 1 piece of fruit, 1 cup of skim milk, and ½ cup of orange juice.)

- **9:30 a.m.:** Grab a healthy snack before lunch. (Example: 1 piece of fruit and 16 ounces of water.)

- **12:00 p.m.:** Eat a healthy lunch and fill up with plenty of fluids. (Example: One 6-inch turkey sandwich on whole-wheat bread with lettuce and tomato, 1 chocolate chip cookie, 1 cup of skim milk, 1 piece of fruit, and 16 ounces of water.)

- **3:00 p.m.:** Eat a pre-match meal three to four hours before weigh-in, but don't drink as many fluids as you did during lunch. (Example: 1 cup of chicken noodle soup, 1 granola bar, 1 whole-wheat roll, 1 piece of fruit, and 12 ounces of water.)

- **6:00 p.m.:** Go to your weigh-in.

- **6:05 p.m.:** Just after weigh-in, have a light snack. (Example: 1 apple or other piece of fruit and 12 ounces of water.)

- **7:00 p.m.:** Match time!

- **9:00 p.m.:** Eat a post-match meal within an hour after your match. (Example: 1 piece of lean turkey or chicken with vegetables, lowfat yogurt, and 16 ounces of water.)

After a quick replenishing snack, take time to eat a good full meal within the next two hours. When planning your post-practice or post-match meal, be sure to include both carbohydrates and protein. Your body needs the carbohydrates after exercise to replace energy stores and the protein to start repairing the small muscle tears that occurred during training. Use this guide to help you decide what to eat for a post-practice meal:

- 75 percent: Lowfat carbohydrates, such as whole-grain pasta, mixed vegetables, and whole-grain bread or rice

- 25 percent: Protein-rich foods, including lowfat yogurt, skim milk, and lean meats, such as turkey and chicken

Foods like oatmeal, grilled chicken, fruits, vegetables, tuna fish, lowfat yogurt, lowfat milk, and whole-wheat breads and pastas are excellent choices for any regularly scheduled meal (breakfast, lunch, and dinner).

Drinking Water and Staying Hydrated

In the old days, coaches often led two-hour practices without so much as one water break. Thankfully, numerous scientific studies have educated coaches on the value of water and safe training practices. They now know that you need to put the right fluids into your system at the right times to be well prepared for the challenges of a grueling match or workout.

In the following sections, I explain the importance of water in relation to physical exercise and performance, and I give you some tips for refueling your body before, after, and during practice or competition.

Replenishing your body's H_2O

Keeping your body well *hydrated* (that is, keeping your internal water tank full) before, during, and after exercise is a must for all wrestlers. Why? Because your body uses water for every single bodily process it performs without you even knowing what's happening.

Your body can't survive without water. In fact, the average 150-pound man has 10 to 12 gallons of water in his system. In other words, as much as 75 percent of your body weight is water. Although this percentage does fluctuate, it rarely goes below 50 percent. Hence, the blood running through your veins is almost 80 percent water. Now that's a lot of water!

Here are just a few of the things water does for your system that you may not even realize:

✔ Water is the key to life. Humans can survive more than a month without food but only a few days without water.

✔ Water acts as a cleaner in your body by helping your body get rid of *toxins* (harmful bacteria) that it naturally produces.

✔ Water lubricates your joints (knees, elbows, and hips), keeps your skin healthy, and prevents your skin and body systems from drying out.

✔ Water acts as your body's natural air conditioner. Your body balances your internal temperature by losing water in the form of sweat. You have to replace the water you lose.

✔ Water helps your system properly digest the food you eat.

Every athlete's body loses water through sweat at different rates, so keep in mind that your body is unique and may react a little bit differently than those of your teammates. That being said, in general, you lose about four pounds of water in every intense two-hour wrestling workout. That means you're likely to drop 64 ounces of sweat during your workout!

Your body naturally alerts your brain when you've lost too much water by making you feel thirsty. The problem is that by the time your brain signals thirst, you may have already lost 1 percent of your body weight. A 1 percent loss means your heart has to beat an extra three to five times per minute to push the required nutrients out to your muscles and body systems.

A 2 percent loss of body weight through sweat means your body is *dehydrated*. When you become *dehydrated,* your circulation slows down, thickening the blood and straining your heart. Dehydration becomes especially critical when your fluid losses become so great that your body can no longer sweat, causing your body temperature to rise to dangerous levels. Here are some of the early warning signs that you may be dehydrated:

- ✔ Headaches or an overall sick feeling
- ✔ Dizziness, blurred vision, or feelings of being delirious
- ✔ Extreme thirst
- ✔ Fatigue or clumsiness
- ✔ Muscle spasms or muscle cramps

Because your body tells you to replace only two-thirds of the sweat you lose naturally, you need to drink plenty of water before and during exercise — even if you're not thirsty. Doing so can help you stay hydrated and healthy.

Filling up on fluids to stay hydrated

Hydration is the process of replacing fluids or sweat in the body. In the following sections, I offer some guidelines for how many fluids to drink before, during, and after exercise to stay hydrated and healthy throughout your practices and matches. Remember that your body is different from everyone else's, so you may need more or less fluid than what I suggest, depending on how your body reacts.

The easiest way to tell whether you're adequately hydrated is to check the color of your urine and your frequency of urination each day. If your urine is dark, it's concentrated with too much waste and you need to drink more water and eat more foods with high water content (such as yogurt, fruit, and vegetables). If your urine is pale yellow, you're likely in a safe zone and adequately hydrated. If you don't urinate often enough, you may not be getting enough fluids. Talk to your coach or doctor if you're not sure whether you're getting enough fluids on a daily basis.

Fluids before exercise

Aim to drink at least 16 ounces of fluids three to four hours before exercise. If your exercise routine lasts less than 60 minutes, water will give you everything you need, but if your exercise lasts longer than that, you may want to drink a low-calorie sports drink, too. When you hydrate several hours before your match or practice, you have plenty of time to release your extra water before the event starts. Also you allow your body to start exercising when it's in water balance, not when it's lacking fluids due to a previous workout.

Fluids during exercise

One way to prevent excessive dehydration during exercise is to continually refuel your system as you sweat. Remember that you can't just rely on your thirst because your body will tell you to replace only two-thirds of what you actually lose. Instead, drink 10 to 16 ounces of water every 15 minutes (slightly more than your thirst level).

As for what to drink, the ideal beverage during exercise lasting longer than 60 minutes contains sodium, potassium, and carbohydrates for fuel. Look for a sports drink that contains these ingredients. If sports drinks aren't available, for every two hours that you wrestle, eat 120 to 220 calories of carbohydrates and drink 10 to 16 ounces of fluids.

Store shelves are stocked with sports drinks, and every company wants your dollar. Be a smart shopper and don't let fancy marketing techniques distract you. Find a drink that tastes good and includes carbohydrates, sodium, and potassium. Stay away from carbonated drinks and anything with caffeine. Drinks that try to sell you on vitamins, ginseng, herbs, protein, calcium, and other minerals aren't necessary as long as you incorporate plenty of fruits, vegetables, and whole grains into your daily diet (see the earlier section "Eating Healthy Before and After You Exercise" for details).

Fluids after exercise

After you exercise, your goal is simply to fix the fluid imbalance in your body. Weigh yourself before and after your workouts to determine how much water weight typically leaves your body during exercise. As a rule, drink 16 to 20 ounces of water for every pound lost during exercise. Your body may take 24 to 48 hours to completely replace its sweat losses.

After a practice or competition, you can replace your fluids with either water or a high-carbohydrate sports drink. Many athletes prefer sports drinks simply because of flavor, so if water is too bland for you after a workout, just make sure the sports drink you choose contains 50 to 70 grams of carbohydrate per 8 ounces of fluid with either no protein or up to ¼ of the carbohydrate content.

Chapter 6

The Mental Aspect: Wrestling in the Right Mindset

Wrestling is obviously a physical sport. Hence, I dedicate all of Chapter 5 to discussing how to take care of your body. What you may not know is that wrestling is just as much, if not more, a mental sport. You may be better conditioned, more rested, better nourished, and more hydrated than your opponent, but if you're not mentally ready to go and completely focused on the match, she'll beat you every time.

The best thing about wrestling is that it's a one-on-one sport in which you give your best against your opponent. However, doing so is also one of the most difficult aspects of the sport because all eyes are on you when you take to the mat and no one else can help you win the match. Thus, you better be mentally as well as physically prepared.

This chapter helps you strengthen your mental muscles. Here, I give you some tips on how to keep your mental edge during a match and at practice, and I offer some suggestions on how to develop a winning strategy. I also touch on the traits of a good teammate and suggest some things to focus on to become a leader who represents character and sportsmanship.

Mentally Preparing to Wrestle

A standard wrestling match lasts just six minutes. If you stay focused and mentally tough for five minutes and 55 seconds, you'll lose the match in the last 5 seconds. To win, you have to develop a disciplined approach to every second of the match.

In this section, I lay out some tips for how to develop a positive, effective mental approach to practices and matches. Then I dive into goal setting to help you figure out what you really want to get from your time on the mat.

Understanding the difference between practice prep and match prep

Before you can start preparing yourself mentally for wrestling, you need to understand that preparing for practice is different from preparing for match day. During practices, you work hard and focus on improving different moves and techniques. Match day is when you have to execute everything you've worked on. Match day is the toughest day you'll face as a wrestler because it tests how physically and mentally strong you are.

Improving as a wrestler in practice is 90 percent physical and 10 percent mental. All you have to do is show up, listen to your coach, and let your physical conditioning and strength get you through. Match day is just the opposite; being victorious against your opponent is 90 percent mental and only 10 percent physical.

Here are just some of the mental challenges you face on match day and a few tips for how to win the mental game:

- ✔ **Staying calm under pressure:** The spotlight is on you, but don't let that get to you; just focus on your plan of attack and make it happen.

- ✔ **Keeping your mind focused at all times:** You can do so by executing one move at a time. Also try not to worry too much about your opponent; instead, focus on wrestling in your unique style.

- ✔ **Forgetting your mistakes:** Great athletes have a certain level of *amnesia* (memory loss) that allows them to maintain focus only seconds after making a big mistake. If you make a mistake, forget it and move on to what you have to do next to win the match.

- ✔ **Believing in yourself:** Have enough self-confidence to dictate the flow of the match by being the aggressor (that is, the offensive wrestler).

- ✔ **Managing negative thoughts that pop into your mind minutes before the match and controlling your fears:** Take deep breaths and visualize what success looks like.

Just because match day is more mental than practice doesn't mean you can forget the mental aspect during practice. Approach practice with the same intensity with which you approach your matches. Don't wait until match day to really turn it on and only go half speed at practice. After all, having the right mental approach to practice can prepare you for the pressure of the match. A great wrestler wins his match on Saturday because of the intensity and focus he gives in practice Monday through Friday.

Three concepts that can help you develop great practice habits — and therefore great match habits and success — are accountability, coachability, and discipline. If you can understand these three concepts and make them part of your mental approach in practice, you'll be ready to go during the match.

Accountability

Accountability is when you take responsibility for your actions and the things that happen to you. When things don't go well, the accountable athlete looks to herself for what needs to change instead of pointing a finger at others. The following checklist can help you become a more accountable athlete. Notice which behaviors you do already and which ones you need to work harder on.

- ✔ Finish what you start.
- ✔ Be willing to complete physically demanding practices.
- ✔ Ask for help if you don't understand what your coach wants you to do.
- ✔ Pay attention to the details.
- ✔ When you have a list of jobs to do, tackle the hardest ones first.
- ✔ Work just as hard when no one is watching as you do when your coaches are watching.

When you develop accountability first to yourself at practice every day and then to your teammates, you help establish habits of hard work that can develop your team into one that's ready for both matches and practices.

Coachability

Being *coachable* means that you make eye contact when your coach speaks to you and you show gratitude for his coaching. When your coach points out something that he wants you to improve upon (a technique, for example), a coachable athlete simply nods and does her best to listen and put his suggestions in action. To get the most out of practice, you need to listen to your coaches and work hard to learn everything they try to teach you. If you aren't coachable, your teammates will perceive you as having a bad attitude, and that attitude may spread throughout the rest of your team.

Keep these points in mind to help you develop and maintain a high level of coachability:

- ✔ Understand that when a coach corrects you, he's just trying to make you a better wrestler. Don't get upset or take the correction personally.
- ✔ Have the confidence not to feel criticized or singled out when you get coached.
- ✔ Look your coach in the eyes when he talks to you and show that you appreciate his advice.

As an athlete, you should be more concerned if you're not getting coached. The lack of coaching may be a sign from your coach that he thinks you're as good as you're ever going to be. If you feel that you're not getting coached, just take a minute after practice and ask your coach what you need to do to improve or what he perceives are your areas of weakness. This simple question tells your coach that you're focused on getting better.

Discipline

Discipline is a great equalizer. For a wrestler, *discipline* means sticking to your strengths, being committed to doing your best, and wrestling to win even when you face a superior opponent or have to adjust on the fly to a unique circumstance. You need discipline to get yourself pumped up and enthusiastic for every practice and match, and you need it to help you make the right split-second decisions on the mat.

So how do you become a disciplined athlete? Here are a few characteristics you need to develop to improve your discipline as a wrestler:

- **Excellent attention to detail:** Listen to the finer points when you're coached or corrected. Improving the little things can make a big difference, so try to become a master at every aspect of wrestling.

- **Motivation to give your maximum effort all the time:** You must have the drive inside to want to do your best. Only you know how hard you're working, so never cheat yourself.

- **Strength and character to overcome temptations and pressures that are counterproductive to becoming the best wrestler you can be:** Maybe your friends want to stay out late the night before a match or steal a candy bar from the concession stand; you know the difference between right and wrong, so always do what's right.

- **Reliability and trustworthiness:** Be the kind of wrestler that your teammates can depend on and trust in all aspects of life. At the end of the season, you want your teammates to say, "Now there's a wrestler we could trust and count on every day."

- **Consistent respect for authority, the rules of wrestling, officials, your teammates, and yourself:** Be a great example of sportsmanship and the type of athlete who treats others how he wants to be treated regardless of the circumstances.

If you stay in the sport long enough and work hard both physically and mentally at developing the characteristics in the preceding list, you can reach your full potential as a wrestler.

Psyching yourself out: Mental drills

The key with mental training is to convince yourself that you'll be in situations that require you to mentally win before you can go out and win physically. If you're able to maintain mental toughness, you have a chance to find success. But if you fail to prepare yourself mentally, you can't expect to adapt well to difficult circumstances, and thus, you can't expect to find success.

In the following sections, I share three key components of mental training that you should use, practice, and think about frequently. These key components are concentration, confidence, and self-control.

Concentration

Concentration is the ability to mentally focus on the task at hand without getting distracted by things outside of your control. As a wrestler, you need your mental focus to last for six intense minutes per match. In order to develop your concentration, start a couple of pre-contest routines that become consistent for you. For example, you may develop a few positive words that you repeat to yourself before every match, or you may listen to the same song to get you pumped up. Whatever routines you choose to follow, be sure to practice them in the weeks before the match so that you're used to doing them on match day. Going through these routines can help you avoid common wrestling distractions, like those that follow, leading up to the match:

- ✔ **Anxiety or nervousness before a match:** Athletes deal with anxiety in different ways, so try to find a technique that helps you deal with anxiety that negatively affects your performance (deep breathing, music, visualization, and so on).

- ✔ **Fatigue or lack of conditioning:** Be well rested and take care of your health so it doesn't negatively affect your on-the-mat performance.

- ✔ **Your opponent:** Focus on your plan, not what your opponent looks like or says to you.

- ✔ **Parents, fans, coaches, scorekeepers, and referees:** Focus on what *you* need to do and how you need to do it. Don't allow yourself to be distracted by anyone or anything else at a match. Remember that officials are human, so they'll make mistakes, too. Just move on and don't live in the past; it won't help you win.

- ✔ **Your own negative thoughts:** Speak only positive words to yourself as you prepare for the match. Whether you think you can or you think you can't, you're right. So stay positive!

Confidence

Confidence refers to your belief in yourself and your ability to win. When you have confidence, you can be enthusiastic and positive even when things aren't going your way. Confidence in wrestling comes from knowing that you have physically prepared better than your opponent and from feeling good about a few moves that you plan to use during the match.

To improve your confidence, you can use *visualization* to mentally picture every moment of your upcoming match. Visualization can help you remember good performances, good moves, and successful plans that won you matches in the past. Make visualization a part of your pre-match routine by finding a quiet place 30 to 45 minutes before each match. Then close your eyes and see yourself making the first move, executing a takedown, and winning the match before it even begins. You may also want to visualize a few negative scenarios so that you can anticipate how you'll adjust if things don't go your way, but always spend more time visualizing the positive scenarios.

Self-control

Self-control allows you to identify when you feel a certain emotion and to understand the meaning behind it *before* you act on it. You need to be able to maintain control over your emotions and actions in the face of adversity if you want to perform at your best. The two emotions that you want to avoid during a wrestling match (or at least be able to control) are anxiety and anger because they can quickly and easily affect your performance in all the wrong ways.

- ✔ Physical anxiety comes in the form of butterflies in your stomach, sweating, nausea, and the need to visit the restroom. Mental anxiety happens when you worry about the result of the match, fail to concentrate on the task at hand, or allow negative thoughts to enter your mind.

- ✔ Anger can come as the result of any number of situations — you don't like the official's call, you harbor resentment toward your opponent, and so on. The problem with anger is that it can quickly cause you to lose control in a match because your focus moves from the task at hand (to beat your opponent) to the anger you feel. After you lose your concentration on the match, your performance deteriorates and all your confidence goes out the window.

Relaxation can help you maintain self-control. If you're in a situation and begin to feel physical or mental signs of anxiety, take a few minutes to relax before that anxiety affects your performance on the mat. If you have negative thoughts, acknowledge that they're there and quickly replace them with positive ones.

Setting goals

A key part of mentally preparing to wrestle is setting goals. Goals are important because they help you direct your focus and effort. If you don't have goals, figuring out where you're going is tough. Goals give you a roadmap, a reason for your work, and the strength to persevere through tough times.

Many athletes don't set goals because they're either afraid of failing or simply not confident enough to set high standards and expectations. For these reasons, goal setting can be a difficult process, but here I spell out the process in eight steps to help you get started. By using this process, you can create a clear set of well-thought-out goals that you can then use to inspire you throughout this wrestling season and beyond.

1. **Determine your starting position.**

   Be honest with yourself and figure out how good you are at the beginning of the season so that you can see the improvements you make during the year.

2. **Define your purpose.**

   Basically, what do you want to do, what do you want to have, and what do you want to be? Write down why you want to improve in wrestling, and how good you really want to be.

3. **Describe the prize.**

   Identify the reward you'll receive if you meet your goals. Describe the sense of success, accomplishment, confidence, and satisfaction you'll feel after you meet your goals. Try to comprehend what it would feel like to be a conference champ or how it will feel after you get your first pin.

4. **Diagnose the problem.**

   Figure out why you haven't reached your goals in the past. What obstacles were in your way? How can you remove them this time around? Maybe your practice habits, lifestyle habits, or lack of focus have been obstacles to your success in the past. Do your best and remember that if you keep doing things the same way, you'll get the same results. To change the results, remove your obstacles.

   If you're just starting out, skip to Step 5.

5. **Design the plan.**

   Define exactly how you plan to accomplish your goals, including how long you expect the whole process to take and how you will measure success along the way. Anything worthwhile takes a lot of work and a good deal of discipline. Have your coach or a supportive adult help you map out a plan of attack.

6. **Discipline your personality.**

   Review your personal characteristics, behaviors, and patterns to figure out what, if anything, you need to change to better prepare yourself to meet your goals. See the earlier section on discipline for more details. Do what you're supposed to do, when you're supposed to do it, and do it every time; that's another way to define discipline as a wrestler.

7. **Deposit the work.**

   Determine what you're willing to sacrifice to reach your goals. If you're not willing to do what it takes, then reevaluate your goals. Your daily effort and work is like making deposits in the bank. Keep at it, and soon you'll build up a large sum that will be worth something.

8. **Depend on people.**

   Call on your teammates, coaches, friends, and parents for support, feedback, and guidance to help keep you on track. It takes a step in maturity to ask other people to help keep you on track, but you'll find people are happy to help you.

Goal setting doesn't have to be a difficult chore, especially if you follow these steps. Just be sure to write down your responses as you go through the eight steps, and then share them with your supporting staff (coaches, parents, and friends). In the following sections, I answer a few questions you may ask yourself as you set your goals in order to help the process go a bit more smoothly.

How detailed should my goals be?

Make sure that you clearly establish each of your goals but also leave a little wiggle room for adjustment if you don't meet them. In other words, you can certainly state that you want to win all your matches this season, but as soon as you lose a match, that goal is unachievable. Therefore, stating that you want to have X number of takedowns in a match or never get pinned or always score first may make more sense. If you don't meet one of those goals in a match, you can always strive to meet it in your next match.

Should my goals be really challenging or more modest?

For all your performance-related goals (whether they deal with wrestling, school, or something else), set them where you have a 50/50 chance of reaching them. In other words, be realistic, but don't settle for easy goals that you could achieve without much effort. For example, if you're wrestling for the first time, stating that anything less than a winning record is unsatisfactory may not be very realistic. However, if you lost in the league finals last year, saying that you want to win the league finals this year is probably a safe goal for you.

For all your behavior-related goals, take a more aggressive approach. For example, be on time to practice, work hard every day, stay positive, be a good teammate and citizen in school; all of these represent your behaviors that will pay off in the long run. Be a champion all the time both on and off the mat.

Before you set your goals, talk to people close to you who may be able to help you figure out what's realistic and what isn't. Just don't be afraid to challenge yourself to your upper limits, and don't be afraid of being great.

How many goals do I need?

Too many goals can create confusion, but too few goals can make life too easy. Remember that goals are set to help you push yourself to achieve something that's difficult. I recommend that you set two to four goals for performance and two to four for behavior. Number your goals one through four for each category and put them somewhere you'll see them every day without fail. If you make a long list of ten or more goals, you'll have a hard time figuring out what you're really trying to achieve. So figure out what your top four goals are, write them down, and go from there.

Remembering There's No "I" in "Team"

You may think wrestling is strictly an individual sport, but it's not. Wrestling also has team dynamics and team relationships that demand constant attention. If you don't foster these team relationships, developing the leadership skills that most championship wrestlers have will be impossible. In this section, I explain what being a good teammate really means, and I tell you how to take on a leadership role within your team without disregarding the important qualities of a good teammate in the process.

Surveying the qualities of a good teammate

A good teammate makes others around her better through her approach to practice, her coachability (see the earlier section on being coachable), and her concern for the development of each individual on the team. A good teammate recognizes what motivates and sustains the other wrestlers on the team. For example, you may notice a teammate having a rough time emotionally and go over to help her out, or you may notice a certain coaching point that she doesn't quite understand, so you spend a few minutes after practice to help her learn. Doing the little things and fostering relationships can cause others to say, "Hey, she really cares about me and the rest of the team, and she works her tail off, never questioning our coach and always staying upbeat."

Here are the four main qualities that all good teammates must have:

- **Pride:** A great teammate represents both pride and humility (see the next bullet). The best kind of pride a teammate can have is pride in her team. This kind of pride forms a close bond between team members that's tough to beat. Proud individuals have a strong desire to do the best they can for their team and for each other. Pride in the team also allows teammates to celebrate each other's accomplishments instead of becoming jealous or full of envy for other teammates' successes.

- **Humility:** A humble teammate is one who is quick to give credit to others for her own successes. Instead of pointing fingers, humble teammates give praise to fellow teammates, coaches, and parents for their part in helping them succeed. Great teams are made up of humble team members who completely commit to the purposes and values of the team.

- **Integrity:** Teammates who have integrity keep commitments and do what they say they will do. They behave in a manner that's consistent with what the team values and goals are. Teammates with integrity are honest, courageous, and dependable in good times and bad.

- **Selflessness:** Selfless teammates demonstrate a team-first attitude by always putting the team before themselves. True teammates understand that everyone has a role on the team whether it's that of a starter or a back-up player and that no one person's role is any better than another's. Being selfless is all about having the right attitude in matches and in practice. So don't get angry if your coach decides to let another teammate wrestle ahead of you or be first in line; instead, embrace a commitment toward your team and its goals.

Serving your teammates through servant leadership

True teammates work to serve each other every day. *Servant leadership* essentially is a commitment to make others around you better, not just as wrestlers, but as people. It's important to you as a wrestler because it helps establish a team culture that you and all your teammates want to be a part of — an encouraging, teamwork-oriented culture without negativity or jealousy. You can become a servant leader by doing the following as you interact with your teammates:

- **Listen actively.** Listen to your teammates to understand them better, not to come up with a solution or response.

- **Be empathetic.** Put yourself in your teammates' shoes to better understand what they're going through instead of being harsh and critical.

- ✔ **Be self-aware.** Be aware of your own opinions, but keep them to yourself instead of telling your teammates how they should act. Show your teammates how to act by how you act every day instead of by telling them outright.

- ✔ **Maintain a big-picture approach.** Take a big-picture approach to both negative and positive situations so you don't allow them to lead to small day-to-day squabbles. Remain focused on your team's goals and direction.

- ✔ **Focus on the needs of others.** Focus more on the needs of others than on your own wants despite how difficult that may be.

- ✔ **Commit to helping your teammates.** Concentrate on helping your teammates become the best they can be both as wrestlers and as people. If you're deeply committed to the growth of your teammates each and every day, you'll be amazed by the difference you can make.

Being a good teammate on the mat

To be a really great teammate, look for opportunities during practice and on match day to show your teammates how much you support them. The following sections give you some tips for where to start.

During practice

Support your teammates and keep practice energetic by doing the following:

- ✔ **Work hard during partner drills.** Help your partner get better in drills by making sure you both work hard enough to get better. Don't look for opportunities to take a few minutes off or give less than all-out effort. Never let your partner slack off, feel sorry for herself, or work to a level below her potential. You can only get as good as your partner forces you to be, so work each other hard in drills. Giving every partner drill your maximum effort will make your next match a whole lot easier.

- ✔ **Be willing to do a little extra.** Be aware of certain drills that you do well but your partner struggles with and take a few minutes after practice to help explain the drill so that she can improve her skills in that area.

- ✔ **Provide plenty of encouragement.** If you see a teammate having a bad day, go over and give her a few words of encouragement to help her get through the practice. The next time you have a bad day, you'll want someone to come over and lift you up when you need an extra boost.

Practices can be long and exhausting, but if teammates keep the tempo up and stay focused on the coach and the overall goal (see the earlier section for details on goal setting), the time will fly by and practice will be over before you know it. Good teammates feed energy off each other and help make practice fun.

On match day

As I explain earlier in the section "Psyching yourself out: Mental drills," having a consistent routine can help relieve anxiety and increase focus and intensity before a match, so help make sure your teammates have what they need to get motivated and respect their unique pre-match routines. The better you understand your teammates, the better able you'll be to say and do the right things to show them your support. Some teammates want to be alone and quiet up until their match starts, while others want to be lighthearted and laughing. Respect what your teammates need before the match and cheer like crazy for them during the match.

Developing a Winning Strategy

You can't ever go in to a match without a plan of attack. Remember the old statement "failing to plan is planning to fail"? Well, it's true in wrestling. In order to be a mentally strong wrestler with a chance to win, you have to know what you're going to do during the match before it even starts. In the following sections, I walk you through what you can do to plan your own winning strategy, and I introduce you to some common strategies in wrestling.

Eyeing some common strategies

If you're a beginning wrestler, you need to have an understanding of the importance of having a plan for how to defeat your opponent. As you advance with more experience, your plan will become clearer because you'll be able to understand where your strengths are. Common strategies include the following:

- Start aggressive and try to score first.
- Prevent your opponent from taking you down first from the neutral position.
- Attack a certain leg or side of your opponent. This may depend on whether you're stronger with the right arm or the left or whether your grip with one hand is stronger than the other. For example, if you're right handed, you may want to use your right hand to attack your opponent's lower leg instead of your left.
- Set the tempo of the match based on your opponent's conditioning level. Either try to score a fall right away or wear your opponent down.
- Keep your team in mind as you strategize how to approach your match. Set out to earn a certain number of points for your team or to prevent losing by a certain number of points.

Planning your own strategy

When setting a general strategy for your match, you first need to get to know yourself and your opponent as much as you can. Start by identifying your strengths and weaknesses and those of your opponent. Then study your opponent to identify the best opportunities to score points and the ways in which you may be threatened when you make an offensive move. You can win more matches on preparation than you think if you truly devote to watching and getting to know your opponent. Refer to Chapter 11 for specific takedown strategies. In this section, I cover three main categories — strengths, weaknesses, and opportunities — that you need to evaluate as you set up a plan for your next match.

Review strengths, weaknesses, and opportunities for every opponent before the match. If you're wrestling someone for the first time, don't try to be fancy; use your best moves, the ones you can count on regardless of the opponent.

Strengths

Recognize your strengths and the strengths of your opponent. Consider the following factors:

- Physical traits, such as strength, reach, height, and stamina
- Technique strengths, such as the takedowns and other moves you and your opponent use most often and the position you each prefer in the referee's starting position (see Part III for details on specific wrestling moves and starting positions)

Weaknesses

Don't spend all your time thinking about how great you and your opponent are. Every wrestler has flaws, and you need to know yours and be able to figure out your opponent's. Usually, weaknesses are the opposite of strengths, so look at strengths first and then see what weaknesses you and your opponent have. *Remember:* A weakness isn't necessarily a problem unless you don't know what it is.

Opportunities

After you evaluate your and your opponent's strengths and weaknesses, get together with your coach to decide how best to score points and win. Match your best traits with your opponent's worst traits. For example, if your opponent is weak in the neutral position, try to get her in that position as often as possible. If your opponent has slow reaction times and you're really quick, use takedowns that allow you to penetrate and use your quickness.

Winning and Losing Gracefully

As a wrestler, you're undoubtedly a competitor. In fact, you probably chose wrestling because it's a one-on-one test of toughness, technique, effort, desire, and will. But despite your desire and preparation to win every match, you're going to win some and you're going to lose some. I hope you'll win many more than you lose, but regardless of how any one match turns out, you need to be able to learn from your mistakes, bounce back, and be ready for the next match.

In the following sections, I give you some pointers on how to win and lose gracefully, including how to display good sportsmanship and how to learn from every match. As the old coaching line goes, "Successful people aren't the ones who never get knocked down but the ones who never fail to get back up."

Being a good sport

As I'm sure you know, sore losers and overly expressive winners don't represent good sportsmanship, but graceful losers and complimentary winners do. As an athlete, you have a responsibility to display good sportsmanship at all times by respecting the game, your opponent, and the officials through both your verbal and nonverbal communication. To be a good sport at every match, keep the following pointers in mind:

- **Honor your obligations and promises.** If you tell your coach that you promise to work hard, then do it. If you promise to attend all workouts over winter break or on a Saturday, then make sure you're there. From a broader perspective, you've committed to a season of wrestling, so make it through.

- **Maintain self-control both emotionally and physically.** See the earlier section "Psyching yourself out: Mental drills" for details.

- **Accept responsibility for your behaviors and the punishments that may come with them.** If you come late for practice or miss for an unexcused reason, accept the extra conditioning or suspension your coach may dole out.

- **Always be fair when dealing with your teammates, opponents, and the officials.** You know the illegal moves, so don't try to get away with one. In practice, give your best effort to help your teammates get better; it's not fair to them or yourself if you're not trying your best.

- **Play by the rules.** Don't look for ways to get around the rules or slightly change them for your benefit.

- **Focus on being the best wrestler you can be at each match.** In other words, don't try to fill the other roles of coach, official, or fan.

✔ **Keep winning and losing in perspective.** Remember that losing is never fatal and winning is never final; what counts the most is how you play the game.

✔ **Strive to make your team, your community, and your school better by how you act as an athlete both on and off the mat.** Profanity, negative comments, and intimidating acts toward opponents, coaches, fans, or officials reflect poorly on you, your family, your team, and your school or community.

Showing good sportsmanship as a wrestler is easy to do. Just try out these tips the next time you take to the mat:

✔ Shake hands with the official, the opposing coach, and your opponent before and after the match. Use a firm handshake and look them in the eyes.

✔ Thank your coach after the match for all the work she did to help you get ready for the match.

✔ Take no more than five minutes to feel bad or great about your match. Then get back out there and cheer on your team.

✔ Be aware of your body language. Don't throw your hands in the air, slouch your shoulders, or make facial expressions that represent disgust.

Learning from every match

Feeling great and remembering what you did well are easy to do after you win. As long as you repeat what you did well and continue to get better, you'll be on your way to winning your next match. Learning from your losses is a little more difficult but just as, if not even more, important.

Don't look at a loss as the end of the world. See it as a learning experience. If you're having a difficult time learning from your failures, try to change your perspective and see losses in a different way. Here are some tips that can help you do so:

✔ Don't take a loss personally, don't blame yourself, and surely don't blame anyone else. Take responsibility for your mistakes, but focus on getting better next time instead of what you did wrong last time.

✔ Don't think that just because you lost a match, you're finished and you'll never win another one. Sometimes losing a match is the one thing that allows you to see your own flaws and correct them. Keep trying, remain optimistic, and always believe in yourself.

✔ View a loss as an isolated incident and don't let it affect you any more than a win would.

✔ Stay focused on your goals and be realistic. Have high expectations for yourself, but don't panic if you don't meet one of your goals right away. Instead, focus on getting better. For example, if your opponent was simply a better wrestler than you, work harder to be just as good the next time you face her. (See the section "Setting goals" for more details.)

✔ Concentrate on what you did well during the match. Maybe you had a great reversal, or you did a great job combating your opponent's best move. Focus on the positives and always take something good from your match.

✔ Evaluate your approach to find out why you lost the match. Maybe you were too aggressive, or maybe you lost focus for a few seconds. Take a look at your strategy and make some adjustments until you find what works for you (see the section "Developing a Winning Strategy" for details).

✔ Bounce back before your next match and come out hungry for another opportunity to show your best stuff. Don't waste time worrying about the past match; focus on your next one.

Chapter 7

Grappling with the Fundamentals and Basic Movements

*W*hen you hit the wrestling mat for your first match, you have to be prepared to do battle with your opponent — that is, if you want to win. Having a basic understanding of the fundamentals and basic movements in wrestling can help you master the different moves, such as breakdowns, escapes, and attacks, that I explain in Part III. After you have a firm grasp on these fundamentals, you can focus on the fun part — pinning your opponent.

This chapter focuses on the fundamentals and basic movements that can help you get started in wrestling. You'll depend on these fundamentals for the rest of your career, and if you learn them right the first time, you'll have a much easier time mastering the more detailed moves that I explain in Chapters 8 through 12.

Standing Your Ground: The Importance of Stance

Wrestling is an intensely physical sport, and your body is the only piece of equipment you have to use against your opponent. As a result, your *stance* (your body position on the mat) is essential in wrestling. A proper stance is important for both defensive and offensive moves. In fact, many coaches say, "Without a good stance, a wrestler doesn't have a chance."

A good wrestling stance refers to the position of balance, equal weight distribution, strength, relaxation, and focus that allows you to move in all four directions quickly and powerfully. In the following sections, I outline the basic movements involved in a good stance and then take a closer look at how to perform the two main stances in wrestling: the square stance and the staggered stance.

Grasping the parts of a proper stance

Whether you're moving around the entire mat or just a small area, the point of the stance is to keep you in good position. Figure 7-1 shows an example of a strong stance. Don't worry if yours doesn't look like the one in the figure, though, because every wrestler's stance is as unique as the wrestler himself. As long as your stance is strong, it can create plenty of offensive opportunities, as well as good positioning overall to keep you from getting scored on.

Figure 7-1:
A good stance can help you move around the mat.

The two stances that I discuss later in this section — the square stance and the staggered stance — have the same basic fundamentals. The two most important are

- ✔ **Body position:** Understanding your body position is critical to being a successful wrestler. *Position* refers to mat awareness, self-awareness, and your placement on the mat in relation to your opponent. Maintaining good body position involves being aware of your overall position, providing yourself with a defensive barrier, and setting yourself up for offensive moves.

  The term *position* comes up frequently in wrestling. For instance, the *neutral starting position* is the most common starting position (see Chapter 8 for details). The stance you use for the neutral starting position can be either a square stance or a staggered stance. I explain both in the next section, and you'll return to one or both of them often during a match.

- ✔ **Posture:** Good *posture* is the foundation for all wrestling positions and all athletic movements in general. Posture is the body position that gives you the balance you need to be a formidable opponent. Falling off balance in the middle of a match can be the opening your opponent needs to score or take you to your back for the pin. Training your body to move with good posture can help you keep your balance, guard your position, and move quickly and effectively on the mat.

The way coaches teach body position, posture, and stance make wrestling an excellent youth sport. After you develop and master your wrestling stance, you can use it for many other athletic movements and fundamentals. For example, every sport requires balance and spatial awareness whether it be baseball, softball, gymnastics, tennis, golf, basketball, or football.

One of the keys to a good stance is that it must allow you to move out of it and actually wrestle. In the following sections, I break down the basics of the stance used from the neutral (or *up*) position, starting with the toes and working my way up to the head, to provide a clear road map so you can master the stance. Keep in mind the basic fundamentals of body position and posture as you read, and then go to work practicing your stance daily.

Your opponent will do everything possible to take you out of your stance, but as you practice and improve, you'll master drills that can help you maintain good positioning throughout your matches. See Chapter 14 for details on these drills.

Feet

Your feet provide the foundation that allows you to move all over the mat with quickness and efficiency. Keep these guidelines in mind as you position your feet for your stance (refer to Figure 7-1 for an example of what your feet should look like):

✔ **Stand with your feet slightly wider than shoulder-width apart.** This position gives you a strong foundation on which to build the rest of your stance.

✔ **Make sure that your entire foot is in contact with the ground.** Doing so allows you to get maximum traction from your shoes and stay on the ground from your toes to your heels. If you're up on your toes, your opponent can easily push you off balance.

✔ **Turn your feet slightly out at a 45-degree angle.** Most of your power comes from when you step off the inside balls of your feet; if your feet are straight ahead, you miss the chance to use all your power. So by pointing your feet out slightly, you allow yourself to push off straight ahead or move side to side and backward as necessary. Imagine pushing a car up a hill in the snow. You'd point your toes slightly outward to get more power and traction off the insides of your feet. The same is true in wrestling.

Knees

Lower-body flexibility is extremely important in wrestling, especially in terms of maintaining a strong stance. After all, a good stance requires ankle, knee, and hip flexibility. The key to lower-body flexibility is knee strength and position. To set up a good stance, follow these two knee-related guidelines (refer to Figure 7-1 for a visual):

✔ **Bend (flex) your knees.** Bend your knees to a point where your chest is over your knees and your butt extends slightly behind your heels.

✔ **Point your knees in the direction of your toes.** As you do so, both of your key movement joints (ankles and knees) should face the same direction, adding stability to your stance (see the preceding section for more on feet placement).

Whether or not you, as a young athlete, can bend at the knees is one tell-tale sign that coaches look for to determine your overall level of athleticism. Strength training and building your muscle endurance can help increase your lower-body flexibility, but bending at the knees and keeping them flexed during practices and matches are just as important. ***Remember:*** Keep the *Z* in your knees, and you'll be just fine.

Hips

The hips play a major part in connecting your lower half with your upper half; thus, proper hip placement helps tie your stance together. In a good wrestling stance, your hips are slightly turned forward, and your back is slightly curled or hunched (refer to Figure 7-1). Unlike in a linebacker's stance in football, you don't want a flat back that's in a perfectly arched position with the shoulders back; rather, you want your shoulders to be forward with a hunch in the back.

Arms

Your arm position and posture are critical in the stance. After all, 100 percent of the takedowns, counterattacks, and other moves you do in wrestling involve grabbing some part of your opponent's body with your arms and hands. Similarly, your opponent is constantly working to take control of your arms to take you down, so you need to keep your arms out of reach at all times.

In a good stance, you need to hold your arms tightly to and touching the sides of your body (refer to Figure 7-1). Imagine that you have to hold a grape in place between your elbows and your ribs or hips. That's how tight your arms need to be to your body in your stance!

Hands

In wrestling, your hands are your main weapons against your opponent. So naturally, a strong grip will become increasingly important as you mature and grow into a great wrestler. Your hands are equally important now as you focus on stance.

As you set up your stance, cup your hands slightly with the palms facing up toward the ceiling and keep them close to one another and always inside your legs as you move around the mat. Keeping your hands inside the width of your feet helps you keep your center of gravity low and centered. The farther away from your core or belly area you move your hands and other extremities, the greater your chances of becoming off balanced and vulnerable to an attack.

Head

The key to maintaining a good head position in your stance is to always keep your eyes up and on your opponent. Focus on the middle of your opponent and the job at hand — getting your opponent to the mat. Don't get caught watching his hands or feet; if you do, you may be tricked by a move that you can't see.

The square stance

The *square stance* is the easiest stance for beginning wrestlers to master. Primarily a defensive stance, the square stance provides you stability, and stability makes it difficult for your opponent to score points on you or take you to the mat. This low-risk benefit makes the square stance the safest option for new wrestlers. On the flip side, this stance doesn't offer much offensive mobility.

As stances and body position go, the wider your feet (your base), the more stability you have. On the other hand, the wider the base, the more difficult it is to move from side to side. Hence, the best time to use the square stance is when you need a little extra balance. For example, if you're in the neutral position and you expect your opponent to really push hard on you from side to side, you can get into the square stance so that you can withstand the pressure your opponent brings your way. Few wrestlers start in a square stance, but they quickly move to it when they feel they're beginning to lose balance.

To get into the square stance, follow these steps:

1. **Stand with your feet shoulder-width apart.**

2. **Bend your knees until your chest is out over your knees and your forearms can rest on your thighs.**

   Also, be sure to keep your elbows bent and your arms close to your sides so that your opponent can't grab them. See the earlier sections "Knees" and "Arms" for details.

3. **Evenly distribute your weight in your feet, lower your hips, and have a slight hump or arch in your back.**

4. **Place your hands out in front of you, palms facing each other slightly, ready for combat.**

   Remember to keep your hands close together and inside the width of your legs (see the earlier section "Hands" for details).

Figure 7-1 shows an example of the square stance.

To move from the square stance in order to either attack your opponent or counter one of his moves, remember these tips:

- **Use short shuffle steps.** Doing so allows you to circle or move from side to side to keep a wide distance between your legs.

- **Always face your opponent.** Stay square to your opponent with your chest facing his chest. If you can't see your opponent or if he gets to one side of you, he's on the attack. Staying square to your opponent eliminates his chance of attacking anything other than the middle of your body, where you're strongest because that's your center of weight and balance.

The staggered stance

The sooner you master *the staggered stance,* the sooner you can become an effective offensive wrestler. Although the staggered stance is riskier than the square stance in that it gives your opponent easier access to score on you, it also gives you a much better opportunity to attack your opponent.

In the staggered stance, one leg is in front of the other. To determine which of your legs should be in front, try the staggered stance for a few minutes with your left leg in front. Then switch so that your right leg is in front. Most likely, one leg will feel more comfortable in front than the other. Don't continue to mix up which leg is in front. Instead, get to where you're very comfortable with one of your legs out in front all the time.

To incorporate the staggered step when you're on the mat, work through these steps:

1. **Stand with your feet slightly wider than shoulder-width apart.**

2. **Bend your knees so that your chest is over your knees, your butt is slightly past your heels, and your forearms can rest on your thighs.**

   Also, be sure to keep your elbows bent and your arms close to your sides so that your opponent can't get a good grip on them. See the earlier sections "Knees" and "Arms" for details.

3. **Evenly distribute your weight in your feet, lower your hips, and have a slight hump in your back.**

4. **Step one of your feet in front of the other so that your legs are slightly staggered.**

   The leg that you step in front is your *lead leg,* the leg you'll use to step into your opponent. The leg that stays behind is called the *power leg* or *trail leg;* it's the dominant leg in most cases.

5. **Place most of your weight on the front foot.**

   Your trail leg should be slightly behind and to the side of your lead leg with the toe pointed out and slightly away from you.

Figure 7-2 shows an example of the staggered stance.

Figure 7-2:
A staggered stance gives you more mobility but also puts you more at risk.

To move from the staggered stance (which you have to do to attack your opponent or to counter one of his moves), remember these tips:

- ✔ **Always move one foot first and then the other.** Moving both feet at the same time means you're hopping, and you never want to have both feet off the ground. If you do, you lose any chance of being in control.

- ✔ **Take small steps.** To move forward, start by taking a small step with the lead leg. To move backward, start by taking a small step with the trail leg.

- ✔ **When moving from side to side, make sure that your trail leg quickly follows your lead leg so that you can maintain a good, strong base.** When your feet are too far apart, you lose balance and give your opponent an easy opportunity to score against you.

Getting a Move On: The Mechanics of Movement

Movement is an essential part of wrestling. After you get in your stance, movement allows you to move around the mat, force your opponent off balance, and get into position to attack your opponent. Having a firm grasp of the general mechanics of movement can help you perfect your technique in all areas of wrestling. With a good understanding of movement, you're better prepared for practicing drills and competing on the mat.

The following sections discuss three important parts of movement — motion, leverage, and agility — that can help you effectively move around when wrestling and get in position to defeat your opponent. I also discuss the importance of balance when moving around a wrestling mat.

Motion

A successful wrestler is in constant motion. If you've ever watched a boxing match, you know what constant motion looks like. Like a good boxer, a good wrestler moves around his opponent in a circling pattern, constantly moving his hips up and down and waiting for the perfect time to attack.

Skilled wrestlers use motion to defend, attack, and set up moves, as well as to execute those moves. Hence, motion in wrestling isn't limited to circling your opponent; it also includes constantly moving the hands, grabbing the back of your opponent's neck, lightly slapping his head, swatting his arms away from you, and using other techniques that distract an opponent or eliminate defensive obstacles to the takedown. After all, a moving target is tougher to hit than one that's standing still, and wrestlers who are constantly moving tend to force their opponents into body positions that they don't want to be in (and thus earn plenty of points for takedowns; see Chapter 11).

Just make sure you don't sacrifice good stance for speed. Maintaining good body position during movement is more important than speed on the mat because a careful wrestler with great technique will beat a fast but reckless and undisciplined wrestler every time. See the earlier section on stance for details on body position.

When incorporating motion into your wrestling stance, keep these very important points in mind:

- ✔ **Beware of extreme positions that cause you to lose balance.** Extreme positions are those positions that force you to place all your weight on one foot and get off balance. Keep your feet shoulder-width apart and your forearms positioned near the thigh and knee area.

- ✔ **Keep your body compact with a low center of gravity.** *Center of gravity* is basically your center of weight and balance. When you drop your center of weight lower, your opponent has a harder time taking you down. Crouch down with your knees bent to get as low as possible while maintaining the ability to move in all directions.

- ✔ **Always keep at least eight inches of space between your feet.** Never cross your feet in a movement. If your feet cross at any time or if they get too close together, your opponent will easily be able to knock you off balance.

- ✔ **Keep your feet in contact with the ground to maintain a powerful position so that you're ready to take on an attack.** Never let both feet come off the ground at the same time when you're moving around the mat.

- ✔ **Take small steps, except when attacking.** The bigger steps you take, the longer your foot is off the ground, and the longer you have to balance on one foot. Keep your steps small so that your feet stay in contact with the mat (see the preceding bullet).

- ✔ **Keep your elbows tight to your side.** Doing so helps you move in a more compact way on the mat.

Leverage

Leverage is an important concept to understand because of how it can help you as a wrestler. Leverage is what allows or enables the person who is "in control" of the other during a match to have that control. *Leverage position* means that your hands are inside your opponent's hands and that your head is lower than his head. The goals of movement in wrestling are twofold:

✔ To make sure that you don't give up leverage so that your opponent can't control you

✔ To get more leverage so that you can control your opponent

Follow these steps to gain leverage from the neutral position in a wrestling match:

1. **Get your hands inside your opponent's hands or your elbows inside his elbows.**

   Keep your arms as close to your body as possible. Doing so allows you to maintain better balance because your limbs are closer to your chest and, therefore, closer to your midsection. Figure 7-3 shows an example of hand leverage.

2. **Get your head or center of gravity below your opponent's head.**

   Keep your head closer to your midsection than your opponent's head. Doing so gives you more balance and brings you closer to his susceptible body parts (his legs, thighs, ankles, and hips) so that you can possibly move into a takedown; refer to Figure 7-3.

3. **Get into a good strong base with your center of gravity under control.**

   A good base is one from which you can easily move but from which your opponent can't easily move you. Your butt is low, your knees are bent, and your feet are a bit wider than shoulder-width apart. Think of someone next to you trying to push you over by placing his hands on your hips from the side. If you stand tall, your partner will easily be able to make you sway, but if you drop your hips and widen your feet, you'll be much more stable. See Figure 7-3 for an example.

Figure 7-3:
Inside hand
leverage
puts you
at an
advantage.

You can get leverage on your opponent by having better technique, more strength, more agility, or more desire, but the easiest way to get leverage is to get your opponent off balance with movement (see the preceding section for details). Three signs can tell you when you know your opponent has lost balance, thus giving you an opportunity to score. Look for these signs and be ready to attack when you see them:

✔ An opponent is off balance when he raises his head.

✔ An opponent is off balance when he crosses his feet.

✔ An opponent is off balance when he moves his elbows and arms wide and away from his side.

See Chapter 11 for everything you need to know about how to attack an off-balance opponent.

Agility

Agility is an essential element of many sports and activities, but it's especially important in wrestling. After all, successful movement on the mat is a direct result of your agility and ability to quickly change directions. Agility is the effective and quick combination of stopping, changing directions, and going fast again, all while maintaining body control. An agile wrestler develops skills such as balance, special awareness, rhythm, and visual and mental focus. Becoming an agile athlete is a must if you want to be a great wrestler.

The essential movements a wrestler must make on the mat are similar to the movements athletes make in other sports. And like other athletes, you need to practice these movements daily and repeat them again and again. This repetition can allow you to increase your agility and eventually move efficiently on the mat during a match. Here are several other reasons why you want to develop agility:

✔ Agility provides a strong foundation for muscle control and skill development and helps improve your overall athleticism.

✔ Changing directions is a common cause of injury, so understanding and developing your agility can help decrease your risk of injury.

✔ Agility development helps your overall performance in both quick-attacking offensive moves and reactive defensive moves.

Balance

When discussing the basics of movement on a wrestling mat, you can't overlook the importance of balance. Being off balance in wrestling spells trouble. Balance means that you're not easily moved, turned, or pushed off your feet. One of the keys to balance is abdominal, or *core,* strength because it allows you to be solid in your position (see Chapter 14 for some abdominal-strengthening drills).

In the following sections, I describe the two most important tools you have at your disposal in your fight to maintain balance, and I explain how to use them.

Your eyes: Focus on your opponent's hips

Your eyes allow you to see everything that happens on the mat so you can figure out what you need to do in order to attack your opponent. For this reason, you need to keep your eyes focused on the hips or belly button area of your opponent to avoid getting distracted. When his hips move a certain direction, you know you need to react. If you focus on the hips, you'll see your opponent's distraction movements in your peripheral vision, and you won't lose your balance or give him an opportunity to score on you because you got distracted.

To be a successful wrestler, your feet and hands must follow your eyes at all times. To help you make sure they do, work hard to maintain a good base while keeping your elbows tight to your chest. When you want to change directions, let your head be the first body part to move, and let your eyes direct which way your head moves.

Don't get caught looking anywhere but at your opponent's hips. He may try to distract you with false steps, jab steps, hand slaps, arm movements, or any combination of these techniques. His goal is to get you to react to these movements, and the first step you take to react may get you off balance. As soon as you're off balance, your opponent has accomplished his first goal, and he may eventually put you on the mat.

Your feet: Keep your opponent on his toes

A key element to being in a proper stance is having your entire foot on the mat (see the earlier section on stance for details). The bottom of your shoe from the toes to the heel gives you balance and a strong base, so your objective is to get your opponent to have a weaker base by getting him on his heels or toes. After all, an opponent who's on his toes, moving around and reacting to you, is an opponent who's off balance and open for a takedown.

Why is staying on the mat and not getting on your toes so important? To answer this question, consider another one: Why do you wear snowshoes in ice and snow? If you live in a cold climate and have been in the snow on a hike, you know that snowshoes help you get traction on slippery snow and ice because they increase your contact area with the ground. The more surface area you cover on the ground, the more stable you are. Now imagine trying to walk on snow and ice in high heels. Not an easy task, right? The bottom line: Use movement to get your opponent on his toes while you keep your base wide and the soles of your feet on the ground.

Changing Levels

When you're moving on the mat from your stance, one of the most important (yet often-overlooked) moves you have to make is called a *level change*. A level change is when you raise or lower your hips while remaining in a good stance to set up an attack, execute an attack, finish an attack, and counter the moves of your opponent. (Simply speaking, *changing levels* is bobbing up and down in a repeated fashion.) Although mastering this skill takes a good amount of practice, knowing how to change levels properly can help you attack your opponent while staying alert in your stance.

Figure 7-4 shows an example of what changing levels looks like. You start in a good, strong stance in a tie-up position with your opponent and then change your levels to get into position for a takedown. (See the section "Standing Your Ground: The Importance of Stance" for details on proper stance.)

Figure 7-4: From a neutral position (a), use level change to get into position for a takedown (b).

To effectively move on the mat, whether you're taking an opponent down or countering an attack, you have to lower your hips while maintaining a good wrestling stance with good knee alignment and knee bend. For some wrestlers, this skill is difficult to perfect, not because they can't change levels but because they have a hard time keeping a good posture while moving up and down. Although many wrestlers consider lowering or raising their heads to be changing levels, it isn't; changing levels involves moving the hips (not the head) while maintaining a good stance (refer to Figure 7-4).

When changing levels, remember these important points:

- ✔ **Keep your head and eyes up and face your opponent.** Doing so allows you to sense what his reaction will be to your level change and when you should initiate that change.

- ✔ **Bend at the knees, not at the waist.** Doing so helps to ensure that your head stays away from your opponent so that he can't grab the back of your neck for control.

- ✔ **Keep a strong wrestling stance with good balance while lowering your hips.** Doing so helps make sure you don't get off balance during your level change. See the earlier section "Grasping the parts of a proper stance" for details.

When you set up for a takedown, you have to lower or raise your level to get leverage on your opponent. You can set up different moves through changing levels because a change forces your opponent to react by matching that level, and your opponent can become off balance as a result. (Check out my discussion on leverage earlier in this chapter for more details.)

Penetration: The First Step to a Takedown

The *penetration step* is the first offensive move you make into your opponent that puts you in position to score. To score a takedown, you must attack either your opponent's upper body in an upper-body attack or his legs in a low-, mid-, or high-level attack. For most low- and mid-level attacks, you have to use the penetration step to get inside your opponent's defenses and within range to complete the attack. (See Chapter 11 for details on these different attacks.)

The most important aspect of the penetration step is maintaining excellent body position (or stance; see the previous section) throughout the attack. In the penetration step, your hips must be forward and under your upper body to give you a good base of support with which to finish the takedown. The step itself must be deep enough so that your penetrating foot lines up with the middle of your opponent's feet.

You should only take the penetration step when you're close enough to smell your opponent's breath (is that garlic you smell?). Trying to use the step from too far away will put you in a less than effective position and may even lead to a takedown by your opponent.

To take a penetration step, follow these steps:

1. **Start in a strong, balanced, staggered stance in a tie-up position with your opponent, as shown in Figure 7-5.**

   See the section "Standing Your Ground: The Importance of Stance" for details on how to maintain a strong stance.

Figure 7-5:
Strong,
balanced
starting
position.

2. **Change levels by bending at the knees while keeping the head and eyes up (see Figure 7-6).**

   See the section "Changing Levels" for tips on how to change levels successfully.

3. **Step with your lead leg so that it lines up in the middle of your opponent's feet under his hips (see Figure 7-7).**

Make sure you practice this skill many times a day. The penetration step allows you to attack your opponent and stay in a powerful, balanced wrestling position. (Refer to Chapter 14 for a penetration step drill to help you master this technique.)

Figure 7-6:
Bend your
knees to
change
levels.

Figure 7-7:
Step with
your lead
leg into your
opponent.

Back Step: Planning for a Takedown

You may come to a point in a match when time is running out and you need to try one last shot to get the final takedown for the victory. Enter the back step. The *back step* is a fundamental move you can use to gain control of your opponent when you're in a tie-up position. You can use this move in place of other, less dramatic moves, but I show it to you here as a technique you can use to score a takedown.

The objective of the back step is to get your hips under the hips of your opponent to lift him and take him to the mat. The keys to performing this move successfully are getting low and using the momentum of your opponent to take him to the mat.

Here, I show you the back step without a partner to give you a clear picture of what this move entails. To add the back step basic move to your repertoire, follow these steps:

1. **Get control of your opponent's near arm by placing your hands on his forearm in a forearm lock (see Figure 7-8).**

   The forearm lock simply means that you have a firm grip on your opponent's forearm for control.

2. **With control of your opponent, pivot on your left foot and then turn your back into your opponent (see Figure 7-9).**

3. **Drive your right knee down to the mat while maintaining control of your opponent and turn 180 degrees into your opponent.**

   Turning while you change levels allows you to use your hip strength and expose your opponent's shoulders to the mat. Don't take a step that's too wide or narrow; keep four to six inches between your two feet, as shown in Figure 7-10.

   Check out the section "Changing Levels" for details on how to change levels.

Figure 7-8:
Control
your
opponent's
near arm.

Figure 7-9:
Pivot on
your left foot
(a) and turn
your back to
your oppo-
nent (b).

Figure 7-10:
Drive your
knee to the
mat and
maintain
control
of your
opponent.

Back Arch: One Way to Get out of a Pin

The *back arch* is a fundamental wrestling movement that you'll undoubtedly have to use at some point when your shoulders are close to the mat and your opponent is close to pinning you. The back arch is a way to keep your shoulders off the mat when your opponent is on top of you; in other words, it helps you keep yourself from being pinned. Chapter 14 goes over a drill you can use to develop your back-arch skills; in this section, I focus on how to get into this fundamental position.

To get into the back-arch position, find a partner to help you and then follow these steps:

1. **Lie flat on the mat facing the ceiling.**

2. **Have your partner help you climb up onto your head with your belly button facing the ceiling.**

3. **Raise up on your toes while keeping your head on the mat.**

   Figure 7-11 shows you what the back-arch position looks like.

Figure 7-11:
A completed
back arch.

TIP

Make these steps a daily warm-up exercise for you. Get in the back-arch position and extend your hips as high as possible. Doing so can help you develop flexibility and a familiarity with the position. (See Chapter 11 for details on the back-arch throw, a move that takes the basic back-arch position to the next level in a takedown.)

Lifting: Using Your Core Strength and Proper Technique

Several different wrestling moves require you to know how to lift your opponent off the mat. In general, lifting your opponent is a very effective way to get a takedown, but it's not a skill you want to use in your first match. Lifting requires a great deal of lower-body and core strength. In addition, you must master proper technique to avoid injuring yourself or your opponent. In this section, I share some tips with you to help you become more comfortable with lifting an opponent off the ground.

Before you try out the lifting technique, grab a partner and get in a position to the side of your partner with your hands firmly wrapped around his waist. To practice lifting, follow these steps:

1. **Stand with your hips under your shoulders and your head and eyes up as you gain control of your partner.**

   Keep your partner tight to your body with a firm grip and ensure that your hips are under your partner's hips throughout this step (see Figure 7-12).

2. **Pop your hips into your partner to get enough power to lift him off the mat and use your legs to lift him up.**

   Popping your hips means thrusting them forward into the side of your partner. Use your arms to control your opponent, but do the lifting with your legs. Figure 7-13 shows an example of this step from two different angles.

Figure 7-12:
Control your
partner
around
the waist.

Figure 7-13:
Begin to
lift your
partner.

3. **When you get your opponent off the mat, turn his body by using your head, neck pressure, and the grip you have against his body (see Figure 7-14).**

4. **Maintain control of your partner and lower him to the mat (see Figure 7-15).**

   After you start lowering him to the mat, drop to a knee to keep your chest in contact with your opponent.

Throwing or slamming an opponent is illegal. So you have to drop to at least one knee in order to stay in contact with him as you go to the mat. Remember that the overall goal of lifting is the takedown. (See Chapter 11 for details on takedowns.)

Expect a good opponent to wiggle onto his chest to prevent the pin, so you'll likely have to use one of the pinning combination moves from Chapter 12 to end the match.

Figure 7-14:
Turn your partner's body as you lift him up.

Figure 7-15:
Lower your
opponent
down to
the mat.

Part III
Hitting the Mat and Using Your Moves

The 5th Wave   By Rich Tennant

MICHAEL ENTERS HIS FIRST
GECKO-ROMAN STYLE WRESTLING MATCH

©RICHTENNANT

In this part . . .

Wrestling involves lots of moves and techniques, and I show you how to use most of them in this part. I include more than 200 pictures, along with my step-by-step guidance, in order to give you a clear road map for each move you need to know.

I start by showing you the basic starting positions and then move into breakdowns, escapes, and reversals. I finish up with attacks and counterattacks, takedowns, and some of my favorite pinning combinations to help you get your opponent on the mat and secure the pin.

Chapter 8

On Your Mark, Get Set: Starting Positions

. . . .

In This Chapter

▶ Identifying the different starting positions and knowing when to use them

▶ Beginning in the neutral position

▶ Figuring out how to set up in the referee's starting position

. . . .

Ready. Set. Go. In wrestling, every match has three periods of two minutes each (unless, of course, a wrestler completes a pin, at which point that wrestler wins the match). You start each period in a *starting position* (clever name, huh?). To be a successful wrestler, you must understand the basics of the different starting positions you (and your opponent) may have to use. By knowing the strategies and strengths associated with each position, you can become a formidable opponent.

In this chapter, I discuss the three basic starting positions you encounter in a folkstyle wrestling match: neutral position, bottom of the referee's starting position, and top of the referee's starting position. (*Folkstyle* or *scholastic wrestling* is a style of amateur wrestling practiced at the high school and middle school level; see Chapter 2 for more details.) From these three positions, you move into the escapes, breakdowns, reversals, and other moves that I describe throughout the rest of Part III.

For details on what happens during a wrestling match before and after you line up in your starting position, turn to Chapter 4.

Getting Started with Starting Positions

The first period of every match starts in the neutral position. To start the other two periods, you either revisit the neutral position or set up in the bottom or top of the referee's starting position, depending on your (or your opponent's) preference. Here's a quick peek at what these three starting positions look like:

✔ **Neutral position:** In this position, you stand on your feet, face your opponent in the neutral position (which I talk about later in this chapter), and shake her hand. The referee checks to make sure you're positioned correctly and then blows the whistle to start the first period of the wrestling match.

✔ **Bottom of the referee's starting position:** In this position, you have to place both your knees behind the rear starting line on the mat and keep both knees in contact with the mat. You also have to place the palms of your hands on the front starting line with both palms in contact with the mat. Finally, you must face the referee.

✔ **Top of the referee's starting position:** In the top position, you must place one knee on the mat outside your opponent's knee without touching her knee. You can place your other foot or knee behind your opponent's feet; just don't let it touch your opponent. Loosely wrap your arm around your opponent, placing the palm of your hand on your opponent's belly button. Place your head on your opponent's back with either your chin or your ear in contact, but don't apply any pressure in an effort to hurt your opponent. Finally, cup your opponent's elbow with your hand.

Grasping the basics of these three starting positions gives you the foundation you need to dominate your opponent each time the whistle blows. The following sections explain how you determine which starting position to line up in, depending on the type of meet you're competing in, and offer tips for developing a starting strategy based on your strengths as a wrestler. The rest of this chapter delves deeper into the three starting positions.

Understanding the different ways starting positions are determined

The way starting positions are determined depends on the type of wrestling competition you're participating in. The following list breaks down the two types of competition and explains how to determine the starting positions for each one (see Chapter 4 for more details):

✔ **Dual meet:** A *dual wrestling meet* is when only two schools are competing against each other. A dual meet competition has a home team and a visiting team. The color green represents the home team, and red represents the visiting team (each wrestler wears an anklet in her team's color). At the beginning of a dual meet, the referee tosses a disk with a red side and a green side into the air. The toss determines which team gets to choose the starting position for the second period (both teams must start in the neutral position for the first period).

> The team that wins the toss chooses odd or even matches in the dual. If they choose odd, their wrestlers get to choose the starting position for the second period in the odd matches (and vice versa with even matches). If they decide to defer the choice, their opponents get to determine the starting position for the second period and they get to choose the starting position for the third period (see the next section for tips on when to choose and when to defer).

- ✔ **Tournament:** A *wrestling tournament* consists of numerous wrestlers from different schools or clubs competing against each other in their respective weight divisions. In a tournament, the referee tosses the disk after the first period of every match (rather than at the beginning of the meet) to determine which wrestler gets to select the starting position in the second period (or defer the choice until the third period).

For my discussion in this chapter, I assume that you're wrestling in a dual meet.

Knowing your strengths and developing a strategy

Say your team wins the toss and you get to choose whether to pick the starting position for the second period or to defer the choice for the third period. What should you do? This section is here to help you decide.

If you're in a close match, having the choice of starting positions gives you an opportunity to choose your best starting position where you're able to score easily. Each starting position has a host of strengths and weaknesses that depend on your strengths and weaknesses as a wrestler. For example, you may want to start in the neutral position if

- ✔ You're good at completing takedowns. After all, takedowns are worth two points each and you can only complete them from the neutral position. (See Chapter 11 for everything you need to know about takedowns.)
- ✔ You like beginning on level ground with your opponent.

On the other hand, you may prefer to start in the top position if

- ✔ You feel confident that you can pin your opponent. Pinning is easier to do when you're already in a dominating (top) position.
- ✔ You have plenty of strength and endurance to control (or ride) your opponent throughout the period.

Or you may want to start in the bottom position if

✔ You're quick on your feet and good at maintaining your balance and anticipating your opponent's moves. Your opponent will have a hard time maintaining control of you if you're in continuous fast motion.

✔ You're good at performing escapes and reversals. Both moves can earn you valuable points in the heat of a close match.

Finally, you may want to choose to defer your choice until the third period if you anticipate a close match, because doing so allows you to choose your best position in the last period.

Leading with the Neutral Position: It's Not So Neutral

The first starting position you need to know is the *neutral position*. The neutral position is the mandatory starting position for the first period of a wrestling match, but you or your opponent can also select this position for the second or third period of a match. (See the section "Understanding the different ways starting positions are determined" for details on who gets to choose the starting position for each period.)

The neutral position is a good starting position for beginning wrestlers to choose in the second or third period because scoring a takedown to control your opponent is easiest to do from this position. But it can also work in favor of more advanced wrestlers who are more agile and skilled in takedowns. In either case, you can earn two points by taking your opponent down from the neutral position.

In the neutral position, you're facing your opponent and standing on your feet. Follow these steps to start in this position:

1. **Place your preferred foot (lead foot) on your team's line at the center of the mat and face your opponent.**

Which foot you use as your lead foot is entirely up to you. To find out which foot you're more comfortable with as your lead foot, jump up in the air and look at your feet when you land. The one out in front is likely your natural lead foot.

Whether you place your lead foot on the red or green line depends on your team's color (the color of your anklet). Traditionally, the home team is green, and the visiting team is red.

2. **Position your other foot so that it's shoulder-width apart from and parallel or slightly behind your lead foot (see Figure 8-1).**

Figure 8-1:
Place your
lead foot on
the line at
the center
of the mat
and your
other foot
behind your
lead foot.

3. **Bend your knees slightly and position your arms so that they're in front of you and at waist level.**

   In the neutral position, you're in a semi-crouched position with your arms in front of you.

Lining Up in the Referee's Starting Position

Another starting position you need to know is the *referee's starting position*. This position is important because it shows up in almost every folkstyle wrestling match. You and your opponent may choose to start in the referee's starting position for the second and/or third period of your match.

If you decide to start in the referee's starting position, you also have to decide whether you want to be the top or bottom wrestler. (The top position is known as the *offensive starting position,* and the bottom position is known as the *defensive starting position.*) Whether you start on the top or bottom depends on your (and your opponent's) strengths and weaknesses, as well as the score of the match. I discuss how to line up in these positions in the following sections.

Starting on the bottom

If you decide to start on the bottom (or your opponent decides to start on the top), you have the opportunity to earn an extra point for escaping or two extra points for performing a reversal. An *escape* is a wrestling move you use to get out of the defensive position (the bottom) of the referee's starting position, to avoid getting thrown off of your base, and to take control of the situation. A *reversal* is a wrestling move that you use to reverse positions with your opponent; in essence, a reversal allows you to go from being controlled to controlling your opponent. Chapter 9 explains different escape moves you can use. Chapter 10 discusses reversal moves you may want to try.

If you're in the bottom position, you have to be the first to take your position on the mat. In the bottom of the referee's starting position, you're basically on your hands and knees at the center of the mat. To line up in this position, follow these steps:

1. **Place both of your knees on the mat behind the rear starting line and face the referee (see Figure 8-2).**

    The *rear starting line* is the line on the mat farthest from the scorer's table. (The other line is the *front starting line.*)

2. **Position the palms of your hands on the mat in front of the front starting line and bend your elbows so that you don't lock your arms (refer to Figure 8-2).**

    Locking your arms makes you susceptible to injuries. Plus, bending your elbows gives you more power to push off the mat when you attempt an escape (see Chapter 9).

3. **Point your feet back, put your weight into your hips, and sit on your ankles (see Figure 8-3).**

    This step gets you ready to spring up into a stand-up position or move into another escape maneuver (see Chapter 9).

4. **Keep your chin up and look straight ahead (refer to Figure 8-3).**

    Your head generally works like a boat's rudder; keeping it up keeps you from heading straight into the mat.

Figure 8-2:
Place your hands and knees on the mat and face the referee.

Figure 8-3:
Sit back on your ankles, arch your back, and slightly bend your elbows.

Starting on the top

Wrestling is all about control and pinning your opponent. The great thing about the top position is that you're starting with control and it's up to your opponent to regain it.

Starting on top in the referee's starting position gives you the opportunity to break down your opponent and maneuver into a pinning combination. A *breakdown* is a move you can use to get your opponent off of his base and onto his stomach. By using a breakdown, you make it difficult for your opponent to use an escape or reversal on you (see Chapter 9 for details on escapes and Chapter 10 for details on reversals). As a result, a breakdown can ultimately lead to a ride and then a pin. Chapter 9 discusses different breakdown moves you can use.

A *ride* is a maneuver you can use to maintain control when you're in the top of the referee's starting position. It involves pressing your body weight against the back of your opponent while moving from side to side, and it can lead to a pinning combination. A *pinning combination* is a move that turns your opponent onto his back and possibly leads to a pin. (See Chapter 12 for the skinny on pinning combinations.)

In the referee's starting position, lining up on top is more difficult than lining up on bottom because you literally have to position yourself around your opponent. For this reason, you have to be the last to line up on the mat.

In the top position, you get to choose whether you want to line up on your opponent's left or right side. To determine which side to line up on, you need to weigh your opponent's strengths and weaknesses against your own. If you're a beginning wrestler, I recommend that you line up on the side that's most comfortable to you.

In the top of the referee's starting position, you basically cover your opponent with your body. To line up in this position, just follow these steps. In this example, I assume that you're lining up on your opponent's right side.

1. **Give your opponent time and space to set up in the bottom position.**

   Stand outside of the center circle and wait for the referee to tell you to line up in the top position.

2. **Step behind your opponent and place your right knee on the mat outside your opponent's right knee and your left foot or knee behind your opponent's feet (see Figure 8-4).**

Don't touch your knees to your opponent.

Figure 8-4:
Position
your knees
to the side
and behind
your oppo-
nent and
wrap your
arm around
his waist.

3. **Wrap your left arm around your opponent's waist (refer to Figure 8-4).**

   Loosely place the palm of your left hand on your opponent's belly.

4. **Turn your head toward your opponent and place either your ear or your chin on the midline of your opponent's back (see Figure 8-5).**

5. **Cup your opponent's right elbow with your right hand.**

   Make a *C* shape with your right hand and let your thumb grip the inside or outside of your opponent's elbow, whichever is more comfortable.

   You must remain motionless after the referee says, "Set." Don't move until the referee blows his whistle to signal that wrestling can begin. Starting early or in the incorrect position is a technical violation that will cost you points after the first warning (see Chapter 4).

Figure 8-5:
Place your chin on your opponent's back and cup his arm just above the elbow with your hand.

Chapter 9

Breaking Down Breakdowns and Escapes

In This Chapter

▶ Figuring out how to stay on top with breakdowns

▶ Getting out of the bottom position with a few escapes

*E*very wrestling match is a series of starting positions, aggressive moves, and defensive maneuvers. During this chain of events, wrestlers may have to set up in the referee's starting position several times. (***Remember:*** The first period of the match starts in the neutral position, and a toss determines who chooses the starting position for the second and third periods. See Chapters 4 and 8 for more details.)

In the *referee's starting position,* the top wrestler "covers" the bottom wrestler with his body. The bottom wrestler sits on his ankles with his knees on the ground and his toes pointed back; his hands are positioned about ten inches in front of his knees. The majority of his weight rests on his ankles. The person in the top position can choose to line up on the left or right of the opponent. Either way, the top wrestler places one of his knees on the outside of his opponent's knee and places his other knee behind his opponent's feet. He wraps one arm around his opponent's waist with the other hand cupping the opponent's elbow. (Check out Chapter 8 for more in-depth information on the referee's starting position.)

If you're in the top position, your goal is to break down your opponent, get points, and move into a pinning combination for the *fall* (or pin). If you're on the bottom, you need to know how to escape from your opponent to earn points, move into a reversal, and ultimately pin your opponent. Mastering the fundamental moves from both positions is key to becoming a formidable wrestler. After all, to stay one step ahead of your competition, you have to know what maneuvers you need to use and what moves your opponent may use.

In this chapter, I discuss a few basic ways to break down and escape from your opponent. These fundamentals provide a solid foundation on which to build your arsenal of moves and countermoves.

Staying on Top: The Breakdown

A *breakdown* is a wrestling move that you can use when you're on top in the referee's starting position to get your opponent off his base and onto his stomach. By using a breakdown, you make it difficult for your opponent to use an escape or reversal on you. As a result, a breakdown can ultimately lead to a *ride* (a maneuver to keep control in the top position) or a pin.

In this section, I discuss a few of the most common breakdowns, such as the tight waist, far ankle; the cross face, far ankle; the far foot, far knee; and the knee block. If you're in the top position, you can choose any of these breakdowns to use (depending on how comfortable you are with them after practicing). If one doesn't work, you can try another; however, if your opponent has time, he may start an escape by the time you try your second breakdown, at which time breaking him down becomes more difficult. After you successfully break down your opponent, you can try to use a pinning combination to get him on his back (see the later section "Escaping from the Bottom Position" for details on escapes and Chapter 12 for different pinning combinations).

Although you don't gain any points for a breakdown, you need to know which breakdown to use when so that you can keep control after the whistle blows — no matter what your opponent does. If you don't know what to do, your opponent can easily escape, use a reverse move, and possibly pin you!

To be successful, you need to start each breakdown as soon as the referee blows the whistle. If your first attempt at a breakdown doesn't work, just continue to *ride* your opponent (stay on top of him) and set up another breakdown.

Tight waist, far ankle

One of the most common breakdowns among beginning wrestlers is the *tight waist, far ankle,* which you can use when you're on top in the referee's starting position. In this move, you take one arm across your opponent's midsection and use your other arm to control and lift one of his legs, causing him to collapse under his own weight.

To perform the tight waist, far ankle, just follow these steps from the top of the referee's starting position. (I assume that you've lined up on the left side of your opponent; see Figure 9-1.)

1. **Move your left hand from your opponent's elbow so that it's under and across his midsection.**

2. **As you do Step 1, move your right hand from your opponent's navel down and grab his far ankle at the top of his shoelaces.**

   To do Steps 1 and 2 simultaneously, you have to reposition your hands quickly to ensure that you keep the top position (see Figure 9-2).

3. **Lift your opponent's ankle slightly away from his body and up as high as possible.**

   Doing so makes it difficult for your opponent to defend himself.

4. **Move from your knees onto your toes and apply pressure to the center of your opponent's back with your chest to bring him to his stomach.**

   As you apply pressure to your opponent's back, drive him forward with your legs; doing so makes him fall flat on his stomach because his hands can't withstand the weight.

Figure 9-1:
Lining up on the left side for the top of the referee's position.

Cross face, far ankle

The *cross face, far ankle* is similar to the tight waist, far ankle (see the preceding section). However, it involves a maneuver that's slightly more difficult; it requires you to *cross face* your opponent, which means you literally move your arm across your opponent's face.

To perform this move, follow these steps from the top of the referee's starting position. (I assume that you've lined up on the right side of your opponent.)

1. **Move your right hand from your opponent's near elbow across his face and grab his far arm above the elbow (see Figure 9-3).**

2. **As you do Step 1, move your left hand from your opponent's stomach down and grab his far ankle at the top of his shoelaces (refer to Figure 9-3).**

   Steps 1 and 2 allow you to gain control by turning your opponent's head away from you with the cross face and then capturing his opposite arm.

Figure 9-3:
Cross face
your oppo-
nent to gain
control of
his far arm
and grab his
ankle with
your other
hand.

3. **Lift your opponent's ankle slightly away from his body and up as high as possible.**

   Doing so makes it difficult for your opponent to defend himself.

4. **Move from your knees onto your toes and apply pressure to the center of your opponent's back with your chest to bring him to his stomach.**

   As you apply pressure to your opponent's back, drive him forward with your legs; doing so causes him to fall to his stomach because he can't support his weight with his hands.

Far foot, far knee

Another effective move that you can use to break down your opponent is the *far foot, far knee*. As with all breakdowns, its purpose is to gain control of your opponent so that you can transition into a pinning combination.

Follow these steps from the top of the referee's starting position to perform the far foot, far knee. (I assume that you've lined up on the right side of your opponent.)

1. **Move your right hand from your opponent's elbow underneath his body to grasp his left knee (see Figure 9-4).**

    When doing this step, turn your shoulders toward your opponent so that your shoulder touches his hip. Doing so provides you with more power to break him down.

2. **Move your left hand from your opponent's stomach down to grab his far foot (refer to Figure 9-4).**

3. **Pull your opponent's left leg toward you, keeping your shoulder that was touching your opponent's hip underneath his body (see Figure 9-5).**

    This step helps you knock your opponent off balance and makes it difficult for him to defend the breakdown.

4. **Move onto your toes and drive with your legs toward the leg you're controlling (refer to Figure 9-5).**

Figure 9-4:
Reposition your hand from your opponent's elbow to his far knee and grab his far foot with your other hand.

Figure 9-5:
Pull your
opponent's
leg toward
you and
drive him
onto his hip.

Knee block

The *knee block* is a great maneuver to use when your opponent is making it difficult to break him down by keeping a wide base. With this move, you basically tip him off balance by tripping his knee with yours to get him to the mat.

To perform the knee block, just follow these steps from the top of the referee's starting position. (I assume that you've lined up on the left side of your opponent.)

1. **Jab your left knee into your opponent's left knee to get him off balance as you begin to pull him toward you (see Figure 9-6).**

Figure 9-6:
Jab your
knee into
your oppo-
nent's knee
to knock him
off balance.

2. **Pull your opponent's left arm down, driving his left shoulder toward the mat (see Figure 9-7).**

Figure 9-7:
Pull your
opponent's
arm down
toward
the mat.

3. **Maintain control of your opponent's midsection as you start to roll him over your knee and toward the mat (see Figure 9-8).**

4. **Finish the move by bringing your opponent's shoulder into contact with the mat (see Figure 9-9).**

Figure 9-8:
Pull your opponent over your knee.

Figure 9-9:
Finish the move.

Escaping from the Bottom Position

An *escape* is a wrestling move that you can use when you're on the bottom in the referee's starting position to avoid getting thrown off of your base and to take control of the situation.

As the bottom person in the referee's starting position, you're sitting on your ankles with your knees on the mat and your toes pointed back; your hands are positioned about ten inches in front of your knees with the majority of your weight resting on your ankles. When your opponent lines up in the top position, one of his knees lines up with one of your knees and his other knee lines up behind your feet. One of his arms wraps around your trunk with his hand on your stomach, while his other hand cups one of your elbows (refer to Figure 9-1).

Knowing how to escape when you're on the bottom of the referee's starting position is important so that you can evade your opponent's attempts at breaking you down to your stomach. An escape (which earns one point) can lead to a reversal (which earns two points) and possibly move into a pin (see Chapter 10 for more on reversals and Chapter 12 for more on pins).

In this section, I cover a few of the most common wrestling escapes, such as the feet-out stand-up and the switch. Which escape move you choose depends on your comfort and skill level. But no matter which escape move you try first, you must be ready with another one in case your first attempt doesn't work. If your opponent successfully breaks you down to your stomach, don't give up; get back to your base, which is on your hands and knees, and try another escape move.

Feet-out stand-up

The *feet-out stand-up* is a simple and common escape move that takes you from the bottom of the referee's starting position to standing. In the *feet-out stand-up,* you essentially push yourself up against your opponent's chest while gaining wrist control of your opponent to help break his grip.

Follow these steps from the bottom of the referee's starting position to perform the feet-out stand-up. (I assume that your opponent has lined up on your left side; see Figure 9-10.)

1. **Adjust your feet away from your opponent (see Figure 9-11).**

   This movement allows you to push off your feet and into your opponent in order to stand up.

2. **Plant your right foot on the mat to get into a lunge position (with your right foot on the mat and your left knee on the mat); at the same time, push back into your opponent.**

   Which leg you bring up depends on your opponent's positioning. If your opponent is on your left side, plant your right foot on the mat first. If your opponent is on your right side, plant your left foot first.

3. **Use your right hand to grab your opponent's right hand.**

   Keep your elbows tight to your sides so that your opponent can't reach under them to gain control.

4. **Continue to push back into your opponent and use your grip on his wrist to pull yourself up (see Figure 9-12).**

   To keep your balance as you move to your feet, keep your feet staggered with bent knees.

Figure 9-11:
Slide your
feet away
from your
opponent.

Figure 9-12:
Push into
your oppo-
nent and
stand up.

Sit-out

The *sit-out* is a simple and common escape move that takes you from kneeling on the mat in the bottom of the referee's starting position to the sitting position. You can perform it in several ways, many of which turn into reversals (and two points). The *short sit-out,* which is the move I focus on in this section, takes you from kneeling in the bottom of the referee's starting position to sitting in front of your opponent.

To perform the short sit-out, follow these steps from the bottom of the referee's starting position. (I assume that your opponent has lined up on your left side; refer to Figure 9-10.)

1. **Use your right hand to capture your opponent's right hand and put your left hand on the mat, keeping your left arm straight.**

   Keep your right arm tight to your side so that your opponent can't reach underneath it.

2. **As you perform Step 1, use your hips to propel both of your legs out in front of you.**

   Steps 1 and 2 need to happen simultaneously (see Figure 9-13).

Figure 9-13:
Grab your opponent's right hand and propel your legs in front of you.

3. **Secure your center of gravity at your core by aligning your rear under your shoulders as you sit down.**

   During this step, make sure you keep your knees bent and in front of you with your feet set on the mat, as shown in Figure 9-14.

4. **Roll onto your left side by thrusting your right hip upward and pushing off your left knee (see Figure 9-15).**

5. **Escape from your opponent by getting up on your right knee, raising your head off the mat, and pressing it into your opponent's right hip (see Figure 9-16).**

Note: The *long sit-out* is similar to the short sit-out except that you propel your legs out as far as possible.

Figure 9-14:
Secure your
position by
checking
and cor-
recting your
balance.

Figure 9-15:
Roll onto
your side.

Figure 9-16:
Finish the
move.

Sit-back

The *sit-back* is a unique escape because it pushes your opponent back into a sitting position. The goal is to sit on your opponent instead of sitting in front of him.

To perform the sit-back, follow these steps from the bottom of the referee's starting position. (I assume that your opponent has lined up on your left side; refer to Figure 9-10.)

1. **Use your right hand to seize control of your opponent's right hand while rotating your feet slightly away from your opponent (see Figure 9-17).**

   Your opponent's right hand is on your stomach.

2. **Pivot on the toes of your right foot and drive back and into your opponent, opening your upper body to the right (see Figure 9-18).**

Figure 9-17:
Gain
control
of your
opponent's
right hand.

Figure 9-18:
Drive back
and into
your
opponent.

3. **As you continue to drive back, sit on your opponent's lap.**

   Doing this step pushes your opponent onto his rear end.

4. **Pull your opponent's right hand up into your armpit as you lean your right shoulder down toward the mat.**

5. **Get your hips outside your opponent's hips toward his head.**

Switch

The *switch from the referee's position* is an escape move that you can use to get out of the bottom of the referee's starting position. It involves turning into your opponent and driving your arm over his arm and under his leg. The key to the move is the first movement of your hands.

To implement this switch, follow these steps. (I assume that the opponent has lined up on your left side; refer to Figure 9-10 earlier in this chapter.)

1. **Move your left arm across your right arm and post both hands firmly on the mat (see Figure 9-19).**

   This step opens up your hips to sit and helps to clear your opponent's hand from your elbow.

2. **Sit down hard; as you hit the mat, reach your right hand underneath your opponent's right leg (see Figure 9-20).**

3. **Pull on your opponent's left leg with your right hand and drive your left hand up and around his body to completely release yourself from his control (see Figure 9-21).**

Figure 9-19:
Post your
left hand
over your
right hand.

Figure 9-20:
Sit down and reach your hand under your opponent's leg.

Figure 9-21:
Complete the switch escape.

Chapter 10

Reversing Your Fortune: Reversals

*I*n wrestling, you use a *reversal* to turn the tables on your opponent. In other words, you go from being dominated by your opponent to dominating her, from being underneath your opponent to being on top in control. The most common use for this move is when you're on the bottom in the referee's starting position (check out Chapter 8 for details on what the referee's starting position looks like).

Understanding how and when to use reversals can help you gain control and earn points in a wrestling match, not to mention help you feel confident when you're on the bottom in the referee's starting position or any other defensive position. In this chapter, I discuss a few basic reversals you can use in a folkstyle wrestling match whenever you find yourself in the defensive position.

Don't confuse a reversal with an escape. Though they're similar maneuvers, you execute them differently and they have different point values. An *escape* is a move that occurs when the bottom or defensive wrestler (the wrestler on the bottom position in the referee's starting position) escapes to the neutral position; an escape is worth one point. A *reversal,* on the other hand, is worth two points and happens when the bottom wrestler goes from being controlled to controlling her opponent. This chapter walks you through some reversal moves, while Chapter 9 discusses some escape moves.

Understanding Reversals and Their Importance on the Mat

At some point in a wrestling match, you're bound to be in the defensive position, such as the bottom of the referee's starting position (see Chapter 8). To be a successful wrestler, you have to know how to regain control when you're caught on the bottom. You can do so with a reversal. By effectively executing reversals, you can become a well-rounded wrestler who earns points in a variety of situations.

Before you can successfully perform a reversal, you need to grasp a few wrestling fundamentals (which I discuss throughout this chapter as I explain the different reversal moves you can do):

✔ **Hand control:** With *hand control,* you're holding one or both of your opponent's hands with your hands. This fundamental is important in reversals because your opponent's hands are her single greatest weapon. That is, your opponent will either seize control or release control with her hands.

✔ **Good base:** Another important fundamental in reversals is to work from a good base. A *good base* means your body is being supported by your arms and legs; in other words, you're not broken down to your stomach. You can still work on a reversal when you're broken down, but you have to get back to your base before doing so.

Mastering a Basic Wrestling Move: The Hip Heist

The *hip heist* is a fundamental wrestling move that's essential to many wrestling maneuvers, including reversals. The basic premise is to flip your hips and scissor your legs to move your hips from pointing down toward the mat to pointing up toward the ceiling. This movement is powerful and quick, and you can use it from the bottom of the referee's starting position.

In the following example, I assume that your opponent has lined up on your left side in the referee's starting position with you in the bottom position; see Figure 10-1. To perform a hip heist, follow these steps:

1. **From the bottom position, slide both of your feet out to the side away from your opponent (see Figure 10-2).**

2. **Turn your right shoulder and lean into your opponent as you grab your opponent's right hand to release his grip (see Figure 10-3).**

Figure 10-1:
You begin on the bottom in the referee's starting position.

Figure 10-2:
Slide both
feet away
from your
opponent.

Figure 10-3:
Grip your
opponent's
hand to
release his
hold on you.

3. **Force your right elbow back toward your opponent's chin while keeping your left leg underneath your body in a balanced position (see Figure 10-4).**

   If you perform this step effectively, you break your opponent's grip around your waist.

4. **Force your right elbow down toward the mat and finish in a balanced position with both feet on the mat and your navel facing the sky (see Figure 10-5).**

   This step allows you to execute a reversal and free yourself from the control of your opponent.

Figure 10-4:
Turn your body and bring your leg through.

Figure 10-5:
Finish the
move with
your torso
facing up.

Rolling on Top of Your Opponent

A *roll* is a common and effective type of reversal to use when you're in a defensive position. Though wrestlers can use several different types of rolls in a wrestling match, the main premise is the same no matter which one you use. With a roll, you basically roll (go figure!) your opponent over you and maneuver your body so that you end up on top.

Having a few different rolls in your arsenal is important because, if you rely on the same move over and over, you can become too predictable. For the most part, you use rolls from the bottom of the referee's starting position (although you can perform some situation-specific rolls in more advanced wrestling situations; see the next section on Granby rolls for details). In this section, I discuss two common rolls: the side roll and the cross-wrist roll.

Side roll

The *side roll* is an effective reversal maneuver to use if your opponent is on one side and you feel his momentum begin to lean toward the other side.

In the following example, I assume that your opponent has lined up on your left side in the referee's starting position with you in the bottom position; refer to Figure 10-1. To perform an inside roll, just follow these steps:

1. **Grab your opponent's right wrist with your right hand and pull his arm tight across your waist (see Figure 10-6).**

Figure 10-6:
Capture your opponent's right wrist and pull it across your waist.

2. **Pull down on your opponent's arm as you lift your left knee and drive your right elbow toward the mat (see Figure 10-7).**

   Doing so gives you room to drive your right hip toward the mat and use your opponent's momentum to help you start flipping him to the mat. You have to get your right elbow to the mat so that you can eventually flip your opponent.

3. **Roll your opponent over using his momentum and the force of your arms, legs, and hips (see Figure 10-8).**

4. **Reach your left arm between your opponent's legs, grab his right leg, and maintain your hold on his right arm.**

   Wrap your arm around his right leg so that you have his leg in the crook of your elbow and put all your weight on top of his chest as you move toward the pin, as shown in Figure 10-9.

Figure 10-7:
Get your elbow to the mat.

Figure 10-8:
Roll your
opponent to
the mat.

Figure 10-9:
Capture his
right leg and
right arm to
finish the
reversal.

Cross-wrist roll

Another effective reversal roll you need to know is the cross-wrist roll. The *cross-wrist roll* is a bit harder than the side roll because you must reach your hand across your stomach. This move is especially useful if your grip strength is better with one hand than the other.

In the following example, I assume that your opponent has lined up on your left side in the referee's starting position with you in the bottom position; refer to Figure 10-1. Follow these steps to execute the cross-wrist roll:

1. **Grab your opponent's right wrist with your left hand and post your right hand on the mat (see Figure 10-10).**

2. **Drive your hips down and into your opponent as you pull on his right arm; at the same time, use your weight to flip him over and roll him onto the mat.**

   Figure 10-11 shows what this step looks like in the middle of the flip. Figure 10-12 shows what the end of this step looks like.

Figure 10-10:
Capture your opponent's right hand with your left hand.

Figure 10-11:
Flip your
opponent.

Figure 10-12:
Roll your
opponent
onto
the mat.

3. **Reach your left arm between your opponent's legs, grab his right leg, and maintain your hold of his right arm.**

   Wrap your arm around his right leg so that you have his leg in the crook of your elbow and put all your weight on top of his chest as you move toward the pin.

Reversing for More Advanced Wrestlers

This section focuses on a few reversal moves that are for the more advanced wrestler. The *Granby roll* is a powerful reversal technique that requires a great deal of practice and the ability to execute an upper-shoulder roll (see Chapter 14). The Granby reversal from both the bottom of the referee's position (see Chapter 8) and the sit-out (see Chapter 9) is an advanced move that beginning wrestlers shouldn't use because of its detail. In the Granby roll, you roll on the top of your shoulders, making it a very risky move because it reveals your back to the mat. If you don't perform it correctly, your opponent may have an easy time pinning you. The first two sections explain the two ways you can use this move.

Like the Granby roll, the ankle pick from a tripod position is an advanced technique that you should try only if you've been wrestling for a while and you're ready to take your skills to the next level. The last section explains more about the tripod position and tells you when to use this move.

The Granby roll is named after Granby High School in Norfolk, Virginia. Billy Martin, a teacher and wrestling coach at Granby, led the school to 21 state titles and was inducted into the Wrestling Hall of Fame. Martin was the first to use the Granby roll, which is now used by many elite-level wrestlers.

Granby roll from the bottom in the referee's position

The ideal time to use the Granby roll is when your opponent is pulling you toward the side he lined up on because this move requires that you take him the opposite direction that you did in the side roll and the cross-wrist roll (see the previous sections).

In the following example, I assume that your opponent has lined up on your left side in the referee's starting position with you in the bottom position; refer to Figure 10-1. To perform the Granby roll, follow these steps:

1. **Grab your opponent's right wrist with your right hand, post your left arm on the mat, and slide your feet out and away from your opponent (see Figure 10-13).**

2. **Shift your weight into your opponent (to the left) to prepare for your upper-shoulder roll (see Figure 10-14).**

3. **Tuck your head and roll on the top of your shoulders while continuing to grip your opponent's right wrist (see Figure 10-15).**

If you lose your opponent's wrist, you lose control of your opponent.

Figure 10-13:
Post your left arm and move your feet away from your opponent.

Figure 10-14:
Shift your
weight
into your
opponent.

Figure 10-15:
Keep hold
of your
opponent's
wrist as you
roll on top
of your
shoulders.

4. **As you finish your shoulder roll, grab your opponent's right leg (see Figure 10-16).**

   Doing so sets you up for an effective pinning combination (see Chapter 12 for details).

Figure 10-16:
Finish the reversal on the mat.

Granby from a sit-out

The *Granby roll from a sit-out* is a reversal that you can only use when you and your opponent are in a *sit-out position,* in which you're seated with your back to your opponent while he's in a *double underhook* position (with both of his arms under your armpits). Figure 10-17 shows you what this looks like.

Like the Granby roll from the bottom in the referee's position, this is an advanced move that has a high risk of failure (you may get pinned) when done incorrectly. This move also requires you to do an upper-shoulder roll (see Chapter 14), which takes a great deal of practice.

In the following example, I assume that your opponent is behind you in a double underhook position and that you're rolling to your left. Follow these steps to execute a Granby roll reversal from a sit-out:

Figure 10-17:
The sit-out
position
with a
double
underhook.

1. **Use your right hand to capture your opponent's right hand and keep your left arm tight to your side.**

   This step keeps your opponent from being able to reach underneath your arm and allows you to begin an upper-shoulder roll (see Figure 10-18).

2. **Maintain a tight grip on your opponent's wrist and use your hips, legs, and arms to execute an upper-shoulder roll (see Figure 10-19).**

3. **Kick your feet over your head and push with your right hand as you move from your right shoulder to your left (see Figure 10-20).**

   The key is to keep control of his wrist throughout your shoulder roll.

4. **Grab your opponent's right leg as he flips to the mat to finish the reversal.**

   You can then use the right leg and right wrist in a pinning combination (see Chapter 12 for details).

Figure 10-18:
Gain
control
of your
opponent's
wrist to
allow you
the freedom
to roll.

Figure 10-19:
Perform
an upper-
shoulder
roll.

Figure 10-20:
Continue to roll, keeping control of your opponent's wrist.

The ankle pick from a tripod position

The *ankle pick from a tripod position* is one of my favorite reversal moves to use, but it's another one of those moves that only more advanced wrestlers should try. The *tripod position* is when you balance your weight on your two feet and hands (see Figure 10-21 for an example). You may find yourself in this position if you started in the bottom of the referee's position and have elevated your hips off the mat. When your opponent is behind you and in control in the tripod position and his feet come too far forward, use this move to pick up his ankle and take control.

Follow these steps to execute the ankle pick from a tripod position:

1. **From the tripod position, hold your ground and peek back through your legs to see if one of your opponent's ankles is within grabbing distance (see Figure 10-21).**

2. **When one of your opponent's feet comes forward, be ready to grab it (see Figure 10-22).**

3. **Quickly reach back between your legs and grab the back of your opponent's ankle, lifting it off the mat (see Figure 10-23).**

   This step forces your opponent off balance because you're raising one of his stabilizing legs off the mat.

Figure 10-21:
Look back between your legs for one of your opponent's ankles.

Figure 10-22:
Wait for your opponent's foot to come forward.

Figure 10-23:
Grab your
opponent
by the ankle
and lift up.

4. **While continuing to lift your opponent's leg high into the air, move your weight back into your opponent and land on him as he falls to the mat (see Figure 10-24).**

   Keep hold of his ankle when you fall and try to move into a pinning combination (see Chapter 12).

Figure 10-24:
Move your
weight back
into your
opponent as
he falls to
the mat.

Chapter 11

Taking Down Your Opponent: Attacks and Counterattacks

*I*n wrestling, your number one goal is to get your opponent down on the mat. After all, you earn two points when you perform a *takedown* — or take your opponent to the mat and gain top control. Statistics show that the wrestler who scores a takedown first goes on to win the match more than 80 percent of the time. Scoring first also gives you a mental advantage throughout the match. When your opponent knows he's behind, his strategy will likely change (and he'll likely try to wrestle differently than he's used to) and you may be able to take advantage of that change. So as soon as the referee blows the whistle to start the match, think takedown!

In folkstyle wrestling, both wrestlers begin the first period of each match standing and facing each other in the center of the mat in the neutral position (check out Chapter 8 for details on this and other starting positions). In the neutral position, neither wrestler has an advantage, but it's the position from which both attacks and counterattacks happen. Your goal, as soon as the ref blows the whistle, is to take down your opponent with an *attack*. On the flipside, if your opponent makes the first move and tries to take you down, you need to be able to perform a *counterattack* to stop the attack and, at the same time, take your opponent to the mat for a takedown.

By understanding the basic principles of attacks and counterattacks, you set yourself up to score points and win matches. In this chapter, I cover several different attacks and counterattacks to help you get your opponent to the mat. Then I discuss some different strategies to help you decide which moves to use based on your skill set and the situation at hand.

Focusing on the Fundamentals for All Takedowns and Counterattacks

In order to perform a takedown (whether with an attack or a counterattack), you need to have a few basic skills in your arsenal. I cover some of these fundamentals as they relate to wrestling in more detail in Chapter 7. In the following list, I review how these skills are important in relationship to takedowns.

- ✔ **Stance:** In wrestling, your body position (or posture) is called your *stance*. A good stance is important both when you line up in the neutral starting position and when you use an attack or counterattack to take down your opponent. After all, a good stance gives you a feeling of stability.

  What exactly is a *good* stance? A good stance is one that you can react from, one that you can attack from, and one that reduces your risk of being taken down by your opponent.

- ✔ **Motion:** When you're on the mat, you want to be in constant motion for two reasons. First, you want to get your opponent off balance, and second, you want to force him to become susceptible to your takedown. For example, by constantly moving around your opponent to the left or right, you may lead him to leave a leg or arm out close to you for you to take control of, thus setting you up for a perfect takedown.

  Movement is especially critical to effective takedowns and attacks because it allows you to put your opponent or one of his limbs exactly where you want it.

- ✔ **Level changes:** Another key component to your success in takedowns and counterattacks is level change. Similar to the constant movement I describe in the preceding section, *level change* means you move your body up and down to try to get your opponent in a position you can take advantage of. For example, if you're going for a low-level attack, you want to make a fake move with your hands and stand up slightly so that when your opponent rises to what he thinks is an upper-body attack, you can quickly lower and attack him right where you originally planned.

✔ **Penetration step:** The *penetration step* is the first offensive move into your opponent that puts you in position to score. One of the most important aspects of the penetration step is maintaining excellent body position throughout the attack. After you know how to use constant motion and level change to get your opponent where you want him, you can use the penetration step to attack your opponent. The penetration step gets you close enough to your opponent that you can make the first move toward your ultimate goal of taking him down to the mat.

Going for the Ankles with the Low-Level Ankle Pick Attack

Low-level attacks are attacks that aim for your opponent's ankle or lower leg. I show you how to perform one of the most common low-level attacks in this section.

In the *ankle pick,* the objective is to grab your opponent's ankle (hence the name of the attack) to gain control and take him down to the mat. This move is sometimes called the *head and heel* because you have to focus on one of your opponent's feet and grab it at the heel while controlling his head and upper body. This move requires perfect timing, but it's a guaranteed take-down when you do it correctly.

Many takedowns, including the ankle pick, begin when you're in the *tie-up* position. The tie-up position is when you and your opponent come together forehead to forehead from a neutral position. You have a grip with your right hand (or left, depending on which one is more comfortable) behind his neck while your other hand grabs his elbow. Your opponent is in a similar position as he fights for control. In the tie-up position, neither wrestler has control of the other. Figure 11-1 shows what the tie-up position looks like.

To perform the ankle pick from the tie-up position, follow these steps:

1. **Move your opponent in a circle by pressuring the back of his neck, forcing him to follow you (see Figure 11-2).**

   Pull your opponent to the left if your right hand is behind his neck; pull him to the right if your left hand is behind his neck. For the rest of these steps, I assume that your left hand is behind your opponent's neck and that you've pulled him to the right.

Figure 11-1:
The tie-up
position,
in which
neither
wrestler yet
has control.

Figure 11-2:
Pull down
and to the
right on your
opponent's
neck.

2. **With your right hand, quickly grab the back of your opponent's left heel on the outside of his foot (see Figure 11-3).**

   This step helps to get your opponent off balance.

3. **Pull your opponent's ankle up as you push his head down toward the mat; stay close to him as he falls to the mat to keep control and get takedown points.**

   Figure 11-4 shows a successful ankle pick.

Figure 11-3: A front and back view of how you can grab your opponent's heel to get him off balance.

Figure 11-4: A successful ankle pick.

Mastering Mid-Level Attacks

Mid-level attacks are attacks that aim for your opponent's knee area. They're the most commonly used attack in folkstyle wrestling. The knee joint is very important in wrestling because it allows the opponent to maintain balance. After you attack your opponent's knee — and if you gain control of it — your chance for a takedown increases significantly.

You can use mid-level attacks no matter what weight class you're in. They provide you a wide variety of moves and options. The following sections discuss four mid-level attacks you can try. All four moves are effective, but the first two (the spear double-leg and the sweep single-leg takedowns) are true staples of folkstyle wrestling that will account for 50 percent or more of your takedowns.

Most mid-level attacks start from the tie-up position. The tie-up occurs as two wrestlers engage each other after starting in the neutral position. (See Chapter 8 for details on the neutral and other starting positions.)

Spear double-leg takedown

The *double-leg takedown* is one of the most common and widely used techniques in folkstyle wrestling. Although this takedown has many variations, the *spear double-leg takedown* happens when you target both of your opponent's legs around the back of the knee.

To add this takedown to your arsenal, follow these steps:

1. **From the neutral starting position, lower your level to get into position for the takedown (see Figure 11-5).**

   See the earlier section "Focusing on the Fundamentals for All Takedowns and Counterattacks" for details on how to get into position.

2. **Stay low to the ground as you take your penetration step; with both hands, grab your opponent behind the legs just above the knees (see Figure 11-6).**

Figure 11-5:
Change your level to get into position for the takedown.

Figure 11-6:
Take your penetration step to gain control of your opponent's legs.

3. **While on your right knee, pull up on your opponent's legs and spear your forehead and eyebrows directly into his belly button (see Figure 11-7).**

4. **Dropping your left knee close to your right, squeeze your elbows tight to your ribs, drive through your shoulders into your opponent, and take him to the mat (see Figure 11-8).**

Figure 11-7:
Ram your forehead into your opponent's navel.

The force of your contact should force your opponent off balance and onto the mat. Stay in contact with your opponent as he lands on the mat. Doing so prevents him from quickly standing up, getting away, and earning escape or reversal points (see Chapters 9 and 10 for details).

Don't hesitate in driving your shoulders toward your opponent. He's helpless when you have control of both of his legs.

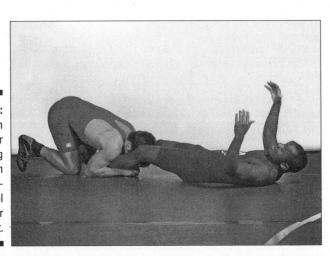

Figure 11-8:
Finish the spear double-leg takedown by maintaining control of your opponent.

Sweep single-leg takedown

The *sweep single-leg takedown* targets your opponent's leg at the knee joint. To perform this takedown, you use a penetration step toward the outside of one of your opponent's feet. (Step toward the foot that's closest to you.) You then grab your opponent's leg, keeping your body on the same side of your opponent as the leg you're attacking. The sweep single-leg takedown is the most common attack in wrestling, in part because it can be very effective if you're quick and aggressive.

Perhaps more important to beginning wrestlers is the fact that the sweep single-leg takedown is such a safe move: You can quickly get away and get back on your feet if something goes wrong or if your opponent counters while you're taking your shot. After you master this takedown, you can use it to score on even the toughest of opponents.

To perform this takedown, follow these easy steps. (Assume that you take your penetration step with your right foot.)

1. **From a tie-up position, lower your level to get into position for the takedown (see Figure 11-9).**

   See the earlier section "Focusing on the Fundamentals for All Takedowns and Counterattacks" for details on how to get into position.

Figure 11-9: From the tie-up position (a), lower your level to set up for the takedown (b).

2. **Take a penetration step with your right foot to the outside of your opponent's left leg.**

3. **Drop to your right knee and wrap your right arm around your opponent's left leg so that your right elbow bend is at the back of his left knee (see Figure 11-10).**

4. **Stand up as you lift your opponent's left leg toward you (see Figure 11-11).**

   Your entire body is on the left side of your opponent in this step.

Figure 11-10:
Take control of your opponent's leg.

Figure 11-11:
Lift your opponent's leg.

5. **Use your right shoulder and the control you have over your opponent's leg to drive him to the mat for a takedown (see Figure 11-12).**

   Wrap your right hand inside your opponent's right thigh to help you get him all the way to the mat.

Figure 11-12:
Use your shoulder to provide force for the takedown.

High crotch

The *high crotch* is when you take a penetration step to attack one of your opponent's legs. What differentiates it from the sweep single-leg takedown is that you use an inside grip anywhere from the back of the knee to the inside of the upper thigh to control your opponent. After you master the high crotch, your opponents will have an extremely tough time defeating you when you're in the neutral position.

To add this takedown to your repertoire, follow these steps:

1. **From a tie-up position, circle your opponent to get his right leg in front of his left (see Figure 11-13).**

   You want to attack the front leg because it's easier to reach and because reaching for the closer leg is less risky to your own balance than reaching for the farther one.

2. **Bend your knees as you lower your hips and pull your opponent's right elbow over your left shoulder to get closer to his right leg (see Figure 11-14).**

Figure 11-13:
Use movement to expose your opponent's right leg.

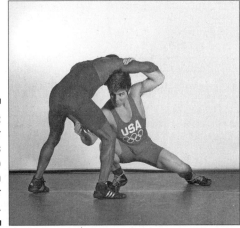

Figure 11-14:
Grab your opponent's elbow to pull him closer to you.

3. **Shoot your right arm between your opponent's legs around the buttocks, pull back on his right knee, and hold it tight to your chest with both arms.**

   If your opponent is caught off balance, he'll fall down right away. If he doesn't, you may need to continue with the fireman's carry, which I explain in the next section.

Fireman's carry

The *fireman's carry* is another mid-level attack that you can use often, especially after you master the high crotch, which I explain in the preceding section. The fireman's carry is an extension or continuation of the high crotch, but unlike the high crotch, the fireman's carry will leave your opponent in a position highly susceptible to a takedown.

Imagine carrying someone on your back across the top of your shoulders. That's the position you're trying to get your opponent into for the fireman's carry. This move is a valuable one for all wrestlers to know because it gives you control of your opponent's arm, which, in turn, gives you the opportunity to score points. Being able to score back points immediately following a takedown is crucial against tougher opponents.

To master this takedown, work through these steps:

1. **From a tie-up position, circle your opponent to get his right leg in front of his left (refer to Figure 11-13).**

   You want to attack the front leg because it's easier to reach and because reaching for the closer leg is less risky to your own balance than reaching for the farther one.

2. **Bend your knees as you lower your hips and pull your opponent's right elbow over your left shoulder to get closer to his right leg (refer to Figure 11-14).**

3. **Turn your body so that the right side of your opponent's torso is against the back of your neck (see Figure 11-15).**

Figure 11-15:
Rotate your
body,
bringing
your
opponent's
torso into
contact with
the back of
your neck.

4. **Pull your opponent's right arm and right thigh to your head (see Figure 11-16).**

   If you complete Steps 3 and 4 successfully, your opponent should end up on your back (hence the name *fireman's carry*).

Figure 11-16:
Pull your
opponent
onto your
back.

5. **Squeezing your opponent's right arm and right thigh to your head, do a somersault, taking him down to the mat (see Figure 11-17).**

Figure 11-17:
Squeeze
your
opponent's
arm and
thigh (a)
and do a
somersault
to bring your
opponent to
the mat (b).

6. **As your opponent hits the mat, maintain control as you sit your hip down on the mat and cover up your opponent for the pin (see Figure 11-18).**

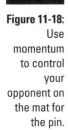

Figure 11-18:
Use
momentum
to control
your
opponent on
the mat for
the pin.

Going with High-Level Attacks

The low- and mid-level attacks I discuss earlier in this chapter are easier to use when you have some space between you and your opponent. If you're closer to your opponent (say, six inches or so), you may need to resort to a *high-level attack,* which is an attack made above the knee. High-level attacks don't require you to drop to a knee, but they do require a very strategic use of your head position on your opponent.

Although many combinations of high-level attacks exist, I focus on two basic ones in this section — the high single-leg takedown and the blast double-leg takedown. As with all takedowns, you need to incorporate good stance, level change, penetration step, and motion into each of these moves (see the earlier section and Chapter 7 for details).

High (snatch) single-leg takedown

With the *high* (or *snatch*) *single-leg takedown,* you basically grab your opponent's leg high on the inner thigh to take control of that leg. Wrestling coaches refer to this common move as both a *high single-leg takedown* and a *snatch single-leg takedown,* so don't get confused if you hear one term and not the other.

The only difference between this move and the mid-level single-leg takedown that I discuss in the previous section is that this move doesn't require you to drop to a knee to attack. The high single-leg takedown is valuable because it's very low risk; after all, you step to the outside of your opponent.

Use this takedown when your opponent is in a staggered stance with one leg out in front of the other. As you attack, go for the leg that's closest to you. (See Chapter 7 for details on stances.)

Work through these steps to master the high single-leg takedown. (Assume that your opponent's left leg is closest to you; thus, it's the one you want to attack.)

1. **From a tie-up position, pull down on your opponent's hands or arms to get him to jolt back and lose balance (see Figure 11-19).**

Figure 11-19:
Pull your opponent's hands down to try to get him to lose balance.

2. **Bend at the knees to lower your head level and grip the inside of your opponent's left leg with your arms (see Figure 11-20).**

Figure 11-20:
Attack your opponent's front leg and gain control.

3. **With your opponent's left leg secured, stand up tall and pull his leg tight to your chest (see Figure 11-21).**

   If you catch your opponent off balance, he'll fall to the mat. If not, you may need to sneak your right foot behind his right heel and trip him to get him to fall to the mat.

Figure 11-21:
Squeeze your opponent's leg tight to your chest.

Blast double-leg takedown

Before you attempt to use the *blast double-leg takedown* in this section, you need to have a firm understanding of the basics of the high single-leg takedown, which I describe in the preceding section. The blast double-leg takedown is similar to the high single-leg version except that you attack both legs. Without dropping to a knee, you use your head to push your opponent back and on his heels. While your opponent is off balance, you use both of your arms to grab the back of his legs behind the knees.

This takedown is very similar to a tackle in American football, in which the defender faces the ball carrier, puts his eyebrows into the ball carrier's chest, grabs behind his legs, and drives him to the ground. The blast double-leg takedown can be a very effective move to catch your opponent off guard. If you practice this technique until you master the timing and explosive power it requires, you'll be well on your way to becoming a takedown machine.

The ideal time to use the blast double-leg takedown is when your opponent is in a square stance (as opposed to a staggered stance) and a step or two slow in reacting to your moves. It's also a great option if you're in better condition than your opponent and can get to his legs quickly.

Follow these steps to work through the blast double-leg takedown:

1. **From a tie-up position with a staggered stance, use motion to try to get your opponent into a parallel stance.**

2. **When your opponent's chest is facing you, lower your head level, grab your opponent's knees, and pick a target on his upper chest (see Figure 11-22).**

   This target is the aim point for your forehead in the next step.

Figure 11-22: Pick a target on your opponent's upper chest.

3. **Put your weight on your back foot, take three steps in a row toward your opponent, and hit your forehead against the target you picked in Step 2 (see Figure 11-23).**

   Pull your opponent's knees toward you as you drive into your opponent.

   Don't use the top of your head for the initial contact. Doing so could cause a concussion or other head injury.

Figure 11-23:
Take three
steps
forward into
your target.

4. **Slide your hands down to the back of your opponent's ankles as you continue to drive into your opponent; let the force of your blast take him to the mat (see Figure 11-24).**

Once your opponent has landed on the mat, finish on top to score another takedown!

Figure 11-24:
Use a
powerful
blast to
force your
opponent to
the mat.

Adding Upper-Body Attacks to Your Arsenal

Upper-body attacks target an opponent's head, arms, shoulders, or hips. They're especially useful when you're in a locked-up position and you and your opponent are holding one another close by the neck or arms. In Greco-Roman wrestling, all moves must be upper-body moves, so Greco-Roman wrestlers have a bit of an advantage when they compete in folkstyle matches.

I discuss two of the most common upper-body attacks — the duck-under and the shrug — in this section. For those of you who are little more advanced, I also cover a slightly more difficult upper-body attack called the back-arch throw. As with all takedowns, good stance, level change, penetration step, and motion are all important factors to remember for each of these moves (see the earlier section and Chapter 7 for details).

Duck-under

The *duck-under* is an upper-body attack in which you duck under the arm of your opponent and pull him to the mat. The penetration step for this move is a rotating step during which you pull the opponent over you. The duck-under starts with a tie-up in which you force the opponent's arm into his body, allowing you to lower your hips and duck your head under his arm.

To master this takedown, practice these steps. (Assume that you're in a tie-up position and your opponent is really pressuring into you.)

1. **Take control of your opponent's upper arms by grabbing the outside of his arms (see Figure 11-25).**

2. **Duck underneath your opponent's right arm while pulling his left arm toward you, keeping your head up and maintaining your balance (see Figure 11-26).**

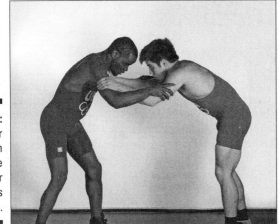

Figure 11-25:
Place your hands on the outside of your opponent's upper arms.

Figure 11-26:
Duck under your opponent's arm and pull him toward you.

3. **Quickly slip to the side of your opponent and try to hook your left arm under his left armpit (see Figure 11-27).**

   Putting your arm under your opponent's armpit is called an *underhook*.

4. **Complete the move by getting completely behind your opponent in a balanced staggered position (see Figure 11-28).**

   Work your right arm into your opponent's right armpit if possible for the *double underhook*.

Figure 11-27:
Quickly
slip to the
side of your
opponent.

Figure 11-28:
Finish
behind your
opponent in
control.

Shrug

A *shrug* is another upper-body takedown you may want to add to your
wrestling arsenal. You can use the shrug when you're in the tie-up position.
You change your body position to force your opponent off balance and to
use his momentum against him. As he pressures into you, find a way to slip
right by him and follow him down to the mat. This option for countering a
head tie-up is very safe and low risk as long as you keep your balance. When
it works, you're likely to gain two points for a takedown.

To perform the shrug, follow these steps:

1. **From a tie-up position, step to the right side of your opponent and reach over his right arm with your left arm (see Figure 11-29).**

Figure 11-29:
Reach over your opponent's right arm (a) as you step to his right side (b).

2. **Slide your left arm around your opponent's torso, point your right ear toward your opponent, and grip the left side of his neck with your right hand (see Figure 11-30).**

Figure 11-30:
Use your hands to gain control.

3. **As your opponent's momentum moves him forward, let him go right past you and get into a balanced position right behind him for control (see Figure 11-31).**

   In this step, you're basically *shrugging* your opponent by you.

Figure 11-31:
Let your
opponent's
momentum
pull him
past you.

If the shrug doesn't work well enough for you to gain control, it should at least enable you to reposition yourself from the tie-up position.

Back-arch throw

The *back-arch throw* is a sudden takedown move that you can use at the end of a match when you need to make a comeback and try something extreme. This move is almost the same as the basic back-arch position, which I explain in Chapter 7, except that you take your hips from the front and put them under the hips of your opponent. You lift his hips with your hips and take him along with you as you get your body into the back-arch position.

To some wrestlers, the back-arch throw may seem like a scary move, but as long as you remember the overall goal — getting your opponent to the mat — you'll be fine. Just make sure to start slow and break the move down into steps before trying it in a match. I suggest that you try the back-arch throw first in a slow-motion walk-through and then progress to a medium-speed move and finally try it at full speed. Only after you've mastered the move at full speed should you try it during a match.

Grab a partner and work on these basic steps to practice the back-arch throw. I assume that you and your partner are standing close together and that both of your partner's arms are under your armpits.

1. **Step between the legs of your partner so that your feet are parallel under your partner's body (see Figure 11-32).**

Figure 11-32:
Starting position for the back-arch throw.

2. **Drop your hips below your opponent's hips by changing levels, squatting down right in front of your opponent, and arching your back (see Figure 11-33).**

See Chapter 7 for details on how to arch your back.

Figure 11-33:
Begin to
arch your
back.

3. **Lift your opponent, flip him upside, and throw him down to the mat (see Figure 11-34).**

Figure 11-34:
Lift your
opponent
and take
him to
the mat.

Answering Your Opponent's Attack with Countermoves

When your opponent attacks you, the first thing you must do is stop his charge or hold on you. Then you can move into your counterattack. Being able to score off your opponent's attack can be a key component to your success. The following sections outline two counterattacks you can use to get a takedown.

Snap down

The *snap down* is an effective way to turn an opponent's attack into points for you. In fact, wrestlers score points with the snap down just as frequently as they do with offensive moves like the ones I describe earlier in this chapter. The best time to use the snap down is when your opponent is leaning into you in an attempt to gain control. This countermove uses your opponent's momentum to your advantage. Work through these steps to master the snap down. (Assume that you and your opponent are starting in the neutral starting position.)

1. **As your opponent moves toward you, lower your level and block the attack with your head and hands (see Figure 11-35).**

Figure 11-35: Block your opponent's attack with your head and hands.

2. **Move your hands to the back of your opponent's neck and powerfully force his head to the mat while you step slightly back and away (see Figure 11-36).**

   You have to step back in this step so your opponent can't grab your leg.

Figure 11-36: Gain control of your opponent with good hand placement.

3. **As your opponent loses balance and falls forward, put your weight on the back of his neck and force him to the mat (see Figure 11-37).**

Figure 11-37: A successful snap down.

Sprawl

While not effective against a high-level attack, the *sprawl* is a very effective countermove to use if your opponent is going for your legs, knees, or ankles. In order to use this move effectively, you must maintain good body posture (that is, keep your knees bent and your hips low).

To perform a sprawl counterattack when your opponent is attacking you low, follow these steps. *Note:* The best way to show you how to do the sprawl is to show you how to do it without an opponent. So the figures for the first step show only me; the last figure shows you how a completed sprawl looks with an opponent on the mat.

1. **As soon as you notice that your opponent is trying to attack your legs, drop one of your hips into your opponent and drive down toward the mat from the neutral position; as you do so, force your legs out behind you to gain balance (see Figure 11-38).**

   Notice that my right hip is dipping low in Figure 11-38.

Figure 11-38: From the neutral position (a), drive down toward the mat, forcing your legs out behind you (b).

2. **Place your hands on or near your opponent's upper back or shoulder area.**

   Doing so forces him to the mat because of his momentum (from trying to aggressively attack your knees). Make sure that you keep your right hip out of reach throughout this step.

3. **After your opponent has hit the mat, stay square to him with all your weight on his back (see Figure 11-39).**

   You have now turned a defensive move into one from which you can gain control.

Figure 11-39:
Stay on top of your opponent, ready to take control.

Strategizing and Planning Your Attack

As I discuss in this chapter, you can use an array of low-level attacks, mid-level attacks, high-level attacks, and upper-body attacks to bring your opponent down from the neutral position, but you certainly can't master them all. In fact, many of the best wrestlers (whether they're competing at the Olympic level, the elementary level, or somewhere in between) work hard to be really good at just one or two takedown moves. So instead of trying to master all the moves I describe in this chapter, focus on becoming confident and comfortable with only a few of them.

The exact moves you use in any given match depend on the experience level of both you and your opponent and on your individual wrestling style. Understanding some of the basic tips that I cover in the following sections can help you set up a game plan for your next match and get you off to a great start at becoming a successful wrestler. Your plan may be to strike first, or it may be to wear down your opponent and use a counterattack. Whatever your plan is, go over it with your coach, go over it in your mind before the match, and then be prepared to use it.

One aspect of being a good wrestler is knowing your opponent. Observe your opponent as much as possible to find possible strengths and weaknesses. In preparing your strategy for a match, use your greatest strengths against your opponent's greatest weaknesses; after all, that's what your opponent is trying to do, too.

Understanding the level of risk

Certain takedowns, when done incorrectly, can quickly backfire, causing you to lose your position, and may even lead to your own takedown. Knowing the risks of different attacks and counterattacks is important so that you can identify which ones to use and which ones to avoid at different times in a match.

Generally speaking, low-level attacks are much riskier than upper-body attacks. In fact, the lower the attack is on your opponent's body (and the closer your head is to the mat), the riskier it is. Why? Because low-level attacks force you to your knees with your head low in order to bring down your opponent. Your opponent may be able to use your low position to his advantage, turning your attack into a counterattack.

In contrast, upper-body attacks and high-level attacks are much safer moves. Your head is higher when you're attacking the upper body or waist area of your opponent, and because of this position, you're less likely to be taken down to the mat if you're unsuccessful in your takedown.

To help you determine which attack makes the most sense in your situation, consider the following:

- **The score of the match:** If the score is close or if you're leading your opponent, use an upper-body or high-level attack. But if you're losing, do whatever you can with your favorite move (regardless of which type of attack it is) to get him down to the mat.

- **The time remaining in the match:** If only a little time is left and you're in the lead, move and change levels constantly to limit your chances of getting into a tie-up position and try not to let your opponent get to your legs.

- **The physical condition of your opponent:** If he looks tired, use lots of movement because he'll likely get sloppy and leave a leg out in front for you to attack low.

- **Your own energy level and previous success:** If you've used a move successfully in the past, go back to it. Be conscious of your own fatigue level, though, and attack only if you have the energy to succeed. If you're tired, try using higher-level moves that are less risky (usually your best ones).

Considering weight class

Your weight impacts which takedown and counterattack moves you attempt. If you're a lightweight wrestler, you may want to try riskier lower-level takedown moves because lighter wrestlers are typically quicker, sleeker, and better able to get into an opponent's ankles or feet than wrestlers in heavier weight classes. On the other hand, if you're in a heavier weight class, you may be more comfortable attacking high because you may be stronger than you are quick.

These weight-related generalizations can work in your favor. For example, if you're in the heavier classes, you can surprise your opponent by using low-level attacks. If you're in the lighter classes, you can surprise your opponent by using high-level or upper-body attacks.

Remembering proximity: How close you are to your opponent

How close you are to your opponent determines whether you use a low-, middle-, or high-level attack:

- ✔ When you're farther away (two feet or more), use a low-level attack.
- ✔ When you're between two feet and about six inches apart, use a mid-level attack.
- ✔ When you're within six inches of your opponent, use a high-level attack.

The penetration step into your opponent that you use for most low-level attacks won't be very effective if you're close to your opponent. The better choice is to use a tie-up to control your opponent's upper body and then use an upper-body attack to gain full control.

Likewise, the farther away you are, the more likely you are to be successful with a lower-level attack. You need space between you and your opponent to take a good penetration step and go low for an ankle or a knee.

Chapter 12

Putting It All Together: Pinning Combinations

*P*inning your opponent is the ultimate goal in every wrestling match. In fact, it's probably the whole reason you decided to don a tight outfit and take to the mat. Of course, winning by points is nothing to turn your nose up at, but winning by a *pin* (also known as a *fall*) — where you get both of your opponent's shoulders or shoulder blades in continuous contact with the mat for two seconds — is one of the most rewarding experiences for every wrestler.

As with most other wrestling moves, being familiar with several different pinning combinations can help you stay one step ahead of your opponent — and eventually force her onto her back. This chapter covers four types of pinning combinations: the half nelson, arm bars, cradles, and leg-pinning combinations.

Introducing the Half Nelson

The *half nelson* is the most common pinning hold you can use. It's an extremely effective way to pin your opponent because you can use it from almost any position as long as you can gain access to the back of your opponent's head. For instance, you can use the half nelson to ride and turn your opponent when he's on his knees, when you're completing a takedown, or when you've just broken him down to his stomach.

The half nelson is just one move in the *nelson series,* which consists of the half nelson, the quarter nelson, and the full nelson. But because the quarter nelson is more of a defensive move (rather than a pinning combination) and the full nelson is illegal in most forms of wrestling, I focus on just the half nelson here. (See the nearby sidebar "Full nelson: The black sheep of the family" for a little history on that move.)

To perform a half nelson from a riding position on top or next to your opponent, follow these steps:

1. **Thread your left arm underneath your opponent's left armpit and put that hand on top of his head, tucking his head down; at the same time, thread your right arm beneath your opponent and grasp his right thigh (see Figure 12-1).**

   As you perform this step, make sure you keep your weight on your opponent's back. Doing so helps you gain control and makes it more difficult for your opponent to fight against the half nelson.

Figure 12-1:
Starting position for the half nelson.

2. **Force your weight over the left side of your opponent, using your control of his left side to force him onto his right side (see Figure 12-2).**

   As you perform this step, stay off your left knee and apply pressure to your opponent's head so that he's forced to look down as you position yourself perpendicular to him.

Figure 12-2:
Force your opponent onto his right side.

3. **Reach underneath your opponent's chest with your right arm as you drive with your chest and legs and move into a chest-to-chest position with him (see Figure 12-3).**

Figure 12-3:
Move into
a chest-
to-chest
position
with your
opponent.

Full nelson: The black sheep of the family

The *full nelson* is another pinning move in the nelson series, but it's illegal in folkstyle, freestyle, and Greco-Roman wrestling because of the strain it puts on the neck of the opponent and the potential it has to cause spinal cord injuries. The only reason I mention it here is to explain what it is so that you can make sure you don't use it.

The full nelson is a hold in which you pass your arms under your opponent's armpits and put both hands on the back of her head. Basically, the full nelson is what you think of when you watch police movies and you see an officer behind the bad guy with the bad guy's hands above his head.

Warning: Don't even think about making this move — ever. Doing so can result in serious injury to your opponent and disqualification for you.

4. **Finish the move by turning your opponent all the way onto his back and completing the pin or earning points for a near fall (see Figure 12-4).**

   A *near fall* is when you have control of your opponent in a pinning situation but you can't quite get his shoulders on the mat. You get two points for holding your opponent near the mat for two seconds and three points for holding him near the mat for five seconds. A near fall is sometimes referred to as *back points.*

   You know you've completed a successful half nelson if you can keep your weight on your opponent's chest by leveraging your body and staying on your toes. Leveraging your body to keep your opponent down increases the possibility of a quick pin because your opponent has a hard time breathing from this position.

Figure 12-4:
Finish the
half nelson.

Mastering the Use of Arm Bars

Many coaches tell their wrestlers never to pass up a bar; in other words, they're encouraging their athletes to stay hyperaware of any chance to use an arm bar. *Arm bars* are effective pinning combinations that you can use to immobilize your opponent by locking his arm behind his back. Arm bars have many options and tricks, but the basic moves are easy to grasp . . . pun intended.

The ideal position to be in before you use an arm bar is on top of your opponent after having broken her down to her stomach when she started in the bottom of the referee's starting position (see Chapter 8 for details on this and other starting positions). The following sections walk you through two different arm bar combinations.

Near-side bar

The *near-side bar* is a valuable pinning combination that you can use to prevent your opponent from moving. With this move, you basically immobilize your opponent by locking one of his arms behind his back. Mastering this technique (along with the double bar in the next section) can make you a dangerous competitor because it allows you to take advantage of your opponent's weak side.

The typical scenario for using the near-side bar is when your opponent attempts to push up from his stomach with his elbows out, leaving him vulnerable from both sides. But you can also use the near-side bar if your opponent maintains a better defensive position and keeps his arms closer to his body as he attempts to push up.

To perform a near-side bar when you're to the side of your opponent, who is lying belly down on the mat, follow these steps:

1. **Use your left arm to pull his left arm up and slide your left hand under his armpit to his back.**

Doing so bars the opponent's left arm above his elbow and clamps it to your chest. The bend of your left elbow should interlock with the bend of his left elbow (see Figure 12-5).

2. **Move your right arm across your opponent's back and pull your opponent's right wrist in to his chest.**

   This step allows you to further immobilize your opponent's arms (refer to Figure 12-5).

Figure 12-5:
Pull your opponent's left arm behind his back and pull his other wrist to his chest.

3. **Apply pressure on your opponent's left shoulder, moving it up to his left ear as you start to move around the front of his head.**

4. **As you move your inside knee to the front of your opponent's head, turn him over (see Figure 12-6).**

   Keeping your head up and your inside knee in front of your opponent's head, arch back into your opponent's back to push his weight up to his shoulders. Doing so allows you to keep your opponent on his shoulders for the pin.

Figure 12-6:
Finish the
move by
turning your
opponent
over for the
pin.

Your ability to keep your opponent's wrist and elbow trapped to your chest is an indicator of success. Doing so also gives the referee a clear view of the pin.

Double bar

The *double bar* is another approach to an arm bar. With the double bar, you essentially move away from the side of your opponent's captured arm to work for the pin. This maneuver is most successful when you're in the top position after you've broken your opponent down and he's on his stomach.

Stick to these steps to perform the double bar:

1. **Trap your opponent's arms by locking both of your elbows through your opponent's elbows, grasping your hands together, and pulling his arms back with your arms.**

   In doing this step, you create a bar with your forearms (see Figure 12-7).

Figure 12-7:
Pull your opponent's arms back and squeeze your elbows together.

2. **Hop onto your toes and rotate over your opponent's head to force all your weight into him; as you do so, roll him onto his back (see Figure 12-8a).**

3. **Rotate your body all the way to your opponent's other side, keeping your elbows tight, and finish the move with your opponent on his shoulders for the pin (refer to Figure 12-8b).**

Keep pressure on your opponent's head with your forearm so that he can't work to his knees or spin out.

Figure 12-8:
Force your
weight into
your oppo-
nent (a) as
you roll him
onto his
back (b).

Rocking Your Opponent to Sleep with a Cradle

The *cradle* is one of the most difficult holds to escape without being pinned, so it's definitely one you want to know how to do. Forget that it's named for its similarity to how one holds a baby. After all, thinking about holding babies certainly won't help you develop the competitive attitude you need to execute this move.

You can use several types of cradles, but, when executed correctly, they all have the same outcome: your opponent on his back with one of your arms under his knee and the other around his head. Knowing how to execute the cradle is essential to your success as a wrestler, but you can't master all the variations at once. So in the following sections, I discuss the two main types of cradles you need to know as you begin wrestling.

Near-side cradle

The *near-side cradle,* also known as the *bow and arrow,* is the most popular cradle move and one that you can easily incorporate into your wrestling arsenal. With this move, you use your head to literally lock in your opponent.

The ideal scenario for utilizing the near-side cradle is either when you've executed a breakdown and your opponent is lying flat on his stomach or when you're on top in the referee's position. (Check out Chapter 8 for details on the referee's position and Chapter 9 for the skinny on breakdowns.) In the example in this section, I assume that you're on top in the referee's position. To perform this move, just follow these steps:

1. **Position your body perpendicular to your opponent's body (on the right side) and place the bend of your right elbow around his neck (see Figure 12-9).**

Figure 12-9:
Position your elbow around your opponent's neck.

A perpendicular position is important because it allows you to grasp your opponent's head and near leg at one time.

2. **Squeeze your opponent's neck, place the bend of your left elbow behind his right knee, and place your forehead into his side (see Figure 12-10).**

Figure 12-10: Squeeze your elbows together and press your forehead into your opponent's rib cage.

Squeeze your elbows together as you place your forehead into your opponent's side. When your opponent bends to relieve pressure, you can grip your hands together so that your arms are locked around his leg and head.

3. **Use your head to bend your opponent's body and roll onto your right elbow to turn his back toward the mat, all the while keeping your grip (see Figure 12-11).**

Drive your head into your opponent, pulling his head and knee together, and lock your hands close to his head to maintain your grip. Locking your hands by grabbing one wrist with the other hand ensures a stronger hold.

Figure 12-11:
Roll onto your side while keeping control of your opponent's neck and right leg.

4. **Continue to roll from your right elbow to your right shoulder and gain control of your opponent's left leg with your left leg to place him in a more uncomfortable position so you can complete the pin (see Figure 12-12).**

Figure 12-12:
Finish the
move for
the pin.

Cross-face cradle

The *cross-face cradle* is a powerful pinning combination that, when mastered, can make you a formidable competitor. With this move, you drive your opponent's face down toward his knee in order to drive him onto his back.

The ideal scenario for utilizing the cross-face cradle is after you've executed a breakdown and your opponent is lying flat on his stomach (see Chapter 9 for more on breakdowns). Just follow these steps:

1. **Position your body so that it's perpendicular to your opponent's body (on his right side) while keeping pressure on the center of your opponent's back with your chest.**

   You want to move from being parallel with your opponent to perpendicular so that you can effectively grab his arm and leg in the next step.

2. **Take your right elbow across his chin and grab his left elbow with your right hand; at the same time, wrap you left arm under his left knee (see Figure 12-13).**

Figure 12-13:
With your
weight
on your
opponent,
grab his
elbow with
your hand
and position
your other
arm under
his knee.

Cross-face your opponent by pressing the inside of your wrist between your opponent's nose and upper lip as you reach for and grab his far arm.

3. **With your chin pressuring your opponent's left shoulder, get complete control of his left leg and lock your hands together (see Figure 12-14).**

Your forearm is still across his face, forcing his chin in toward his chest in an uncomfortable position.

Figure 12-14:
Lock your hands together to bring your opponent into an uncomfortable position.

4. **Place your right elbow on the mat to turn your opponent's shoulders to the mat and move your left leg in between your opponent's legs (see Figure 12-15).**

5. **Roll onto your right shoulder and get control of your opponent's right leg with your left leg, allowing him to slide back down to the mat (see Figure 12-16).**

As you perform this step, continue to drive your opponent's head toward his left knee. Move your feet toward your opponent's head and press your knee right into his side.

Make sure you bury the top of your head into your opponent's temple for the pin, as shown in Figure 12-16.

Figure 12-15:
Begin to turn your opponent's shoulders to the mat.

Figure 12-16:
Finish the move by rolling to your right shoulder and gaining control of your opponent's left leg.

Relying on Your Legs: Leg-Pinning Combinations

As you develop as a wrestler, you may want to rely more on your lower body to help with pinning combinations because you can control more of your opponent by using your legs. After all, your legs are more than twice as strong as your arms because the muscles are so much bigger and longer in your lower body than they are in your upper body. Not to mention, your opponent will try to do anything he can to get out from under you after you break him down, so he will undoubtedly try to use his legs to get out of the mess you've created with the breakdown. If you can use your legs to control his, you'll be much more likely to complete the pin.

In both of the leg-pinning combinations I cover here, you're on your opponent in top control. The difference is that in the leg scizzors, your belly is on your opponent's belly, and in the turk, your belly is on your opponent's back.

Note: The leg-pinning combinations that I describe in the following sections don't lead to pins on their own. But you can use them in combination with any of the other pinning combinations I cover in the previous sections.

Leg scizzors

You can use the *leg scizzors* pinning combination after you've broken down your opponent from the bottom of the referee's position and you're on top of his back with his belly on the mat. (See Chapter 8 for details on the referee's position and Chapter 9 for the lowdown on breakdowns.)

Follow these simple steps to execute the leg scizzors successfully:

1. **Push all your weight into the center of your opponent as you wrap the bend of your left knee around your opponent's left knee just above his knee joint.**

   In other words, lock your leg around his.

2. **Place the top of your left foot on your right calf and lift your legs toward your butt.**

   You finish the move by hooking your legs to gain control of your opponent's left leg. Figure 12-17 shows you how to complete this move successfully.

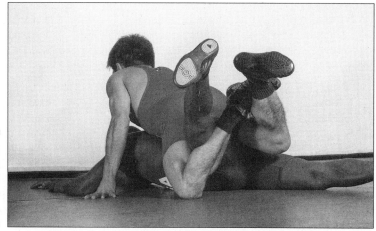

Figure 12-17:
Lock your legs around your opponent's leg.

After you complete the leg scizzors, finish with a pinning combination, such as the cross-face cradle or near-side bar.

Turk

You use the *turk* pinning combination after you've broken your opponent down from the bottom of the referee's position and you're on top of his belly with his back on the mat. The only difference between the leg scizzors and the turk is the position of your opponent on the mat (belly down or belly up).

To do the turk, just follow these steps:

1. **Push all your weight into the center of your opponent; without looking, control his right leg by pinching it between your right inner thigh and your left hamstring.**

   This step is known as *locking the leg*.

2. **Clamp your right leg around his right calf with your right heel controlling his right leg just below the knee.**

   This step is known as *hooking the leg*. Figure 12-18 shows what a successful turk looks like.

After you complete the turk, finish with a pin by squeezing his arms together between your arms.

Figure 12-18:
Wrap your leg around your opponent's leg to complete the turk.

Part IV
The Adults behind You: Coaches and Parents

The 5th Wave   By Rich Tennant

"Let's see — I'll need some children's aspirin for my players and some sedatives for their parents."

In this part . . .

This part serves as a reference for your supporting cast — namely, your parents and coaches. Not only is this section great for them, but it's also important for you to read because the more you know about the sport, the better wrestler you'll become.

I provide valuable information for wrestling coaches on how to coach wrestling, as well as on how to be effective in all areas of managing a wrestling team at any age group. Here you find numerous drills that work well for me and that you can incorporate into your daily practice.

Finally, I commit an entire chapter to your parents. Being the parent of a wrestler isn't easy; as a parent, you need to know a lot of important information ranging from helping your child stay healthy and safe to being an overall well-informed supporter of your child and his team. I show you how to do all this and more in this part.

Chapter 13

Coaching 101: Being the Best Coach You Can Be

In This Chapter

▶ Knowing as much as you can about wrestling

▶ Figuring out how to manage your team

▶ Focusing on your duties as a coach

▶ Mastering effective communication with players, officials, and parents

▶ Dealing with other team-related issues

*F*ew positions come with more responsibility and influence than being a coach. After all, a coach can have a greater impact on the kids he coaches than any other person in the community. Thus, your wrestlers' parents have put a tremendous amount of trust in you, and they expect you to treat their kids with love, compassion, and care.

When you're a wrestling coach, your life can be a rollercoaster of ups and downs. You may feel a tremendous amount of stress and anxiety one week and equal amounts of pride and satisfaction the next. As a coach, you can't expect to receive a lot of pats on the back or thank-you letters from parents when things go well, but you can expect to get a lot of feedback when things go south. I'm guessing you aren't in coaching for the money, but if you are, get out now because you can't expect to earn a lot of money.

Despite the difficulty of the job, coaching is one of the most rewarding jobs in society. Just think about the impact you can have on young people and the sheer joy you can feel when your wrestlers improve and believe in themselves more than they ever did before they met you.

This chapter covers the nuts and bolts of coaching. In it, I include sections on managing your team, understanding your roles as a coach, communicating effectively with your team, fellow coaches, and parents, and keeping everything organized. For the specifics on how to run a productive practice, turn to Chapter 14.

Knowing the Sport of Wrestling Inside and Out

To be an effective wrestling coach (and to gain credibility with your team), you need to have a solid understanding of wrestling as a sport. Although you can coach wrestling without ever having participated in it, having some hands-on background can make coaching wrestling a lot easier.

In this section, I provide a brief review of some things you need to know about wrestling before you start coaching and blow the whistle for the first time.

Understanding the different wrestling styles

Before you try to provide direction to your athletes, you need to understand the ins and outs of the sport, including the differences between the three styles of wrestling and the rules for each one. Here's a quick look at the three wrestling styles (Chapter 2 discusses them in a lot more detail):

- **Folkstyle:** This style is what you're probably coaching if you're coaching scholastic wrestling in the United States. It's the focus of this book.

- **Freestyle:** This style is popular internationally, and it allows wrestlers to use their upper and lower bodies (arms and legs). They can hold their opponents above or below the waist.

- **Greco-Roman:** This style is popular internationally, but in it, wrestlers can use only their arms and upper bodies to try to pin their opponents. They can't use their legs or attack their opponent's legs.

In addition to knowing the basic styles, you need to become familiar with the rules of the sport and the general match procedure, which I cover in Chapter 4.

Developing a plan for competition, training, and conditioning

Most effective coaches (similar to good schoolteachers) enter a season with a well-designed plan of action. Teachers need to have daily plans, unit plans, semester plans, and annual plans; likewise, coaches need to have daily practice plans, weekly or monthly plans, match plans, and season plans. Clear, well-designed plans can help reduce the number of miscommunications and disagreements you have in your season. The following sections help you lay out a road map for the season and for each day during it to help you figure out where you're going and how you plan to get there.

Competition plan

Your *competition plan* is a structured, consistent routine that you and your wrestlers follow during the season to help them reach their full potential on match day. Your competition plan starts before the match and includes both rest and nutrition (see Chapter 5). Here's an example of a good competition plan:

- ✔ **The day before the match:** Don't make your workouts any longer than 90 minutes and stay away from practicing live wrestling drills. Use the day before the match for flexibility, light conditioning, and shadow wrestling (see Chapter 14 for details).

- ✔ **The day of the match:** Plan to arrive at the match site 30 to 60 minutes before weigh-ins and meet with your team to review goals, key points, and the strengths and weaknesses of each individual opponent. Meeting with your team right before the match helps establish a mental focus on the task at hand. But after the weigh-ins and random draw (see Chapter 4), I suggest that your wrestlers prepare individually. After all, some kids will wrestle within 30 minutes, while others will have to wait as long as 90 minutes.

- ✔ **Approximately 30 minutes before each wrestler's match:** Make sure the wrestler is fully dressed by the 30-minute mark. Then have him begin to jog lightly, stretch, ride an exercise bike, or do some other general loosening exercises to build up a sweat and increase the heart rate.

- ✔ **Approximately ten minutes before the match:** At this point, the wrestler should be finished with his 20-minute warm-up routines. You can help him stay focused by providing a few quick reminders and key words like these: *Be quick, be aggressive, have fun,* and *stick to your best moves.*

Training plan

Your *training plan* is the basic routine you follow for regular daily practices throughout the season. In general, you want to begin every practice with loosening and stretching exercises before you move into partner drills and live wrestling.

Table 13-1 walks you through a sample training plan that you can follow for each practice, including the approximate amount of time I suggest that you spend in each segment. (*Tip:* Chapter 14 gives you some specific training drills to help you add variety to your daily routine.)

Table 13-1	A Sample Training Plan
Activity	**Time Spent**
Stretching and flexibility exercises, such as jumping jacks or other dynamic warm-up exercises (See Chapters 5 and 14 for more suggestions.)	10 minutes
Conditioning and basic strength exercises, such as push-ups, jogging, pull-ups, and neck exercises	15 minutes
Water break	2.5 minutes
Technical warm-up drills, including half-speed double-leg takedowns, single-leg takedowns, duck-unders, high crotches, and fireman's carries	25 minutes
Water break	2.5 minutes
Technical drills, including takedowns, rides, escapes, stances, penetration steps, and other basic skills (See Part III of this book for details on these drills.)	25 minutes
Water break	2.5 minutes
Live wrestling with three wrestlers at a time, each session lasting 2 minutes to simulate a full period (While two teammates compete for 3 minutes, the other one jogs until it's his turn to wrestle.)	25 minutes
Water break	2.5 minutes
Cool-down exercises, including dynamic or static stretching (See Chapter 5 for details.)	15 minutes

Regular daily practices shouldn't last longer than 135 minutes, but the amount of time you spend working on specific exercises and techniques varies as the season progresses. For example, the exact amount of time you spend working on each of the segments listed in Table 13-1 depends on many factors, including how close your team is to competition, whether you're practicing in the middle of the season or before it even starts, and how experienced your team is. *Note:* The times suggested in Table 13-1 are for a Wednesday practice before a Saturday match in the first third of the season.

As the season progresses, you may have to adjust the length of each segment based on wrestler fatigue or soreness. In addition, as a coach, you have to closely monitor the health of your team and do just enough to get your wrestlers ready without overworking them to the point that they aren't fresh for the match.

Conditioning plan

Having a detailed *conditioning plan* that includes strength training, cardiovascular training, and practicing specific wrestling drills is an important component of an overall coaching plan. I discuss general strength training and conditioning in Chapter 5, and I show you some basic practice exercises in Chapter 14. To help your wrestlers perform at their best, give them a year-round exercise schedule divided into four main seasons:

- ✔ **In-season:** The time of year when wrestlers are competing and practicing five days a week with their coach (about four months)
- ✔ **Postseason:** The time immediately after the competitive season when wrestlers are focusing on cardiovascular conditioning and strength training (about one month)
- ✔ **Off-season:** The time from the end of the postseason to the beginning of the preseason when wrestlers are focusing on strength training, cardiovascular conditioning, and agility workouts (about five months)
- ✔ **Preseason:** The time after the off-season immediately before the competitive season when wrestlers are focusing on strength training, cardiovascular conditioning, and some actual wrestling drills (about two months)

Table 13-2 gives you some general guidelines for how much of each type of training to do in these four seasons.

The conditioning outline I present in Table 13-2 is for more advanced wrestlers who make a commitment to wrestling as their number one sport and who want to focus on wrestling more than any other athletic endeavor. I recommend that kids age 12 and younger try to be involved in as many sports as possible to reduce the chance that they'll feel burned out later in their career or that wrestling will prevent them from doing other sports they might enjoy.

Table 13-2	Sample Year-Round Conditioning Plan		
	Type of Conditioning	*Example*	*Frequency*
In-season	Strength training	Select 4–6 exercises (such as bench press, push-ups, arm curls, shoulder press, leg extensions, leg curls, and pull-ups) and do each one for 2 sets of 12–16 reps.	2 days per week
	Wrestling-specific drills	Select 3–4 exercises (such as the shuffle, front rolls, army crawls, shadow wrestling, pummeling, and others from Chapter 14). Go to Chapter 14 for specific directions on how many reps to do for each drill.	5 days per week
	Cardiovascular conditioning	Do some medium-distance running, up to 2 miles.	4 days per week
Postseason	Strength training	Select 2–4 exercises (such as the ones I list for in-season strength training) and do each one for 2 sets of 14–18 reps.	2 days per week
	Wrestling-specific drills	None.	
	Cardiovascular conditioning	Bike for 30 minutes.	3 days per week

	Type of Conditioning	Example	Frequency
Off-season	Strength training	Select 6–8 pulling exercises (back, legs, and biceps) for 2 days and 6–8 pushing exercises (triceps, chest, and shoulders) for the other 2 days. Do each exercise for 3 sets of 10–12 reps for the first 3 months and 4 sets of 6–8 reps for the second 2 months.	4 days per week
	Wrestling-specific drills	Limit the number of drills you do to 2 per day (like shadow wrestling and the single-leg drill or others from Chapter 14), but do plenty of agility drills, such as backward running, speed ladders, or jump roping.	3 days per week
	Cardiovascular conditioning	Spend 30–45 minutes either on an exercise bike or running or jogging.	3 days per week
Preseason	Strength training	Select 6–8 exercises (upper back, lower back, legs, biceps, triceps, chest, and shoulders). Do each exercise for 3 sets of 10–12 reps.	3 days per week
	Wrestling-specific drills	Begin shadow wrestling and doing other technical drills from Chapter 14 on your own for 15 minutes a day.	2 days per week
	Cardiovascular conditioning	Bike or jog for 45–60 minutes.	4 days per week

Teaching basic skills for top, bottom, and neutral positions

You need to understand the basics of the three main starting positions in wrestling (top, bottom, and neutral) so that you can break them down into a few simple steps to teach to your team. I discuss how to get into these three positions in Chapter 8, and I provide specific drills you can run during practice to help your wrestlers master these positions (and the skills they need to move out of them) in Chapter 14.

Continuing your own education

Like most sports, wrestling is always going through rule changes, and wrestlers and coaches alike are constantly coming up with new practice and training methods. Being a good coach means continuing your own wrestling education and keeping up-to-date with these changes so that you can then share them with your assistant coaches and wrestlers.

Within two weeks of the end of your season, sit down with your assistants and/or parents and write out two or three specific areas in which your team needs to improve to get better. Then do some research to find the information (new practices, new rule changes, and so on) you need to help your team improve. You can turn to the following resources to continue your education about the changes in wrestling:

- ✔ **Respected coaches:** Consult experienced coaches in your community, state, and nation to make sure you're doing things the right way. Rely on your peers and fellow coaches to help you keep abreast of what you need to know.

  Although being consistent and sticking with your coaching plan is important (see the earlier section "Developing a plan for competition, training, and conditioning" for details), you owe it to your team to visit with respected successful coaches to find out how you can incorporate some of their proven methods into your own plan. *Remember:* Your job as coach is to decide what drills to do and how to set up your training program, so don't be afraid to take risks and try new drills if your practices seem stale and your athletes need a change of pace.

- ✔ **Wrestling governing bodies or associations:** Your state and local wrestling organizations and associations offer numerous resources and opportunities to help you improve your coaching. These organizations usually host wrestling camps and clinics, at which you can learn all about rule changes, new practice methods, training methods, and team management tips. Make sure you take advantage of these great opportunities.

Even if you learn only one new tip from attending a two-day clinic, that tip could make a world of difference to your coaching (and, in turn, to your team). Thus, I recommend that you attend at least two days worth of wrestling coaching clinics each year to brush up on your technique and training principles.

✓ **Books, magazines, and other publications:** I suggest that you read three coaching or leadership publications each year to help you continually mold and refine your coaching style.

Just like your wrestlers, you're constantly changing as a coach from one day to the next. You're either getting better or getting worse, depending on how much time and effort you put into your role. You ask your wrestlers to work hard in the off-season to prepare effectively, and as their coach, you need to do the same.

Managing Your Team

An effective wrestling coach not only understands the fundamentals of the sport but is also able to manage both the program as a whole and the individual wrestlers on his team. This section gives you some tips to help you become a better coach from a leader and team-management perspective.

Building (and maintaining) credibility and authenticity

Two of the most important characteristics of a successful coach are credibility and authenticity. If you have these two traits, you're off to a great start; if you don't, you need to work hard to improve them.

Credibility is the perception that you, as a coach, have something important to offer your wrestlers (in the form of skills, knowledge, insight, information, wisdom, and so on) and that learning these things will help your wrestlers improve. Here are the three aspects that affect your credibility the most:

✓ **Your expertise, or knowledge, as a coach:** Take time in the off-season to expand your own knowledge of the sport. Your wrestlers will know that you're credible if what you do in practice works in matches.

✓ **Your experience as a coach and the years of training you've had to establish a level of respect:** Use your own experiences as a wrestler or coach to make decisions for your team and understand that the more experience you have, the more credible you become.

✔ **Your conviction, passion, and enthusiasm for coaching wrestling:** Show up every day for practice enthusiastic, well organized, and highly energized. As a coach, you can never have a lazy demeanor or low energy level because your players feed off your energy level.

Authenticity is the perception that you're being open and honest with your wrestlers to help them reach their full potential as both people and wrestlers. Here are the four main aspects that affect your authenticity as a coach:

✔ **The level of congruence between what you say you will do and what you actually do:** In other words, make sure you talk the talk and walk the walk.

✔ **Your level of honesty:** Your athletes know when you're not telling the truth, so be open with them.

✔ **Your responsiveness to the needs of your athletes:** You need to be sensitive to the individual needs of each athlete. Don't expect every wrestler to have the same needs and goals.

✔ **Your level of realness:** Be yourself and be genuine with your athletes. In other words, don't try to be someone you're not.

Forming a team in the true sense of the word

Team dynamics (the level and quality of team member interactions) and *team climate* (the mutually agreed-upon expectations of team policies and procedures) affect your team's ability to succeed and work well together. In fact, your team is only a true team if the following four key characteristics are visible:

✔ **Clear and understandable team goal:** A good goal is one that focuses the team on its task and is clear enough for all team members to understand.

✔ **Clearly established team boundaries:** These rules address what each wrestler needs to do to be on the team and differentiates who is on the team from who isn't. Every team member must adhere to team boundaries to remain on the team.

✔ **Shared understanding of who's in charge and who's responsible for accomplishing team tasks:** An imbalance or misunderstanding of the extent of the team's authority leads to lack of clarity and creates a dysfunctional team. When team members feel that they have too much authority, they may undermine the head coach.

✔ **Stability:** Team performance increases as stability of membership becomes more reliable. Stability makes practices, meetings, and other team events more familiar and leads to increased communication and effectiveness. Have clear dates for when tryouts end and be careful about adding team members during the season because they may create unnecessary conflict.

If you don't address these four issues, then instead of a team, you have a group of individuals acting selfishly toward their own goals without a unifying purpose.

Assessing your team's effectiveness

After you form your team, you need to measure how well you and your team are doing in terms of meeting goals and finding success both on and off the mat. The following checklist provides a brief description of the characteristics that define an effective team. If your team lacks one or more of these characteristics, you need to evaluate the reasons why (possibly through speaking with other team leaders) and make adjustments where necessary.

✔ **Clear purpose:** Everyone on the team needs to accept a common vision, mission, goal, or task, as well as an action plan for how to accomplish it.

✔ **Participation:** Your wrestlers should want to be involved with your coaching and your program.

✔ **Civilized disagreement:** You and your team members should be comfortable with disagreement. Don't avoid or smooth over conflict; instead, address it openly, being respectful of everyone involved.

✔ **Open communication:** No one on the team should have a hidden agenda. As the coach, you need to be completely honest with your athletes and their parents. In turn, they should be honest with you. Refer to the "Communicating Effectively" section later in this chapter for more info.

✔ **Clear roles and assignments:** Make sure that all your team members know and understand their individual and group duties and responsibilities. Frequently communicate your expectations to your team.

✔ **External relationships:** Effective teams pay attention to outside groups that play a role in helping the group achieve its goals. Develop good relationships with the school, community, parent groups, and businesses nearby.

✔ **Diversity:** An effective team has members with diverse talents, skills, and styles. After all, a team of 20 lightweights won't score very well. If your team isn't very diverse in terms of skills, try to attract new members with different skills.

✔ **Openness to criticism:** Good teams are open to periodic examinations of how well they're functioning, and they're willing to address issues when they arise.

Highlighting the Key Roles of a Coach

Many people think that coaching is a fairly easy job. Little do they know that being a successful head coach is far from easy. A great deal of behind-the-scenes work goes into becoming an effective coach because the job involves so many responsibilities. In this section, I describe what your main roles are as a coach, and I explain how these roles should guide your interactions, behaviors, goals, and program philosophies.

Being a good role model

As a coach, you have to establish principles for how your team members should treat other people and how they should pursue their goals. Most importantly, though, you have to model (or show) your team exactly what type of behavior you expect. You have a tremendous amount of influence over the kids you coach, and with that influence comes a huge responsibility to watch your own actions and words to make sure they're consistent with what you expect from your team.

Always try to be an example of good sportsmanship for your wrestlers. If you outwardly criticize officials, use foul language, and lose self-control, how can you expect your athletes not to do the same?

Inspiring your team

Coaching requires an ability to inspire and motivate. To be a good coach, you have to help your players believe they can conquer the world, and then you have to establish a plan for how they can do so. After all, your team won't know which path to follow unless you lay out a map and show them what to do.

Setting an inspiring vision for your team is one of your main duties as a head coach. This vision sets a direction that energizes your team, orients your team to its goals, and motivates your wrestlers every day. In setting this vision, your job is to be passionate, never lose hope in your athletes, and always believe that you (and they) can make a difference. You have to be able to create a unique image for what each athlete on your team can become.

Some coaches naturally have *charisma*, a special quality that allows them to inspire allegiance and passion. If this isn't a natural quality of yours, follow these three tips to help you improve your charisma as a coach:

- ✔ Change your focus from yourself to others by listening more and talking less.

- ✔ Improve your ability to make a positive first impression by presenting yourself in a professional manner through how you dress, how you speak, and how you make others feel.

- ✔ Commit to adding value to everyone you talk to by sharing experiences and focusing on serving others rather than on having others serve you.

Focusing on education

You're probably a coach in a youth or middle or high school program. Although you may just want to teach your athletes how to wrestle to the best of their ability and win, your ultimate job as a coach is to teach your athletes life lessons. For example, wrestling can teach young people about the importance of hard work, determination, overcoming obstacles, and teamwork.

Good coaches search for opportunities to adjust the way they teach if their athletes aren't getting better on the mat. Great coaches look for ways to teach important life lessons at the same time that they teach their wrestlers how to improve their game. A famous quote says that doing the same thing and expecting different results is insanity. Always search out new and innovative ways to improve each wrestler in your program both on and off the mat.

Cultivating mutual respect and providing encouragement

Great coaches place a lot of importance on building relationships and encouraging positive thinking. Make sure that you build bridges with administrators, parents, officials, and other coaches and pay attention to developing trust and respect throughout your program. Don't forget that mutual respect between you and others is what sustains a program.

When you coach, don't ever criticize your wrestlers as individuals, but do be critical of their actions. Make sure your team members understand that you will coach, correct, and discipline them but also make sure they know that you respect and believe in them. Your job as a coach is to correct negative actions and behaviors, not to put your players down. So encourage your wrestlers when they do things right and keep a positive outlook even when you correct what they do wrong. If you don't provide some encouragement along with your criticism, you'll take away your team's aggression and spirit in no time.

Evaluating and celebrating

Accomplishing extraordinary things as a team requires hard work from every team member. As the coach, you have to constantly evaluate every aspect of your team and program so that you can help improve people's attitudes, skills, and techniques and team processes when needed.

Evaluate which of your wrestlers are giving full effort and which ones need some extra motivation. Sit down with each wrestler at the end of the season and talk about what he needs to do in order to improve for the next year. Whether he needs to get stronger, quicker, or more intense, tell each wrestler where he stands so he can improve and get better.

In every team, teammates need to feel a sense of recognition and share in the rewards of their efforts. Great coaches understand how to celebrate accomplishments and make their athletes feel like heroes. Develop traditions, such as wrestler of the week, sportsmanship awards, end-of-the-season banquets, or other ceremonies, to celebrate accomplishments that align with program objectives. Not only will team members feel good about themselves, but other teammates will feel more motivated to try and attain recognition the next time around.

Communicating Effectively

Communication (both verbal and nonverbal) happens in many different ways. As a wrestling coach, the first two things you need to do to make sure you communicate effectively with your team are to create clear overall team goals and objectives and then to be consistent when you talk about them. After you've set your goals, pick out a few key talking points that all relate back to those goals and share them with your wrestlers and their parents. Just make sure you don't use any mixed messages (saying one thing but doing another). If you do, you'll likely have to deal with conflict in one form or another.

In the next sections, I help you figure out how to communicate effectively with a few key groups, including your wrestlers, their parents, and officials.

With wrestlers

Your team members deserve a high level of communication from you, their head coach. To start things off, you need to provide clear practice policies, team guidelines, and your expectations at the beginning of the season. You also need to let your wrestlers know how to appropriately communicate any concerns or questions they may have.

To help you inform your athletes what you expect of them throughout the season, I suggest that you create a player policy manual. Hand out your manual and go over it with your entire team on the first day of practice, if not before. In the following sections, I offer some suggestions for what to include in this manual.

As you write your policy manual, remember that you're responsible for making sure your whole team complies with every policy that you write down and for providing appropriate discipline when needed. Hence, I recommend having just a few general policies and expectations so that you have the freedom to address each situation in a unique way and aren't held to a policy statement.

Work wrestler communication into the culture of your team by forming a leadership group of seven to ten team members that you can meet with on a weekly basis to make sure you hear all the voices on your team.

Practice policies

Practice policies are rules and expectations that you give your wrestlers at the beginning of the season so that they know right away what you expect from them. Examples include your rules on practice attire, obscenities, respect for others, and respect for the sport.

Remember to address these rules when you establish your practice policies:

- ✔ Be punctual and properly dressed for every practice and match.
- ✔ Make eye contact with coaches when they're speaking.
- ✔ Compete with a maximum effort, hustle, and listen to your coaches.

Team guidelines

Team guidelines are rules and expectations that deal with other issues besides practice. Setting team guidelines upfront is important because they let your wrestlers (and their parents) know that being part of your program requires appropriate behavior both on and off the mat. Your team is unique, so you need to set your own team guidelines. Here are some important areas you need to address before the season starts:

- ✔ Attendance, academic, discipline, equipment, and drug and alcohol policies
- ✔ Treatment of injuries, return-to-play procedures, and locker room, weight room, and training room procedures
- ✔ Media (including social media), jewelry, and grooming policies and cellphone use

Expectations

Team expectations should be brief and to the point. Be clear enough to provide direction and vague enough to permit interpretation. Start with these four general expectations; if your team abides by them, you're on the right track:

- ✔ Always speak the truth and never lie.
- ✔ Don't take anything personally.
- ✔ Don't make assumptions.
- ✔ Always do your best.

Although this list isn't long, these expectations do capture the essence of what you need from each of your players. I suggest that you use this same list to explain what the players can expect from you as their coach.

With officials

As a coach, you come into contact with officials every time your team takes the mat. The key to communicating effectively with officials — whether you're talking to them before, during, or after the match — is professionalism. Before the meet begins, the officials will talk to the head coaches and discuss any rule changes or special situations for that meet. Use that time to ask any questions you may have. Inform the referee of any recent situations that created difficulty in previous matches, and try to get a good idea for how the referee will call the match.

You establish a reputation with the officials based on your demeanor and level of self-control during matches. In other words, how you interact with officials gets around to other officials. Because you're always working to get the next call, the last thing you want to do is get on their bad side. Plus, officials never change the calls they make, so yelling about them after the fact isn't going to help.

If you notice a discrepancy with the scorer, calmly ask the official to address the issue. If you're dissatisfied with how the official is calling a certain move during the match, calmly ask the official about it between periods if you get the chance. Let the official know that you're addressing the issue for the purpose of clarity, not to criticize or question his judgment. After all, your approach and body language toward the officials determine whether or not he'll discuss a rule with you.

The way you and your team members interact with officials is a representation of you and your program. Never embarrass an official during a match. Doing so reflects poorly on you and is a poor example to your team. Not to mention you probably won't get any close calls for a long time.

With parents

The best way to communicate with parents is to give them all the information they need before the season starts. Poor or inconsistent communication with parents is the number one cause of parent-coach relationship issues.

A great way to communicate the nuts and bolts of your program to your wrestlers' parents (and to set your team up for a smooth-going season) is by creating a preseason program overview and handing it out at the first parent meeting. Your full disclosure at the start of the season shows organization, thoughtfulness, and transparency — all things parents love to see. When creating your preseason overview, make sure to include the following elements:

- ✔ Season schedules for matches and practices with clearly marked start and end times and locations
- ✔ Contact information for the coaching staff with a brief personal biography for the head coach and each assistant
- ✔ Key program objectives, including your program mission statement and the key points that guide your program (character, integrity, trust, and so on)
- ✔ Brief overview of your coaching philosophy
- ✔ Expectations of parents, players, and coaches

- ✔ General practice policies

- ✔ General playing time guidelines

- ✔ Team policies and discipline policies

- ✔ List of the requirements needed to gain specific postseason recognition, such as a varsity letter

- ✔ Five or six program goals (what you hope your athletes will learn under your tutelage)

- ✔ General equipment policies, including how to wash and take care of issued gear and how much each item costs if not returned

Realize upfront that you can never please all your wrestlers' parents all the time. Not surprisingly, the only truly happy parents are the ones whose kids are the starters. As for the rest of the parents, just be sure you always treat them with respect and keep them in the loop.

Addressing Other Miscellaneous Activities

Coaching your team during practices and meets is one of the easier (or at least more fun) parts of being a coach. What separates a great coach from an okay coach is his ability to handle the many other issues that need his attention throughout the course of the season. For example, coaches are also often responsible for noncoaching-related issues, such as fundraising, organizing volunteers and boosters, and handling logistics.

One easy way to handle some of these duties, which I discuss in the following sections, is to delegate and rely on your assistant coaches. But no matter who you get to do a task, you need to keep tabs on everything going on within and surrounding your program. Even if you give a job to someone else to complete, it's still your responsibility, and you need to make sure it gets done right.

Fundraising

Without a doubt, you'll have to raise some money in order to provide your team members with what they need to be successful. So whether you're a youth coach, a middle or high school coach, or a club coach, you need to understand some of the basics of fundraising before you start your season.

A well-organized fundraising program is more than simply getting people or businesses to donate money toward your efforts. Yes, one of the main goals of fundraising is to increase revenue or bring cash into your program, but fundraising has three other equally important goals:

- ✔ To target potential recruits or team members (through such fundraising tools as sport camps, clinics, golf tournaments, and lift-a-thons)
- ✔ To explain to the community what your program is all about
- ✔ To strengthen community or school relationships

Hence, a good fundraising program is about more than just asking for money. It also includes clearly stating to givers where the raised funds will go and why they should donate to your program rather than others.

The basic elements of a successful fundraising program are as follows, and if you address each one of these carefully, you'll be well on your way to adding funds to your coffer:

- ✔ Be specific about how much money you wish to raise and exactly what you will use the funds for.
- ✔ Develop an initial prospect list to make sure you don't ask the same business twice to give for the same purpose. Your donors expect you to know what you're doing and whom you're asking.
- ✔ Have a clear and transparent tracking system for the funds that you raise.
- ✔ Form a board of directors, including at least three people who track the funds and sign off on any donations or expenditures.
- ✔ Select projects that have a purpose; for example, a lift-a-thon can raise funds and also promote healthy lifestyles.
- ✔ Quickly and accurately write thank-you notes to those individuals or groups who donate to your cause.

Logistics

As a coach, you often have to handle important logistical issues, such as transportation, food, and lodging. In some instances, your athletic director will handle many of these issues, but even in such cases, you need to communicate with him to make sure everything is complete. (For example, nothing would be worse than your team not having a bus to get to your meet.) The following sections help you plan, delegate, and execute these logistics.

Transportation

Most schools provide transportation to away wrestling meets, but you still have a part to play in getting your team to meets on time. For instance, you need to communicate with your athletic director to verify that he has scheduled a bus for your team. You then need to make sure your team and assistant coaches know what time the bus leaves.

After you get on the bus, you need to have a roll sheet so that you can make sure everyone is on board, and you need to know how to get where you're going. Be sure to take weather, traffic, and road considerations into account and don't trust that the bus driver knows where he's going. Plan on arriving at the site 30 minutes to one hour before weigh-ins to ensure you get there on time and your wrestlers don't feel rushed.

If your school or club team doesn't provide a bus, be clear to your wrestlers and their parents how your team is getting to the match. Make sure all your wrestlers have a way to and from the match.

Food

If your travel includes meals or snacks, you need to make sure someone coordinates the food. You have a lot on your plate (pun intended) as a coach, so I recommend that you delegate food duties to volunteers and boosters to plan (check out the later section "Volunteers and boosters" for details). They can put together meals or snacks for your team after the meet, which the team should always eat together.

If you want to stop and eat on the way home from a meet, don't just hand out cash and let your athletes choose what fast-food restaurant they want to go to. Eat together. If possible, call ahead to reserve a large meeting room and eat in a secluded area. Only go to all-you-can-eat places after a match, not before. Make sure your athletes are well dressed if you eat in public and remind them that they're representing their school and community. Also remember that restaurants are a great place to give people an excellent impression of your program.

Sometimes the best post-match meal is one that's delivered to your match site. Call ahead and have pizza or sandwiches delivered to the site so that you can get on the road and get back home as soon as possible.

As for pre-match meals, make sure your wrestlers eat them three to four hours before weigh-in. These meals should include protein and some carbohydrates with water to drink. Stay away from fatty or fried foods and carbonated beverages. Check out Chapter 5 for more helpful information about what to eat before and after meets.

Lodging

If your travel includes an overnight stay, you need to make sure your team has a proper place to sleep. Take the following precautions to make sure your overnight trips go smoothly:

- ✔ Develop a rooming list and send it to the hotel early so the keys are waiting for you when you arrive.

- ✔ Try to reserve a section of the hotel to reduce your impact on and contact with other hotel guests.

- ✔ Never allow wrestlers to leave the hotel grounds unless they're accompanied by a coach or parent.

- ✔ Call ahead to get a price break or to make sure you aren't staying the night of a wedding, party, reception, concert, or other event at the hotel that could create a distraction for your team.

- ✔ Have all your wrestlers be in their rooms by 9:00 p.m. and set a lights-out time for 10:30 p.m. Always do a bed check at 9:00 p.m. and again at 11:00 p.m.

- ✔ Remember to take your rooming list to the front desk and schedule a wake-up call. Then go knock on the doors yourself to make sure all your team members are up and moving around.

- ✔ Make sure that you and your assistant coaches never leave the hotel grounds and that you always stick to the same behavioral standards that you've set for your team.

Volunteers and boosters

Volunteers and booster clubs can be a great help to you in many ways, but they can also be a thorn in your side if you don't manage them correctly. In case you're unfamiliar with the difference between these two groups, here's a quick rundown:

- ✔ *Volunteers* are individuals who offer random assistance at one time or another during the season or off-season.

- ✔ *Boosters* are individuals who meet consistently to discuss fundraising opportunities and who help determine where and how the raised money is spent. Booster clubs often have their own tax number and operate a budget independent of the team's school budget.

Note: How much contact you have with volunteers and boosters depends on the age group of your wrestlers, so for the sake of this section, I assume that you're coaching a middle or high school team.

Your athletic director will probably help you get some volunteers, like trainers and concession stand workers, but you may need to find volunteer clock operators and scorekeepers on your own. Plus, if your school doesn't offer transportation, you may need to rely on volunteers to transport both wrestlers and necessary equipment to and from matches.

The first step in managing volunteers and boosters effectively is to decide whether or not you need help and what you need help with. After you identify which roles you need to fill with volunteers or boosters, follow these guidelines to make things go as smoothly as possible:

- ✔ **Identify individual strengths.** Don't assign duties to different volunteers; instead, ask who wants to do what. Your volunteers will enjoy their jobs much more, and they'll be more willing to help again.

- ✔ **Train your volunteers and be clear with expectations, assignments, and roles.** This guideline is important because you want your volunteers to come back. If your volunteers don't feel like they're doing something important, they may decline to help out next time.

- ✔ **Clearly inform all volunteers that their roles are strictly to fill a need for the team.** Their volunteerism doesn't give them the right to start coaching or to guilt you into treating their children differently.

- ✔ **Thank your volunteers and recognize them.** Everyone appreciates recognition. Be sure to thank your volunteers at your end-of-year banquet or other team gatherings whenever possible.

Chapter 14

Running a Productive Practice with Key Drills

The easiest day for any wrestling coach should be the day of the match. After all, if you prepare your wrestlers effectively with organized and purposeful practice sessions leading up to the match, you can feel confident that your wrestlers will bring everything they need to the mat come match day. In other words, match day is simply a public display of what you've been working on day in and day out during practice. Thus, you need to approach practice with the same intensity with which you approach each match — by establishing an environment of competition, hard work, and focus.

Because practice is so important, I spend this entire chapter showing you how to design an effective practice plan, complete with numerous drills that give your wrestlers what they need to succeed on match day.

I start by explaining how to create a general practice plan, and then I move into specific warm-up, conditioning, and fundamental skill drills that you can use during each practice. I finish up with a few more advanced drills that you can try out with those wrestlers who are ready for a challenge. Note that the drills I give you aren't the only wrestling drills out there, but they're a great place to start.

Although this chapter includes a lot of how-to information specifically for coaches, student-athletes can use this chapter (particularly the sections on drills) to improve their wrestling techniques. Many of the drills are safe and simple enough that you can do them on your own if you have the space and a mat.

Getting the Most out of Every Practice

Your primary goal as a wrestling coach is to help your wrestlers become better wrestlers at the end of the season than they were at the beginning. One way to accomplish this goal is to use effective practice sessions and drills. In this section, I give you some basic tips for setting up a general practice plan and for figuring out how long to practice and what drills to include in each practice.

Designing a practice plan

A *practice plan* is basically a road map deigned to keep practice on track. Without a plan, you can easily lose track of time and spend too much time focusing on one drill and forgetting to work on another. As a coach, you have a lot to accomplish in a two-hour (or slightly more) practice, and having a plan can help you fit in everything.

When putting together your practice plan, keep the following points in mind:

- ✔ **Be consistent and set your schedule at least two weeks in advance.** I recommend that you post your practice plan so your wrestlers know what to expect at each practice session. Allowing your athletes to see the plan before practice helps to establish a culture of professionalism and a level of respect between you and your wrestlers.

- ✔ **Clearly state your daily objectives on your practice plan.** Coaches are essentially just teachers. Every good teacher posts learning objectives on a lesson plan; every good coach should do the same.

- ✔ **Keep things fresh.** A good coach can sense when he needs to make changes because wrestlers are tired of doing the same drills or are falling into too much of a routine. Try some new drills now and then to help keep interest up, especially when you're working with kids younger than high school level.

Use the template in Table 14-1 to help design your practice plan. Keep in mind that the time allotments for each segment (and the specific drills you use for each segment) will change from day to day, but the general structure of practice should remain the same.

Table 14-1		Sample Practice Plan	
Practice Segment	*Time Allotted*	*Examples of Drills to Include*	*Section or Chapter Where I Explain These and Similar Drills*
General warm-up and stretching	15 minutes	Shuffle, backward run, lunges, push-ups, arm circles, penetration step/level change drills	Chapters 5 and the later section "Focusing on Basic Movements: A Warm-Up"
Wrestling-specific warm-up drills	25 minutes	Army crawl, front roll, hip heist drill, following-the-hips drill, lift and return, pummeling drill, fireman's carry drill	The rest of this chapter
Wrestling and ability-specific skill drills	35 minutes	Takedowns, escapes, reversals, pinning combinations, and breakdowns	Chapters 7, 8, 9, 10, 11, and 12
Live wrestling drills or practice competitions	35 minutes	Live wrestling against a teammate	Chapters 7, 8, 9, 10, 11, and 12
Conditioning drills	15 minutes	Handstand push-ups, abdominal push-down and pull-down drills, spin drill, hip heist drill, ironman drill	The later section "Staying in Shape: Conditioning Drills"
Cool-down	10 minutes	Same as general warm-up and stretching	Chapter 5 and the later section "Focusing on Basic Movements: A Warm-Up"

Figuring out how long your team should practice

In addition to deciding which drills to include in your practice plan, you have to determine how long each practice will be. The exact length of each practice varies depending on how big (or small) your team is, how advanced (or not) your wrestlers are, where you are in the season, and how soon your next match is. As a general rule, your practice sessions should be no longer than 135 minutes at the high school or collegiate level and 120 minutes at the youth or middle school level. If you can't fit everything you want to teach in that amount of time, you're either running an unorganized practice or you're trying to fit too much into each session.

Always use a watch and stay on time during practice. If your practice plan allows 15 minutes for warm-up, then make sure your warm-up doesn't last 20 minutes. Going over on time early in practice can easily turn a 135-minute practice into a 180-minute practice. Neither you nor your wrestlers (nor their parents) want that!

Your athletes have only so much energy to bring to the mat, so you need to make sure you keep things moving in an organized fashion. You don't want your wrestlers to use all their energy during the first few warm-up drills and not have anything left for the skill-specific drills and conditioning that come later. You also need to plan several water breaks into your practice session to allow your wrestlers to rehydrate (see Chapter 5 for details on the importance of hydration).

Knowing which drills to use in practice

When putting together your practice plan, focus on drills that can help your wrestlers improve. Each drill should relate to a specific wrestling movement. Don't just use drills for the sake of keeping your athletes busy. You don't have time to waste doing drills that won't directly impact your wrestlers' ability to become more effective on the mat.

After you've created the objective for your practice, break each of the main movements down into parts and make a list of them. Make sure you have a drill that relates to those movements.

One of the key challenges of coaching is uncovering the needs of each individual wrestler. What one kid needs to work on may be different from what another kid needs to work on, so be observant at every practice session so that you know what each of your wrestlers needs most.

One of the best ways to show your wrestlers (and you) the importance of the drills they do in practice is to video your practice and match sessions. Doing so allows you to show your athletes where the drill comes into play in a live match.

Focusing on Basic Movements: A Warm-Up

Every practice needs to start with a good warm-up to get your wrestlers' bodies ready for practice. A good warm-up initiates blood flow and loosens the muscles. You can use the following warm-up drills at the beginning of a practice session either before or after a general stretching routine (which I cover in the first section). This list of drills isn't an exhaustive list, but it's an excellent place for you to start.

Always design your drills so that wrestlers can clearly see how the drill will translate to success on the mat and give them a catchy name so your wrestlers immediately know what to do when you call them out. When your warm-up drill requires that your wrestlers stand up, make sure your wrestlers keep their knees bent and stay in a good athletic stance (see Chapter 7 for details on proper stance).

Keep your wrestlers active during warm-up. Never have a line of more than four wrestlers for each warm-up drill. Your athletes need to spend their time warming up, not waiting in line. If you have too many wrestlers in a particular line, move some of them to a different drill.

Stretching to start practice

Before or after your wrestlers do their warm-up drills, they also need to stretch their muscles. Stretching gets their blood flowing and can improve their athletic performance by helping to increase their flexibility and decrease their risk of injury (see Chapter 5 for details on flexibility).

Use the following stretches at the beginning of each of your practices and match warm-ups to help your wrestlers become more flexible and get ready for the real work ahead. Have your wrestlers hold each stretch for 15 to 20 seconds and do each stretch on both the right and left side, where applicable. Also, remind your wrestlers to keep breathing through all the stretches. No holding their breath!

- **Quadriceps stretch:** Stand tall and reach down to grab the top of your right foot. Pull it up so that the back of your heel is near your buttocks.

- **Calf stretch:** From a standing position, keep your left heel flat to the ground as you walk your right foot forward. Keep moving your right foot forward until you can feel your left calf muscle stretching.

- **Hamstrings stretch:** From a standing position, bend down and touch your toes with your fingers. Keep bending with your legs straight until you feel your leg muscles stretching.

- **Hip flexor stretch:** From a kneeling position, step out with your right leg (you're now on one knee) and thrust your hips forward until you feel your muscles stretching.

- **Knee-to-chest stretch:** Lie down on your back, bring your right knee up to your chest, and pull it close to your chest with both hands. Keep pulling until you feel your muscles stretching.

- **Shoulder stretch:** While standing, raise your right hand above your head. Place your left hand on your right elbow and pull your right elbow back behind your right ear. With your right arm now bent, try to scratch your back as low as possible with your right hand. Keep pulling until you feel your muscles stretch.

- **Neck stretch:** While standing, take your right hand over your head and place it near your left ear. Keep your chin up and pull your head to the right. Keep pulling until you feel your muscles stretch.

Shuffle

The *shuffle* primarily focuses on making basic movements from a proper wrestling stance (see Chapter 7 for details). Hence, a wrestler does this drill from the standing position. To use this drill in practice, have each wrestler start on the outline of the 28-foot wrestling circle on the mat and then follow these steps:

1. **Stand in the middle of the circle and have all your wrestlers start in a proper square stance on the circle, facing you.**

   Make sure each wrestler keeps a good knee bend (refer to Chapter 7 for details on proper stance and knee bend). His hands should stay out in front of him as if he were ready to start a match in the neutral position (see Chapter 8).

2. **Instruct each wrestler to shuffle laterally around the circle, staying low and never crossing his feet.**

   As each wrestler shuffles laterally, make sure his feet never cross or get closer than three inches to each other.

3. **After 15 seconds, instruct each wrestler to turn around and face outside the circle and then to continue his shuffle around the circle.**

Have your wrestlers repeat this drill as many as five times in each direction.

As a variation on this drill, you can have your wrestlers go around the circle in the following ways:

✔ Forward jogging

✔ Backward jogging

✔ Jogging while lifting the knees high

✔ Jogging while alternating right and left foot contact on the 28-foot line

Army crawl

The *army crawl* focuses on developing upper-body flexibility and strength and gets wrestlers used to moving on the mat, using only their elbows and upper body. Wrestlers start this drill on their bellies with their elbows and lower body (from the hips down) on the mat (see Figure 14-1). The point of the drill is to crawl forward as fast as possible for a distance of 30 feet and then stand up and hustle back to the end of the line.

Figure 14-1:
The starting position for the army crawl.

To use this drill, line up your wrestlers in a few single-file lines and have the first wrestler in each line get down on the mat in the position shown in Figure 14-1. Then follow these steps:

1. **Instruct the first wrestler in each line to crawl forward as fast as possible.**

   Make sure the wrestler pulls himself forward using only his elbows and forearms. Side-to-side movement will slow him down. Also make sure his head is up with his eyes focused forward.

2. **Allow each wrestler to crawl for a distance of 30 feet and then have him jump up and hurry to the end of the line.**

Have each wrestler do this drill for a period of 20 to 30 seconds five times.

Front roll

The *front roll* is a great warm-up drill to use because it teaches wrestlers how to properly absorb a fall to the mat. Specifically, it shows wrestlers how to tuck their chin and safely roll over on the mat, a technique that shows up in many wrestling moves from beginner level to advanced.

To use this drill, have your wrestlers form several lines (so that no more than four wrestlers are in each line). Stand on the mat in front of your lines and have your wrestlers follow these steps:

1. **The first wrestler in each line stands, facing forward, with his knees bent and his feet parallel to each other (see Figure 14-2).**

Figure 14-2:
Starting position for the front roll.

2. **The wrestler squats down so that his hands come into contact with the mat for support (see Figure 14-3).**

Having his hands on the mat helps stabilize the wrestler and allows him to make sure he rolls straight over in the next step.

Figure 14-3:
The wrestler places his hands on the mat.

3. **The wrestler pushes off both feet while tipping his body forward to the mat and tucking his chin tight to his chest as he rolls over (see Figure 14-4).**

Figure 14-4:
The wrestler rolls over while tucking his chin.

Make sure each wrestler tucks his chin in this step. Your wrestler's head should hardly touch the mat at all; in a proper roll, the back of the neck, not the head, should contact the mat. The wrestler should end the roll back on his feet, facing the same direction as when he started (see Figure 14-5).

4. The wrestler finishes with his hands wrapped tightly around his knees (see Figure 14-5).

The wrestler's momentum allows him to return to an upright position.

Figure 14-5:
The wrestler
finishes in
an upright
position.

Have each wrestler do this drill eight times in a row and repeat all eight reps three times.

Dive roll

The *dive roll* is the second progression in the roll series (after the front roll, which I describe in the preceding section). This drill is the same as the front roll except that the wrestler dives into the roll instead of simply tumbling over. This drill helps wrestlers figure out how to safely land on the mat and use the cushion of the mat to their advantage.

Don't use the dive roll until your wrestlers can safely execute six to ten front rolls in a row. If a wrestler does this drill improperly, it could cause neck or shoulder injury.

To use this drill, have your wrestlers stand in several lines and then have them follow these steps:

1. The first wrestler in each line stands, facing forward, with his knees bent and his feet parallel to each other (refer to Figure 14-2).

2. The wrestler jumps forward, pushing off with both feet and tipping his upper body forward to the mat and through a forward roll, all while tucking his chin (see Figure 14-6).

At first, the wrestler's arms and hands help propel him forward in his jump (see Figure 14-6); then they help absorb the contact with the mat as the wrestler executes a forward roll. The wrestler should end the roll back on his feet, facing the same direction as when he started.

Figure 14-6:
Lunge
forward
and dive
into the roll.

Make sure each wrestler tucks his chin in this step. Your wrestler's head should hardly touch the mat at all; in a proper roll, the back of the neck, not the head, should contact the mat.

To see how to complete the dive roll, refer to the preceding section and Figures 14-3, 14-4, and 14-5. The only difference between the front roll and the dive roll is the start.

Have each wrestler perform this drill eight times in a row and repeat all eight reps three times.

For the dive roll, start your wrestlers off with jumps of one to two feet first. Then develop their skills and confidence so that they can safely perform the dive roll four to five feet in front of their original starting point.

Shadow wrestling

Shadow wrestling is a wrestling technique that you can use from both the neutral position and the bottom of the referee's position (see Chapter 8 for details on these starting positions). It involves penetration steps, movement, and simulated takedown moves. When you use it at the beginning of practice as a warm-up exercise, each wrestler does it on his own without an opponent and focuses on motion, body position, and timing. Not only is this drill an effective warm-up physically, but it also allows your wrestlers to get into a focused mindset early in practice. As your wrestlers work through this drill, instruct them to gradually build up to full speed and check that they're maintaining a good position at all times. (As an added bonus, wrestlers can also use this drill at the end of practice as a cool-down activity.)

To use this drill, tell each wrestler to find an area on the mat to shadow wrestle and then have them follow these steps:

1. **Each wrestler starts in the neutral starting position.**

   See Chapter 8 for details on this and other starting positions.

2. **The wrestler begins to move around on the mat by using various wrestling steps and techniques without an opponent in front of him.**

   For example, the wrestler could practice using a penetration step (see Figure 14-7) or a low-level attack (see Figure 14-8).

Figure 14-7:
Simulating a
penetration
step.

Allow each wrestler to do three or four periods of shadow wrestling for 30 to 45 seconds each.

To get the most out of your shadow wrestling sessions, do the following:

- ✔ Have your wrestlers simulate various takedowns, doing them faster over time.
- ✔ Have your wrestlers work on defensive moves, too. For example, have them simulate proper body position, leg protection moves, and counterattacks.
- ✔ Emphasize quickness and full-speed simulation.
- ✔ Reinforce proper stance, level change, hip positioning, penetration, and attacks or takedowns as you watch your wrestlers shadow wrestle.

Figure 14-8:
Simulating
a low-level
attack.

Staying in Shape: Conditioning Drills

Chapter 5 covers the general idea of conditioning your body through endurance and strength training. Most wrestlers focus on building endurance
and strength during the off-season and then don't have the time during the
season to continue to condition. Lucky for you, I include a handful of conditioning drills in this section that allow your wrestlers to maintain the strength
they developed in the off-season during the season. Some kids get stronger
with these drills, especially if they're at the beginner level or if they didn't do
any off-season strength work. But for the most part, these drills simply help
wrestlers maintain their muscle strength and endurance while they focus on
building their skills on the mat.

Make the drills in this section a part of your daily practice routine. I recommend incorporating them into either your warm-up or your cool-down so that
you don't forget about them.

For the drills that require a partner, match each wrestler with a teammate of
roughly the same size and strength. Some of the drills call for one partner to
sustain the body weight of another, so matching teammates up according to
size and strength helps prevent unnecessary injuries.

Handstand push-ups

The *handstand push-ups drill* is a partner drill that helps develop shoulder and
arm strength. It involves the following steps:

1. **Wrestler A puts his hands on the ground slightly wider than shoulder-
   width apart.**

2. **Wrestler B helps Wrestler A do a handstand by holding his feet in the air while standing behind him (see Figure 14-9).**

   Wrestler A's elbows are bent, and his head is likely in contact with the mat.

Figure 14-9:
The beginning position for the handstand push-up.

3. **Using only his own strength (not his partner's), Wrestler A pushes his body up from the handstand position for a push-up (see Figure 14-10).**

   Have each wrestler do 12 to 14 repetitions of this drill.

Figure 14-10:
The proper
execution of
a handstand
push-up.

Abdominal push-down drill

The *abdominal push-down drill* is a partner drill that helps develop abdominal strength (surprise!). Abdominal, or *core,* strength is a key part of being successful on the mat because it allows wrestlers to stabilize their bodies and maintain balance in the heat of the match. Here are the steps you need to know to use this drill:

1. **Wrestler A starts flat on his back with his head between the legs of Wrestler B and his legs up in the air; Wrestler A grabs the back of Wrestler B's ankles for balance (see Figure 14-11).**

Figure 14-11:
The starting position for the abdominal push-down drill.

2. **Wrestler A raises his legs so that Wrestler B can grab his feet or ankles (refer to Figure 14-11).**

3. **Wrestler B throws Wrestler A's feet down toward the mat at a variety of angles (see Figure 14-12).**

   Wrestler A must keep his legs straight throughout this step and not allow any part of his legs to touch the mat. Wrestler B can push the ankles straight down, to the left, or to the right.

Figure 14-12:
Wrestler A keeps his legs straight as Wrestler B throws his legs down.

4. **As soon as Wrestler A's legs get close to the mat, he kicks them immediately back to the face of Wrestler B.**

   Wrestler A's back should remain flat on the mat throughout this drill.

5. **Wrestler B catches Wrestler A's feet or ankles and throws them down immediately.**

Have each wrestler do 30 to 40 repetitions of this drill.

Abdominal pull-up drill

Like the abdominal push-down drill, the *abdominal pull-up drill* is a partner drill that helps develop core strength. However, the pull-up drill is an advanced drill that requires a whole lot more abdominal strength. Here are the steps you need to know to use this drill:

1. **Wrestler A starts flat on his back with his legs bent and his head between the legs of Wrestler B; Wrestler A grabs the back of Wrestler B's ankles for balance (see Figure 14-13).**

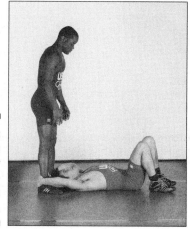

Figure 14-13:
The starting position for the abdominal pull-up drill.

2. **Wrestler A thrusts his legs upward so that Wrestler B can grab the back of his knees (see Figure 14-14).**

   Wrestler A has to use the strength in his abdominal muscles and hip flexors to thrust his torso into Wrestler B.

Figure 14-14:
Wrestler
A thrusts
his legs
upward.

3. **Wrestler A returns his feet to the mat in preparation for another repetition by using his abdominal strength to control the downward motion of his hips.**

Have each wrestler do as many reps as he can do and then repeat that same number of reps three times.

Spin drill

The *spin drill* is a partner drill that helps wrestlers develop hip flexibility and balance. The following steps explain how to use this drill:

1. **Wrestler A lines up in the bottom of the referee's starting position on the mat, where he remains for the entire drill.**

2. **Wrestler B puts his chest on the lower back of Wrestler A, keeping his hands behind his own back (see Figure 14-15).**

Having Wrestler B keep his hands behind his back forces him to use only his abdominal and lower-body strength for balance. Beginner wrestlers may need to place one hand on Wrestler A's head and one hand on Wrestler A's lower back to keep balance.

Figure 14-15:
Starting
position
for the
spin drill.

3. **On the coach's command, Wrestler B spins in one direction (see Figure 14-16).**

Wrestler B changes directions each time the coach gives a command.

Have each wrestler perform this drill as Wrestler B for 15 to 30 seconds four to six times.

Figure 14-16:
The wres-
tler spins
in different
directions
according to
the coach's
call.

Hip heist drill

The *hip heist drill* is the only conditioning drill in this section that doesn't require a partner. This drill develops shoulder strength and flexibility, hip flexibility, and balance. The following steps explain how to do this drill:

1. **The wrestler starts in the bottom of the referee's starting position and slides his feet out to his right (see Figure 14-17).**

Figure 14-17:
From the bottom of the referee's position (a), the wrestler slides his feet out to the right (b).

2. **The wrestler rotates back and to his right, keeping his left foot and left arm on the mat, and ends with his belly facing up, as in an upside-down crawl position (see Figure 14-18).**

Figure 14-18:
The wrestler rotates so that his belly faces up.

Have each wrestler do 12 to 16 reps of this drill in a row two or three times per practice.

Starting with Some Fundamental Skill Drills

Every sport involves certain fundamentals that, if developed, can help you become a master at that sport. The drills I provide in this section are the bread-and-butter drills that every wrestler, regardless of talent level, needs to do consistently. Even though your advanced wrestlers will eventually move on to more challenging drills (see the next section), they can't afford to ignore the basic drills I include in this section. *Note:* This set of fundamental skill drills isn't a complete list, but it offers a solid starting point for your wrestling program.

Base-building drill

Maintaining a good base is key to performing successful point-earning moves like escapes (see Chapter 9) and reversals (see Chapter 10). In both of these moves, wrestlers go from being in a defensive position on the mat to either gaining control of their opponent or getting to the neutral position.

Share the following pointers with your wrestlers to help them maintain a good position:

- Keep your head up.
- Keep your buttocks down.
- Keep a slight bend in your knees.
- Hold your elbows in tight to your ribs.
- Maintain a wide base on the mat (if you're on your knees in the referee's starting position).

See Chapter 7 for more details on how to maintain a strong base.

The *base-building drill* helps develop lower-back and abdominal strength, as well as balance. Wrestlers can do this drill with or without a partner. The following steps show you how to use the solo version of this drill in practice:

1. **The wrestler gets into a belly-down position on the mat, simulating having been broken down by his opponent (see Figure 14-19).**

Figure 14-19:
Starting
position for
the base-
building
drill.

2. **The wrestler pushes up with his right knee, hip, and shoulder to get his chest off the mat (see Figure 14-20).**

Figure 14-20:
The wrestler
pushes up
to get his
belly off the
mat.

3. **The wrestler continues to work his way into the bottom of the referee's position on the mat by maintaining balance and using the strength in his hips, legs, and arms (see Figure 14-21).**

Have your wrestlers perform this drill for 15 to 20 seconds.

Figure 14-21:
The wrestler ends in the bottom of the referee's position.

Changing-levels-for-penetration drill

The *changing-levels-for-penetration drill* is a partner drill that helps wrestlers develop hip flexibility and leg strength. The drill highlights the importance of lowering one's level for an attack and stepping into the opponent on a penetration step. (If you need a refresher on level change and the penetration step, skip over to Chapter 7.)

Here are the steps you need to know to use this drill in practice:

1. **Wrestler A stands in front of Wrestler B, simulating the neutral position; Wrestler B stands with his legs wide enough apart to allow Wrestler A to go through them (see Figure 14-22).**

Figure 14-22:
Wrestler B starts with his feet spread wide.

2. **Wrestler A lowers his hips and steps forward into Wrestler B, using a penetration step (see Figure 14-23).**

Figure 14-23:
Wrestler A moves toward Wrestler B with a penetration step.

3. **Wrestler A penetrates through the legs of Wrestler B by lowering to one knee and using his hands for balance out in front (see Figure 14-24).**

Figure 14-24:
Wrestler A slips through the legs of Wrestler B.

4. **Wrestler A completes the drill by getting up into his original neutral position, facing away from Wrestler B.**

Have each partner do this drill as Wrestler A 10 to 15 times in a row at least twice during each practice.

Following-the-hips drill

The *following-the-hips drill* is a partner drill that helps wrestlers practice how to follow (or *ride*) an opponent by staying low with their knees bent and keeping their hands in contact with the outside of their opponent's hips.

Follow these steps to use this drill during practice:

1. **Wrestler A starts in the bottom of the referee's position; Wrestler B stands immediately behind Wrestler A with his hands on the hips of Wrestler A (see Figure 14-25).**

Figure 14-25: The starting position for the following-the-hips drill.

2. **On your command, Wrestler A begins to move in a circle on the mat to the left and right, leaving his hands in roughly the same area.**

3. **As Wrestler A moves, Wrestler B tries to keep a firm grip on Wrestler A's hips while maneuvering on his feet to try to stay immediately behind Wrestler A.**

Wrestler B's goals are to move quickly, react to every move Wrestler A makes, and keep his hips at the same level as those of Wrestler A throughout the drill.

Have your wrestlers do this drill for 15 to 20 seconds and repeat it four to six times, switching positions each time.

Back arch

The *back arch* is a good partner drill to use to increase your wrestlers' flexibility and neck strength. Follow these steps to use the back arch in practice:

1. **Wrestler A stands facing Wrestler B; they get a firm grip on each other's hands.**

2. **Wrestler A arches his back, keeping his feet steady on the mat, and tries to get his head all the way down to the mat while Wrestler B helps by holding onto Wrestler A's hands (see Figure 14-26).**

   Keep a good arch in your back with your hips high off the mat.

Figure 14-26:
The back arch with partner assistance.

3. **Wrestler A holds the back arch for two to three seconds and then Wrestler B helps lift him back up.**

Have each partner repeat this drill five times.

Lifting drill

The *lifting drill* is a partner drill that helps wrestlers develop the proper technique for lifting an opponent off the mat. Why is using proper lifting technique so important that I include a separate drill just to practice it? Because if your wrestlers use improper lifting technique, they may suffer injuries and lower-back pain that can sideline them for an extended time period. So don't skip over this drill!

Here are the basic steps you need to follow to use this drill during practice:

1. **Wrestler B stands with his feet shoulder-width apart; Wrestler A stands next to him with his left ear on Wrestler B's spine and Wrestler B's left leg in between his legs.**

2. **Wrestler A bends at the knees, keeping his chest up, and takes a firm grip around Wrestler B's waist (see Figure 14-27).**

Figure 14-27:
Starting position for the lifting drill.

3. **Wrestler A lifts Wrestler B into the air by thrusting his hips into Wrestler B and straightening his knees almost to full extension while pulling up with his arms and hugging Wrestler B tightly (see Figure 14-28).**

4. **Wrestler A carefully returns Wrestler B to the mat.**

Have your wrestlers perform the lifting drill 12 to 15 times in a row and then have the partners switch roles.

Figure 14-28:
Wrestler A
lifts with his
hips, legs,
and arms.

Freeing-the-hands-and-wrists drill

The *freeing-the-hands-and-wrists drill* is a partner drill that focuses on helping defensive wrestlers break free from their opponents' control. To use this drill in practice, follow these steps:

1. **Wrestler B stands behind Wrestler A with a firm grip on his waist; Wrestler A maintains a firm grip with his hands on Wrestler B's wrists (see Figure 14-29).**

   Wrestler A is in a defensive position; Wrestler B is in control.

Figure 14-29:
Starting
position for
the freeing-
the-hands-
and-wrists
drill.

2. **Wrestler A lowers his base and uses his strength and change in level to break the grip of Wrestler B (see Figure 14-30).**

   This move releases Wrestler B's grip. At that point, Wrestler A can pull both his hands away and get in position for an escape or reversal.

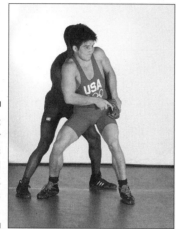

Figure 14-30:
Wrestler A drops his level to break Wrestler B's grip.

3. **Wrestler A rotates his hips and continues to drop his level while pushing Wrestler B's left arm down and pulling up on his right arm (see Figure 14-31).**

Figure 14-31:
Wrestler A rotates his hips and drops his level even more.

The most important part of the freeing-the-hands-and-wrists drill is getting use of the hands back. A defensive wrestler will stay on the defensive unless he can use a technique like this one to break free from his opponent's control.

Moving to Skill Drills for More Advanced Wrestlers

While all wrestlers need to spend practice time working on the basic drills that I discuss in the previous section, only the more advanced wrestlers need to work on the ones I list in this section. Make sure your wrestlers master the foundational drills before they move on to these drills. Although this list isn't exhaustive by any means, it can certainly help you start taking your advanced wrestlers to the next level. If you're working with wrestlers of different skill levels, you can have the less experienced wrestlers stick to the basic drills while the more experienced ones do the drills in this section.

Lift and return

The *lift and return* is a partner drill that helps wrestlers practice how to safely and correctly return the opponent to the mat from the standing position. After all, just because you can pick your opponent off the mat doesn't mean you can take him down recklessly. As a bonus, this drill also helps wrestlers master the art of falling safely and letting the mat absorb the contact.

A *slam* is the act of lifting and returning the opponent to the mat with unnecessary force. Slams are illegal and always result in the loss of a point. In other words, the referee doesn't give any warnings before he takes away a point. Four slams in a match lead to disqualification. See Chapter 4 if you're wondering what other infractions referees can call during a wrestling match.

Use these steps to incorporate the lift and return into your practice:

1. **Wrestler A stands to the side of Wrestler B with his hands in a firm grip around Wrestler B's waist (refer to Figure 14-25).**

   Note that Wrestler A is in control here.

2. **Wrestler A lifts Wrestler B off the mat, using the skills he practiced in the lifting drill.**

   See the section "Lifting drill" for details.

3. **As Wrestler A lifts Wrestler B off the mat, Wrestler A uses his hips to get Wrestler B off balance (see Figure 14-32).**

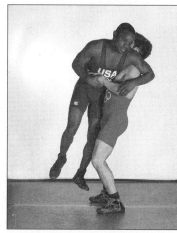

Figure 14-32:
Wrestler A uses his hip strength to force Wrestler B off balance.

4. **Wrestler A takes Wrestler B to the mat by leaning his right shoulder into Wrestler B's upper back and by rotating slightly down during the throw (see Figure 14-33).**

This drill also helps Wrestler B practice how to land after a throw.

Figure 14-33:
Wrestler A finishes by taking his partner to the mat in a controlled fashion.

Have each wrestler repeat this drill eight times and then switch positions.

Pummeling drill

The *pummeling drill* is a partner drill that shows wrestlers how to effectively gain inside leverage on their opponent. (Part of having good *leverage* is getting your hands inside your opponent's armpits; see Chapter 7 for details.) Specifically, this drill helps wrestlers understand the importance of gaining inside control from the neutral position and aggressively positioning their hands inside their opponent's armpits during actual competition.

Here's how to use the pummeling drill in practice:

1. **Wrestler A and Wrestler B face each other in the neutral position, each with one arm in the underhook position and one in the overhook position.**

    The *underhook position* is when a wrestler's arm is underneath the opponent's arm in a tied-up position. The *overhook position* is when a wrestler's arm is around the outside of the opponent's arm in a tied-up position (see Figure 14-34).

Figure 14-34: Starting position for the pummeling drill.

2. **On your command, the wrestlers attempt to get both their arms in the underhook position by digging their hands into their opponent's armpits (see Figure 14-35).**

    During this step, each wrestler's head will move back and forth as he switches from underhook to overhook position. Regardless of which position he's in, each wrestler needs to keep his feet moving throughout the drill.

    When a wrestler has both hands in the underhook position, he's in control.

Figure 14-35:
The wrestlers fight for inside hand position.

Have your wrestlers repeat this drill for 15 to 20 seconds at a time, take a 15-second break, and then repeat it six times.

Upper-shoulder roll

The *upper-shoulder roll* is a solitary drill that wrestlers can do to work on rolling on the top of their shoulders rather than on their backs (which they need to know how to do if they want to use the Granby roll reversal; see Chapter 10). Contacting the mat with the middle of the back (rather than the shoulders) places a wrestler in a risky position that can lead to a fall in a hurry because of body balance and weight distribution. So be sure your more advanced wrestlers practice this drill during practice so they can stay safe on the mat during rolls.

To use this drill, follow these steps:

1. **Each wrestler starts in the bottom of the referee's position.**

2. **Each wrestler rolls down to the mat and then up onto his upper shoulders (see Figure 14-36).**

3. **Each wrestler changes directions and rolls the other way.**

   You can either have your wrestlers change directions on their own or wait for individual commands from you.

Figure 14-36:
The wrestler rolls to the mat (a) and then onto his upper shoulders (b).

Have your wrestlers do this drill one way and then back the other way for 20 seconds. Have them rest for 15 seconds and then repeat the drill six more times.

Fireman's carry drill

The *fireman's carry drill* is a partner drill that breaks down the details of the attack called the *fireman's carry* (see Chapter 11). Here's what you need to know to use this drill in practice:

1. **Wrestler A starts with his right knee on the mat and his left leg out to the side; Wrestler A wraps his right arm between Wrestler B's legs and around his right thigh and uses his left arm to maintain a firm grip on Wrestler B's upper right arm (see Figure 14-37).**

   Wrestler B is practically on Wrestler A's back in this drill.

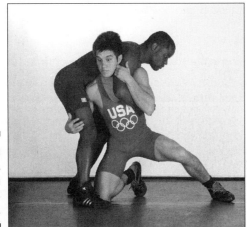

Figure 14-37:
Wrestler A starts with Wrestler B on his back.

2. Wrestler A turns away from Wrestler B's right leg and flips him onto the mat, as shown in Figure 14-38.

Wrestler A needs to keep tight control of Wrestler B's right arm in the triceps area when executing this step.

Figure 14-38:
Wrestler A flips his partner to the mat.

3. Wrestler A uses his momentum to continue the flip and end up on top of Wrestler B for the pin (see Figure 14-39).

Throughout the flip, Wrestler A must maintain control of Wrestler B's right thigh and right arm.

Figure 14-39:
Wrestler A finishes on top for the pin.

Have each wrestler do this drill six times in a row. Then have them switch roles. If time allows, have them switch one more time so they can do a total of 12 reps of this drill.

Lift to sweep

The *lift to sweep* is a partner drill that shows wrestlers how to use proper form to lift their opponents and bring them safely back to the mat. The following steps explain how to use this drill during practice:

1. **Wrestler A is in a position of control on the side and slightly behind Wrestler B; Wrestler A's hands are clasped around Wrestler B's belly (see Figure 14-40).**

Figure 14-40:
Starting position for the lift to sweep.

2. **Wrestler A forcefully jams his left knee into the thigh of Wrestler B, knocking him off balance and lifting him into the air (see Figure 14-41).**

3. **Wrestler A uses this momentum to bring Wrestler B safely down to the mat on his side.**

Have your wrestlers do this drill six times in a row. Then have them switch roles.

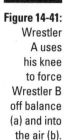

Figure 14-41: Wrestler A uses his knee to force Wrestler B off balance (a) and into the air (b).

Cross-face cradle drill

The *cross-face cradle drill* is a partner drill that helps wrestlers practice an important technique they can use when pinning their opponents. The drill simulates the cross-face cradle combination that I describe in Chapter 12.

Use the following steps to help you incorporate the cross-face cradle drill into your practice:

1. **Wrestler A starts in the offensive position with Wrestler B underneath him on the mat; Wrestler A's right arm is through the crotch of Wrestler B and his left arm is across the face of Wrestler B, grabbing his right upper arm (see Figure 14-42).**

Figure 14-42: Beginning position for the cross-face cradle drill.

2. **Wrestler A connects his hands together by forcing Wrestler B's right knee to his chin (see Figure 14-43).**

   Throughout this step, Wrestler A needs to keep his left forearm below Wrestler B's left ear and squeeze.

Figure 14-43:
Wrestler A forces Wrestler B's right knee to his chin.

3. **Wrestler A falls back to the mat, maintaining his grip and forcing Wrestler B's back to the mat (see Figure 14-44).**

Figure 14-44:
Wrestler A rolls Wrestler B's back to the mat.

Have your wrestlers do the cross-face cradle drill eight to ten times during practice.

Monkey on the back

The *monkey on the back* is a partner drill that helps wrestlers improve their pinning techniques. It shows the offensive wrestler how to stay close to the defensive wrestler before starting a pinning combination. This drill also helps develop balance for both partners and is helpful in developing skills important to riding the opponent (see Chapter 9). Here's what you need to know to use this drill in practice:

1. **Wrestler A is on top of Wrestler B with both of his hands under Wrestler B's armpits (in a double underhook) and both of his feet under Wrestler B's thighs; Wrestler B is on the bottom with his hands on the mat and arms straight (see Figure 14-45).**

   Unique to this drill is that the entire chest of Wrestler A is on the back of Wrestler B.

Figure 14-45: Starting position for the monkey on the back.

2. **On the coach's command, Wrestler B drops, rolls, and moves side to side in an attempt to get Wrestler A off his back; at the same time, Wrestler A works hard to stay in position on Wrestler B's back.**

   Ideally, Wrestler A will stay glued to Wrestler B's back the entire time.

Have each wrestler be the top wrestler for 12 to 15 seconds. Then have the wrestlers switch positions. Repeat the switch four times.

Cejudo single-leg drill

The *Cejudo single-leg drill* is one of my favorites. The single-leg takedown is a specialty of mine (see Chapter 11), and this drill helps me develop my skills for it. Here's what you need to know to do this drill in practice:

1. **Wrestler B is standing with his feet shoulder-width apart, while Wrestler A is on his right knee with his right hand around the inner thigh of Wrestler B (see Figure 14-46).**

   Wrestler A needs to keep his right ear close to the left hip of Wrestler B.

Figure 14-46: Starting position for the Cejudo single-leg drill.

2. **Wrestler A steps his left foot out in front of the right foot of Wrestler B while staying close to Wrestler B's body (see Figure 14-47).**

Figure 14-47: Wrestler A takes a big step with his left foot.

3. **Wrestler A drops his left knee behind the right leg of Wrestler B, quickly releasing his right hand and gripping the back of Wrestler B's right inner thigh with his left hand (see Figure 14-48).**

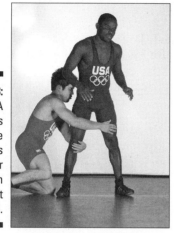

Figure 14-48: Wrestler A drops his left knee and grips Wrestler B's thigh with his left hand.

4. **Wrestler A finishes the drill by placing his left knee close to the right ankle of Wrestler B.**

Wrestler A ends up in the same position he started the drill in but on the other side of Wrestler B (see Figure 14-49).

Figure 14-49: The drill finishes as it started but on the other side.

Have your wrestlers do the Cejudo single-leg drill rapidly back and forth for 20 seconds, making sure to pause on each side. Then have them switch positions. Repeat the switch four or five times. I guarantee that this drill will help your kids improve as wrestlers, especially in the single-leg attack (see Chapter 11 for details on the single-leg and other takedowns).

Chapter 15

Knowing How to Be a Supportive Parent

*B*eing good parents who support their student athletes while letting the coaches, officials, and kids do their jobs to the best of their abilities isn't easy. Unfortunately, in many athletic settings today, parents zap the energy away from the kids just when they need it the most.

The challenge is that you, as a parent, always have a very personal tie to what's happening on the mat and can rarely provide an honest, unbiased perspective while watching from the stands. After all, you want to see your child succeed, right? Ironically, kids have the most fun when parents fulfill their roles as parents and supporters and truly allow their kids to have fun and participate.

This chapter shows you how to be a supportive wrestling parent, first by outlining the rules of the sport, then by explaining your role as a truly helpful parent, and finally by providing useful insight on how to take care of and prepare your wrestler for competitions and practice.

Getting the Lowdown on Wrestling

Before you can fully support your child on the wrestling mat, you need to have a firm understanding of the sport, including the rules and regulations involved. Wrestling is an individual sport for both boys and girls that not only offers many of the benefits of a team sport (like bonding, camaraderie, and respect) but also allows every individual to achieve unlimited success proportionate to his or her own level of training and investment. In the following sections, I cover some general wrestling information that you, as a well-informed and supportive parent, must be aware of before you attend your child's first match.

Eyeing the advantages of wrestling

Wrestling may be the purest form of competition out there because the competitors don't need any equipment (except headgear, shoes, and a uniform; see Chapter 3); it's just one wrestler on the mat against another.

Realize right away that wrestling isn't what you see on television marketed as *professional wrestling*. It doesn't involve theatrics, violence, punching, kicking, body slams, or competitors dressed in outrageous costumes. Instead, the sport of wrestling is based on discipline, hard work, and the skills displayed on the mat with a certified official, regulations to ensure participant safety, and a focus on sportsmanship and mutual respect.

In addition to developing discipline, strength, flexibility, and work ethic, wrestling provides life lessons that can build and strengthen the following character traits:

- ✔ Self-reliance
- ✔ Mental toughness
- ✔ Competitive spirit
- ✔ Responsibility
- ✔ Self-discipline
- ✔ Goal orientation
- ✔ Confidence

Although not all wrestlers are equal in terms of their mental toughness, physical strength, or endurance, wrestling matches competitors by age and weight, so you can rest assured that your child will be equally matched based on age and body weight.

Each wrestling age group (middle school, high school, and collegiate) has strict rules for weigh-ins and weight management to ensure that competitors face opponents of equal body weight. Check out Chapter 4 for a complete breakdown of the different weight categories.

Understanding the rules and types of wrestling

Having some basic knowledge about the rules of wrestling can help you figure out what's going on when your child is grappling his opponent on the mat. For example, if you can tell the difference between an escape and a reversal, you can figure out why a wrestler scores the points he scores. Then when your son or daughter finishes a meet, you can discuss the different moves you saw during the match and show your child that you know what you're talking about. (See Chapter 4 for the lowdown on wrestling rules and scoring.)

Furthermore, from a coach's or official's perspective, nothing is worse than a parent yelling when he doesn't know what he's yelling about. So instead of yelling just to yell, ask your child's coach what your child could do after a reversal to get into better position. By doing so, you're telling the coach that you not only care about your child's wrestling skills but also know what you're talking about.

In addition to knowing about the rules of the sport, you need a basic comprehension of the type of wrestling in which your child is participating. Although wrestling is an international sport seen in nearly every country dating back 5,000 years, not everyone practices wrestling the same way. Today the sport of wrestling basically has three variations. *Folkstyle wrestling* is the style used in U.S. schools, while the other two types — *freestyle* and *Greco-Roman* — are more widely practiced internationally. Each style is a little different in terms of moves and rules; Chapter 2 dives into the ins and outs of each one.

Embracing Your Duties as a Parent and Letting Other People Embrace Theirs

As a parent, of course you want to be involved and supportive of your child. But did you know that doing so can mean walking a fine line between being supportive and being so overbearing and controlling that both your child and his coach lose interest?

In a wrestling match, every individual in the gym has one of four potential roles: coach, athlete, spectator, or official. In the following sections, I explain these roles in greater depth so that you can understand how to play your role as a supportive parent and not play someone else's role. After all, when you understand your role, you help make your child's involvement in sports the enjoyable and fulfilling experience it was meant to be.

Athlete's role

Your child, the athlete, is competing in the wrestling match. He has practiced and prepared for weeks or months to get ready for this moment. Here are some of the athlete's responsibilities:

✔ Participate in the meet for fun and pure enjoyment.

✔ Be gracious in victory and defeat.

✔ Respect and abide by the rules of the sport.

✔ Accept the decisions made by the officials and coaches.

✔ Show respect and sportsmanship to teammates, officials, and coaches at all times.

✔ Be a disciplined, coachable wrestler with a high standard of character.

These roles are the athlete's, not yours. Perhaps you were once an athlete, but for today you're a parent, so you need to focus on fulfilling the rules I outline in the section "Parent's role" and leave the roles of the athlete to your child.

Coach's role

Becoming more educated about the role of your child's coach can increase your understanding of your role as the parent. The coach has the difficult task of treating each athlete equitably while providing appropriate instruction to allow each individual to reach his personal level of potential. In addition to this monumental task, your child's coach is also responsible for doing the following:

✔ Put the welfare of the athlete above winning.

✔ Love all the athletes and display a passion for the sport.

✔ Model high character, respect, professionalism, and fairness in all interactions.

✔ Follow all the rules of the sport and every local, regional, state, and national regulation to the letter of the law.

✔ Place the needs of the team above the needs of an individual.

✔ Be approachable and willing to talk to parents when parents have questions or concerns about their children.

✔ Teach effective strategy and techniques and lead effective practices that prepare athletes well and push them to improve daily.

Official's role

The official, also known as the *referee,* is responsible for enforcing the rules of play and maintaining general control of the match. A referee isn't perfect, and yes, he will make mistakes. Understand that the job of referee isn't an easy one and trust that the local official's association has a process in place to promote the best officials and to educate the inexperienced and average ones. Chapter 4 covers the roles of the referee in more detail.

Don't make comments either directed at the referee or in reference to one of his calls. Remember that your role is that of a parent, not the referee.

Parent's role

In general, your role as a supportive parent is to love your child and do whatever you can to keep him actively engaged in the sport or activity he enjoys. In case you need a list to make your role a little clearer, take a look at these suggested parental duties:

✔ **Make the athletic experience as educational and positive as possible for your child and other members of the team.** Use timely opportunities to teach life lessons through what happens on the mat, whether positive or negative, and remember that the sport environment is merely an extension of the classroom.

✔ **Allow the coaches to coach, the officials to officiate, and the athletes to wrestle.** Stay in your role as a parent. Enjoy watching your child, but let everyone else do his or her job to the best of his or her ability.

✔ **Positively cheer for all the wrestlers on the mat regardless of their team affiliation and learn to appreciate good wrestling from all participants.** This point means you cheer for your team and not against the other team.

✔ **Attend as many matches as possible and inform your child's coach at least one week in advance if your child has to miss a practice or match.** Effective communication is a two-way street. You expect your child's coach to communicate a change in practice or match schedules, so if your child needs to miss a practice, be respectful of your child's coach by informing him 48 hours in advance so that the coach can plan accordingly.

✔ **Accept the goals, roles, and achievements of your child.** Your child naturally wants to please you as the parent. Don't put undue expectations on your child and try to make him focus on your expectations rather than his. Your playing days are over; now it's your job to help your child find his passion one step at a time. Be satisfied that he is part of a team instead of sitting at home on the couch.

✔ **Be your child's greatest advocate and appropriately communicate with his coach.** Your child's coach deserves respect. When you're considering a parent-coach conference, keep in mind that timing is important (showing up in the middle of practice, for example, is obviously a bad time). If you want to talk to the coach, e-mail or phone him and ask for a time when you can have a private conversation.

As for what you should (and shouldn't) discuss with your child's coach, here are some appropriate topics for parent-coach discussions:

- **Your child's mental and physical treatment or condition:** Your duty is to be concerned about your child's health at all times, so these topics are fair game.

- **Suggestions for ways your child can improve:** Be direct with a coach and ask what your child needs to do to get better. Then accept what the coach has to say.

- **Concerns about your child's behavior or attitude:** Your coach will appreciate your interest in this area, and the conversation may also lead to subtle reasons why your child may not be playing.

Here are some inappropriate topics that shouldn't come up in your parent-coach discussions:

- **Your child's playing time:** A coach is hired to coach and make decisions on who plays and who doesn't. Period.

- **Team strategy, match strategy, or wrestling technique:** Your coach is also hired to be the expert on strategy, tactics, and planning. If you have concerns in this area, address them with his superior.

- **Other teammates or parents:** Never start the rumor mill. If you have a concern with another kid or parent, directly address the parent instead of taking the cowardly way out by talking behind someone's back.

Realizing What Your Child Needs from You

The number one thing your child needs and expects from you is that you model appropriate behavior at all times in all relationships surrounding the team and during practices and competitions. I'm confident that you, like most parents, want to be a great parent for your competitor, but you may not know how to meaningfully help him reach his goals and improve performance.

Although much of what your child needs from you depends on his age, some basic acts of support go a long way toward helping your child no matter how old he is. In the following sections, I share some tips for how you can give your child all the support he needs before the season and during and after competition.

The chances of your child earning a collegiate wrestling scholarship or competing professionally are very small. In fact, 70 percent of all young people are done with sports by age 12. Thus, doing everything you can to reinforce life lessons, enjoy the sport for the sport's sake, put your focus on your child and his teammates, and maintain a healthy perspective at all times is essential. If you act inappropriately by yelling at the officials or coaches, all you do is embarrass your child.

Before the season

At the beginning of the season, make sure you're extra supportive of your child's decision to wrestle. I encourage you to ask yourself the following questions and write down your responses:

- ✔ Why do I want my child to wrestle?
- ✔ What will make the season a successful one from my perspective?
- ✔ What are my goals for my child and my child's team?
- ✔ What do I hope my child will gain from the experience?
- ✔ What do I think my child's role will be on the team?

After you answer these questions for yourself, ask your child the following four questions and remember to listen to what he has to say:

- ✔ Why do you want to play?
- ✔ What does a successful season look like to you?
- ✔ What goals do you have for yourself and the team?
- ✔ What do you think your role will be on the team this season?

Compare your answers to your child's. If inconsistencies exist, change yours to match the desires of your child. Don't expect your child to adjust to your expectations. If you do, you've already set the stage for disappointment and a frustrating experience for both of you. After all, one of the only guarantees you can count on during every athletic season is conflict. When conflict arises, whether it involves playing time, relationships, or coaching, you and your child need to have a mutual perspective on your expectations surrounding the overall athletic experience.

As a parent, you need to be able to let your child go at the beginning of the season so that he can play his sport with his teammates and coach. Yes, you need to get to know the coach and the general team guidelines and you need to stay alert to your child's emotional and physical safety throughout the season, but you also need to be able to let your child be a part of his team and sport without your constant interference. In fact, the sooner you can release your child to his coach and the sport, the better. When you release your child to the sport, you give him ownership in his successes and failures, and you allow him to learn and grow from the team sport experience.

Here are some warning signs that you're too involved in your child's experience and that you haven't yet released him to his team or coach. (***Note:*** You won't notice some of these warning signs until after your child starts competing in matches, but you need to be aware of them before the first match so you can identify them as soon as they happen.)

- ✔ You try to continue to coach your child when he knows more about the sport than you do.
- ✔ You're overly nervous before your child's contests.
- ✔ You have a difficult time recovering after your child suffers defeat.
- ✔ You make mental notes or written reminders on paper of what you need to remind your child about after practice or a match.
- ✔ You become verbally critical of your child's coach or the officials during a contest.

During each match

As a parent, you need to remember five important points when you go to watch your child compete. Though the list is short, complying with all five points may be difficult at times. But as long as you remember why you're following these five points — to give your child what he needs to grow as an athlete and a person — you shouldn't have a problem following them every time you sit in the stands to watch your child wrestle.

- ✔ **Arrive on time.** Because of the random-draw nature of wrestling, your child won't know when his match starts until shortly before it begins. Show up early so you don't miss a thing.
- ✔ **Model appropriate behavior and don't embarrass your child.** Maintain self-control and don't use body language to communicate disgust or

frustration. Your child needs to see a confident look in your eyes and hear positive words of reinforcement. As a parent, you need to focus on reinforcing your child's strengths and avoid using negative reminders like, "Don't miss that single-leg move like you did last week."

✔ **Focus on the team and show support for the team's goals, not just those of your child.** Cheering on teammates and supporting other parents and athletes can help take your focus off your own child so that you don't get too stressed out during the match. By cheering on the whole team, you also show your child that you care about the progress of the team, not just your child. Don't leave the gym immediately after your child wrestles; stay and cheer on the rest of the team.

✔ **Don't coach from the stands.** Nothing is more confusing to a young wrestler than listening to two different voices that are providing different coaching points during a match. The only voice an athlete should hear during a match is the voice of his coach, so sit down and let the coach do his job.

✔ **Let the officials do their jobs.** Officials are there to enforce the rules of wrestling, make objective judgments, and maintain overall control of the match. No parent should interact with a game official during or after a match. If you do, you're teaching your child and his team members that challenging any authority that you don't agree with is permissible.

Wrestling presents a unique environment because it gives your child the spotlight for an entire match; he can't hide. If you, as the parent, model respectful behavior and act appropriately, your child will enjoy and cherish your attendance at every match. But if you behave poorly and embarrass your child for whatever reason, the coach or even your child may ask you to stay home next time. How shameful would that feel?

After each match

The most influential and impressionable time for a young athlete is right after the match on the ride home when the parent and child are in a one-on-one situation. As a parent, you get to choose how to communicate with your child after a competition win, loss, or draw.

If you treat this time haphazardly by criticizing your child, you can actually squelch your child's confidence and deflate his spirit. Instead of having a confrontational conversation with your child, give him unconditional support without any questions, accusations, or criticisms.

If he asks you for an opinion or a few pointers, provide them cautiously, but never provide unsolicited criticism, coaching, or correction if you want your child to stick with his activity. Despite what you may want to say about how your child messed up during the match, say this instead and you won't regret it: "I love watching you compete."

If your child has suffered an especially tough defeat, make sure you give him time and space before you try to talk to him. If your child does reach out to you, provide quiet understanding and receptive listening, always reminding your athlete of the big picture and giving him a dose of perspective if needed. Your child may resent uninvited post-match conversation, so be sure to keep your criticism and correction to yourself until you're asked to share them.

The one time I do suggest correcting your child immediately is if he exhibited a behavior during the match that's also unacceptable in your home (such as poor sportsmanship, profanity, negative body language, or disrespect of authority). I suggest that you suspend your child as long as it takes for him to get the point. Despite what you may think, you're doing him and his team a favor. Sit him out until he shows you he can control himself.

Making Sure Your Child Is Healthy, in Shape, and Mentally Prepared

As a parent, you're ultimately responsible for your child's health and well-being. You have to protect your child, no matter what. To prepare (and protect) your child for the physical sport of wrestling, make sure you take the following steps:

- **Be proactive about safety issues and make sure that both you and your child are aware of the risks involved in wrestling before he gets started.** The main issue here is general hygiene. Educate your wrestler to cover all open wounds, immediately report skin rashes, and wash well after practices and meets.

- **Make sure the coaches working with your child have updated training in basic emergency protocol, such as first aid, CPR, and concussion training.** Check to make sure coaches have a fully stocked first-aid kit on hand at every practice and match.

- **Caution your child about overuse injuries.** Make sure your child doesn't participate in just one sport all year round but also tries other activities. In adolescence, developing all muscles and joints equally is important. I recommend your child engage in two or even three sports or activities in addition to wrestling to help his body fully develop. Sticking to just one sport means year-round development of the same muscles, which can hurt overall muscle development. Encourage your child to be involved in as many activities as possible.

✔ **Verify and demand safe facilities and practice environments.** Make sure the places where your child practices and competes are clean and uncluttered and that they have easy access to phones and emergency services.

✔ **Protect your child from dangerous coaches.** Make sure your school or organization carries out background checks, including fingerprinting, on all coaches.

✔ **Know exactly who is influencing your child.** If volunteers or other parents have access to your child's practices, each person should have to follow the same screening procedures that the head coach had to follow.

In addition, you need to make sure you talk to your child about some other important topics related to his health, well-being, and success as a wrestler, such as proper nutrition, injuries, and conflict resolution. The following sections provide you a brief list of things that you as a parent can do to prepare and protect your child in wrestling. Naturally, you may need to add to or tweak parts of this list depending on the age of your wrestler, but regardless, it gives you a great place to start.

Providing proper nutrition

As a parent, you're responsible for making sure your child eats the right foods so that she has plenty of energy when she takes to the mat. I cover nutrition in detail in Chapter 5, but in this section, I share some good information that every supportive parent needs to know about proper nutrition and energy. If you need a little direction on providing basic nutrition for your wrestler, follow these pointers.

✔ **Make sure your wrestler drinks enough fluids.** Have your child drink according to a schedule; for example, have her drink 12 ounces of water every 30 to 45 minutes during the day. If water is too boring, you can use flavored sports drinks that are lightly sweetened and noncarbonated to help prevent dehydration and fatigue.

✔ **Monitor what your child eats before and after exercise.** Planning and preparing pre- and post-exercise meals are easy ways to support your wrestler. Have your child eat a full pre-match meal with lots of fluids, plenty of carbohydrates, some proteins, and just a little fat roughly three hours prior to a match. After your child finishes exercising (whether that exercise is a full practice, a meet, or just training), make sure she eats a high-protein snack or shake within 45 minutes and follows that with a full meal within the next two hours.

For your kid's pre- and post-exercise meals, try including whole wheat pasta, vegetables, chicken, fruit, cereal, lowfat yogurt, toast, and juice in any combination. When in doubt, feed your child carbohydrates because they're the main energy source for exercise and fuel for the brain. High-carbohydrate foods include grains, rice, pasta, milk, yogurt, cereals, fruits, and vegetables.

✔ **Combine different types of foods when possible during meals.** Carbohydrates aren't the only type of food your child needs to be healthy. She also needs proteins (poultry, meat, fish, cheese, and beans) to build muscle and fats (in moderation) for energy.

✔ **Keep your wrestler full.** In addition to preparing healthy meals, make sure your child gets plenty of energy from lowfat snacks, such as granola bars, energy bars, pretzels, trail mix, fruit, peanut butter and crackers, bagels, and low-sugar sports drinks, throughout the day.

✔ **Be careful with supplements and vitamins.** The ingredients of many over-the-counter supplements are not regulated by the FDA, so you have no guarantee that they're safe. A good diet is the best supplement possible.

Treating injuries

In most cases, a certified athletic trainer isn't present at matches until your child gets to the high school level, and even then, a professional may not be on site. Your child's coach will be trained to dial 911 in cases of emergency or head trauma, but you and the other adults present will have to deal with other nonemergency bumps and bruises on your own. As a responsible parent, you need to know how to treat injuries, including what to do immediately after the injury, how to help your child rehabilitate, and when to let your child return to play.

Until wrestlers reach the college level, their parents should be involved in all injury-related processes, including documentation, recovery, and the decision for your child to return to play.

Immediate care

For those youth injuries that aren't serious enough to warrant a 911 call (such as muscle pulls, strains, soreness, and minor surface bumps and bruises), you can manage them effectively by following the *RICE method:*

✔ **Rest:** Depending on the severity of the injury, your child may need to rest for anywhere from one day to one month. The keys to help determine the severity of an injury are discoloration, swelling, and range of motion. If the injured area becomes discolored, enlarged, or unable to operate through a full range of motion, call your doctor.

✔ **Ice:** Ice helps eliminate immediate pain by reducing swelling and blood flow to the affected area. Use ice massages, ice baths, ice wraps, or some other form of cold treatment immediately after the injury. Ice should always be applied tight to the affected area with some sort of wrap.

✔ **Compression:** Compression reduces swelling and brings comfort especially to muscle strains and skin-surface injuries. Use an elastic wrap, towel, compression sleeve, or other tight wrap to compress the affected area in between ice treatments.

✔ **Elevation:** Elevation helps to decrease inflammation. While you follow the advice in the preceding bullets, be sure to position the affected body part above the heart to reduce blood flow.

If you can hold your child's swelling to a minimum during the days immediately following the injury, recovery will be faster and your wrestler can get back out into action sooner.

Sore muscles go hand in hand with athletics, so sometimes you may have a hard time deciding whether your child is suffering from normal soreness or a more serious muscle strain. For the most part, general soreness happens immediately after intense exercise and lasts for a day or two. You can assume your child has a muscle strain if your athlete is in so much discomfort on the second or third day after activity that he can't run or move normally. Either way, the treatment is the same. In addition to following the RICE method, follow these tips:

✔ For the first 72 hours following the injury, apply ice continually as much as possible.

✔ After 72 hours, alternate between applying ice and heat treatments for 20 to 30 minutes three to four times daily.

In case of any type of head injury, always visit the doctor immediately. A head injury is a brain injury, so treat it as such. Go to Chapter 5 for complete information about concussions and return-to-play protocol for head injuries.

Rehabilitation

After the initial pain and swelling reduce to manageable levels (return to normal range of motion with limited or no pain), you can help your child start to participate in activities to regain strength, range of motion, and flexibility. Although your child may be slightly uncomfortable and have to call on an increased level of pain tolerance as he begins to increase motion, balance, and strength, blood flow to the affected area can help to reduce further inflammation.

Most of the time, your child's doctor will give him a rehabilitation plan based on what part of the body he injured. Or he may have your child visit a physical therapist. No matter what your child has to do for rehab, remember that it's about gradually using resistance to allow the affected body part to return to a pain-free full range of motion.

To give you an idea of what I mean by gradually increasing the resistance, consider the following rehab plan, which goes from barely any resistance at the beginning to your kid's weight in resistance at the end. For this rehab plan, I assume that your kid has injured his elbow or biceps (both common injuries in wrestlers). For each exercise in this list, have your child start by standing with his arm relaxed down by his hip and his elbow fully extended.

- ✔ Curl the fist on his affected arm up to his chin 50 times. Try to have your child do this exercise in a pool if one is available to use water as resistance.

- ✔ Curl his fist to his chin with a light resistance exercise band for five sets of ten repetitions (reps).

- ✔ Curl his fist to his chin with a light dumbbell for five sets of 25 reps.

- ✔ Curl his fist to his chin for three sets of 15 reps with a dumbbell that's heavy enough that he can barely do the last few reps of the third set.

- ✔ Do three sets of ten pull-ups until he no longer feels pain. Being able to pull his full body weight with no pain is a great indicator that your kid may be ready to get back to his usual routine.

For best results during rehabilitation, have your child apply heat to the affected area for 30 minutes followed by a light 10- to 15-minute massage of the area before any activity. Then have him apply ice to the area for 20 to 30 minutes after the activity.

If your child's injury becomes chronic (repeated) and the recovery process seems to stop and pain remains, follow up with a physician for further evaluation. You're the expert on your child, so take control of the rehabilitation process and make sure he gets professional help when he needs it.

Return to play

Depending on how severe the injury is and whether or not your child can still be functional on the mat, your child may have to miss practices and competitions. As a general rule, don't let your child return to play until he's pain-free and has returned to his pre-injury range of motion and strength.

If your kid goes to a doctor with an injury, he'll need a doctor's note in order to get back on the mat. As a general rule, doctors will be conservative before signing a release note. Your doctor wants to be 100 percent sure that your child is recovered; don't get upset if your doctor refuses to sign a release and makes your child wait for a follow-up appointment before he can get back in the action.

Dealing with conflict

Teaching your child how to appropriately deal with conflict as a member of a wrestling team can be a key way for you to help both your athlete and his coach. After all, conflict will arise at some point (or, more likely, multiple points) during the season among teammates, coaches, or other parents. (Not to mention having a good conflict-resolution process is a lifelong skill everyone should have.)

When your wrestler comes to you about a conflict he's having with a third party (teammate, other parent, or coach), refer to the following conflict-resolution plan to help your child move past the issue and refocus on the task at hand:

1. **Discuss the issue with your child to get a sense of what the main issue is and whether you need to address it further (or whether it was simply a misunderstanding).**

    If you need to address the issue further, continue to Step 2, but don't do so until you've had time to sort through your thoughts and feelings. Follow the 24-hour rule, meaning that you should take at least a day to decide if and how you want to act. Sometimes this reflection time lets you cool down and think sensibly as opposed to acting emotionally right away. After all, people are more likely to listen to others who have self-control.

2. **Seek out a trusted adult to provide a second opinion on the issue after you've communicated the important facts.**

    If you and the trusted adult agree that you need to take further action, move on to Step 3.

3. **Address the third party (the person with whom your child has a conflict) face to face about the issue.**

    Establish a nonthreatening environment by inviting conversation. Don't say, "Hey, I need to talk with you right now, I've got a problem with you." Instead try this, "Do you have a minute to chat with me about a concern? It's probably no big deal, but if you have a minute I'd appreciate it."

If a face-to-face meeting isn't possible, call the third party on the phone. Never use e-mail for this step.

If you feel like you haven't gotten anywhere after speaking to the main players in the conflict, move on to Step 4.

4. **Respectfully communicate your concerns up the chain of command in the organization.**

   If your issue is with another athlete, talk to the parent and then the coach. If your issue is with the coach, talk to the coach and then the program director or athletic director.

   You may want to write down your thoughts to make them clear, rational, and organized before you present them to people higher in the organization.

   If you're still not satisfied with the way the organization has handled the conflict, move on to Step 5.

5. **Reconsider the value of keeping your child on the team.**

   Making a big-picture change (and putting your child on a different team in a different league) may be better for everyone involved.

Staying active during the off-season

As a parent, you need to support your child by keeping him active and engaged in physical activity all year long — not just during wrestling season. In fact, I suggest that parents become actively involved in their kids' training processes. Whether you join your kids in lifting weights, running, or doing flexibility workouts, being active is a great lifelong habit for both children and adults to adopt.

When your kids see that you too are active, they'll be much more willing to put down the video game, get off the couch, and exercise. Refer to Chapter 5 for detailed information on training principles regarding strength, flexibility, and cardiovascular conditioning.

Part V
The Part of Tens

The 5th Wave   By Rich Tennant

"You could have told me Morty was a wrestling champ in college. When he asked if I'd like a chicken wing, I assumed it was something that came from a chicken."

In this part . . .

The chapters in this part serve to close out the book in traditional *For Dummies* fashion by providing you with a few key lists that you can use as you begin (or continue) your wrestling career.

I use this part to share some of my secrets. First, I let you in on my top ten tips for how to be a successful wrestler. Then I include advice on where to go for training and wrestling development on a national scale. I suggest the top camps in the country, where you can go to take your game up a few notches.

Chapter 16

Ten Tips for Wrestling Success

*T*echniques and fundamentals are as important in wrestling as they are in any sport, but much of your success on the mat depends on whether you make smart decisions. What often separates the average from the great in wrestling and other sports is how much focus and passion you have, how well you pay attention to detail, and how well you handle the mental battle.

Furthermore, much of your success depends on your mastery of the intangibles like practice tempo, attitude, self-confidence, and commitment. In this chapter, I give you my top ten tips for wrestling success, and none of them have to do with your size, strength, or natural talent.

Mastering Technique with Plenty of Practice

The only way to get better at wrestling is to work at it, but you can't just work hard during matches. To be successful, you have to work hard in practices, too. So don't tell your coach that you're a *gamer,* meaning that you only give your best effort during a match. A great wrestler is committed to showing up at practice and living by this credo: Practice doesn't make perfect; perfect practice makes perfect. Keep the following points in mind to help you maintain a committed, practice-centered perspective day in and day out:

> ✔ **Commitment is complete and starts in the heart.** Being 90 percent committed to something is impossible. Either you're in it all the way, or you're not. To find success on the mat, you must be committed to the smallest details of technique and practice all the time.

✔ **Commitment precedes achievement.** Sometimes athletes wait to see how things go before they commit 100 percent to a program. But that mentality won't result in success. You must bring your A game to practice every day before you can expect to enjoy success on match day.

✔ **The only true measure of commitment is action.** Great wrestlers practice what they preach. If you're working hard every day to improve, your coaches and team members will see the results in your actions during practice.

✔ **Saying the right words is easy; backing them up is much more difficult.** Saying you're going to practice hard every day is easy to say, but if you want to be successful, you have to practice each and every day with consistent maximum effort.

✔ **Perseverance is key.** Your first few matches may challenge your commitment to working hard, but you can't give up. You have to keep trying to improve. If you quit when the going gets tough, were you really committed in the first place?

Building Strength and Conditioning

Each and every wrestler is made differently. Your body matures at a different rate than other wrestlers'. Some wrestlers mature sooner than others, and some are simply more coordinated and flexible. Regardless of where you start, one way to improve your body's wrestling ability is by following a good strength and conditioning program.

The program you follow to build strength and condition your body for wrestling is probably going to be different from any program you've done in the past for other sports. As you set out to start your strength-building/conditioning routine, follow these tips to get the most out of it:

✔ Ask your coach for advice if you don't know where to start.

✔ Always work out with at least one other partner and an adult nearby to stay safe.

✔ No matter what program you choose, commit to it 100 percent, and you'll notice a difference in your muscle tone and fitness within three months.

Refer to Chapter 5 for more details on how to build a safe and effective strength/conditioning program.

Being Prepared and Focused

Some wrestlers are naturally focused and well prepared for reaching their full potential, but understand that you may need to work hard to improve your preparation and focus in order to become the best wrestler you can be. The following pointers can help you do so:

- **Spend your time wisely.** Organizing your time is critical to staying focused and prepared. Make sure you know what's next on your agenda both on and off the mat and be purposeful and resourceful as you plan your days. Arrive early for practice, get your homework done right when you get home from school, and schedule your meals in advance. Doing so can help you build and maintain a prepared and focused mindset.

- **Build on your strengths.** A prepared wrestler knows her strengths and those of her opponent. For example, you may have strong hands capable of breaking nearly every hold or a strong lower body enabling you to execute the toss series really well (see Chapter 10). Focus on building the techniques and moves you do well, but also spend plenty of time working to improve your areas of weakness.

- **Focus on what works for you.** Your best move may be someone else's worst move, and that's fine. Concentrate on what you need to do to be in the *zone*, or completely engaged all the time, and keep doing it.

- **Do the tough things first.** Be disciplined and understand how to do the difficult tasks or things you don't like to do first. Doing so allows you to continue working on things that are challenging for you and get them out of the way. In wrestling, you must work on some drills and techniques day in and day out that can help you score points and be effective even though they may not be the most fun.

- **Make good decisions.** Every day, you have to make decisions based on what's best for you as a student athlete. If you come to a difficult crossroads, just ask yourself this question: Will my choice help me become a better student and wrestler? If the answer is either unclear or on the negative side, be confident enough to say no and head down the other path. Although the alternate path may be less popular at the time, it'll almost certainly be better for you in the long run.

- **Write things down.** Make a clear to-do list every day and keep it with you at all times. You may be surprised by how little time you waste and how focused you can become when you start every day with a plan.

Developing Mental Toughness

Being mentally tough is easy when things are going well and you're motivated. But true mental toughness comes out when things aren't going your way or when you fail. Mentally tough wrestlers can bounce back after a tough situation and keep fighting. Here I give you a few tips to help you develop your mental toughness:

- ✔ **Face failure head-on and then move on.** When faced with failure, many people either internalize it and blame themselves or blame someone else. Fight the temptation to place the blame in either of these areas. Instead, take full responsibility for the failure (if it was indeed your fault) without taking it personally and letting it get you down.

- ✔ **Don't give up — ever.** Always keep hope alive in a match. Keep trying, keep fighting, and stay optimistic almost to a level beyond understanding. Believe in yourself all the time, even when a practice or match gets tough.

- ✔ **See failure as an isolated incident.** One mistake or bad choice doesn't mean that failure lasts forever. Don't base your overall attitude on a single incident and allow yourself to sink into a negative mindset. Remember that failure is never final and hang in there.

- ✔ **Always bounce back.** Being mentally tough means that you never stop fighting your opponent. Keep moving forward no matter what and realize that any failures you have today will provide the lessons that lead you to success down the road.

- ✔ **Forget about the past.** Acknowledge past experiences, but know that what happened yesterday or a second ago is ancient history in the mind of a mentally tough wrestler. Don't waste time in the past; instead, learn from your mistakes, strategize your next move or match, and break down your rearview mirrors.

Being Passionate

Passion isn't a *tip* for success; it's a *requirement* for success. *Passion* is loving what you do and enjoying every minute of it through the good times and the bad times. In some sports, you may be able to have success without passion simply because of your athletic or natural ability or because of your teammates. Wrestling isn't one of those sports because of all the work and sweat involved. Not to mention, you're out on the mat one on one against your opponent. Only passionate wrestlers stick with the sport long enough to have success.

Passion sometimes requires patience. If you're new to the sport, you can't expect to be passionate about it until you fully understand the game and have at least a small measure of success. So don't give up yet!

Here are a few signs you can look for to evaluate whether or not you're truly passionate about your wrestling endeavor:

✔ Passionate wrestlers are confident and make their teammates better.

✔ Passionate wrestlers attract the attention of others because they enjoy what they do, share their love of the sport, and expect the best from their teammates.

✔ Passionate wrestlers stay hopeful and cheer on their teammates until they're red in the face whether their team is ahead by 20 or behind by 20.

✔ Passionate wrestlers are outwardly positive, eager for instruction, and respectful of the rules of the game.

✔ Passionate wrestlers look forward to practice and remain unnaturally enthusiastic through even the toughest drills.

Showing a Positive Attitude

Having a positive attitude is a choice you have to make if you want to be a successful wrestler. In fact, a positive attitude is probably the single most important issue that impacts the potential success of a team. Attitudes determine actions, and the best wrestlers show a great attitude even though they may be having a bad day.

Attitudes are contagious, and no one, including your teammates, wants to be surrounded by someone who's always negative. If you're not a naturally positive person, follow these steps to improve your attitude:

✔ **Feed yourself the right "positive food."** Read positive books, listen to positive music, and try to look on the bright side as much as you can until doing so becomes natural. When you face a tough situation, take a positive perspective and realize that things will work out regardless of how difficult things may seem.

✔ **Surround yourself with positive people.** Choose to hang out with friends who lift you up by being positive. Don't spend your time with people who bring you down.

- ✓ **Achieve a goal every day.** Create your own opportunities for successes one small step at a time. Take a one-hour-at-a-time approach and recognize small advances when they happen. For example, if you're having a hard time with the high crotch move, it may be because you haven't yet perfected a penetration step. So instead of getting frustrated, break the move down into smaller parts and get good at the penetration step first. A small improvement in your step that gives you confidence may just be the thing that allows you to use the high crotch move successfully. Small successes lead to big successes over time when you maintain a positive attitude. (See Chapter 7 for details on the penetration step and Chapter 11 for details on the high crotch.)

- ✓ **Make your goals visible.** Write down your goals and your accomplishments and find ways to celebrate every positive change you make in your life.

Strategizing Tactics

In order to be successful, you need to stick with a consistent strategy for how you plan to approach defeating your opponent. Maybe your strategy always starts with wearing your opponent down with quickness in the first period before being really aggressive in the second, but you also need to be able to change it if it doesn't work. Chapter 6 covers developing a strategy in detail.

Staying Composed on the Mat

Successful wrestlers have an ability to maintain a level of self-control when everything around them is out of control. Having self-control means staying composed on the mat and being proactive rather than reactive.

Staying composed on the mat means you understand that you're responsible for yourself and that your behavior is a direct result of your decisions, not your conditions. Composed wrestlers take responsibility for and control of their behaviors instead of letting their emotions and circumstances drive their actions. They find success by keeping their values always present and understanding that no wrestler can defeat them mentally without their consent. So control your match and your opponent and maintain composure; don't react to the match or your opponent. And remember that if your opponent, the official, the fans, or your surroundings cause you to lose self-control or composure, you need to improve your mental toughness.

Sticking to a Training and Competition Plan

Chapter 5 provides details on helpful topics such as diet, exercise, rest, and living a healthy lifestyle. What is consistent is that these are all intangible things that have nothing to do with wrestling technique but that have everything to do with how you prepare your body for wrestling itself. Some wrestlers don't have to work as hard as others to win a match, but all wrestlers have to work hard to reach their full potential. I would be the first one to tell you that eating right, staying away from negative influences, training every day, and getting enough rest isn't easy, but because I have stuck to a training plan, I have been able to reach my full potential, which in my case is an Olympic Gold Medalist. The old saying goes, "If it were easy, everyone would do it," meaning that only people who are willing to hold themselves to a consistent high standard will reach their full potential and become true champions. Not everyone can be an Olympic medalist, but everyone can reach his full potential.

Staying focused on your training and competition plan requires more discipline than motivation. Wrestlers who have discipline do what they're supposed to do even when they aren't motivated to do it.

To help you maintain discipline, do the following:

✔ Surround yourself with good people who hold you accountable to doing the right thing and making good decisions in every aspect of life.

✔ Stay passionate about your sport through the ups and downs (see the earlier section "Being Passionate" for details).

✔ Be disciplined every day in everything you do from brushing your teeth to dressing for class.

✔ Say what you're going to do and then do what you said you would do . . . every time.

Creating a New Lifestyle

If you want to take your wrestling ability to the next level, you have to commit to a new lifestyle. In other words, you need to get rid of old habits and start making new ones that align with your goal to be the best wrestler you can be. Reading through this book, especially Parts I and II, can give you an idea of what you need to do to be a successful wrestler and what habits you need to adopt (or drop).

To create your new lifestyle, follow these steps:

1. **Make a list of the commitments or changes you need to make to be a successful wrestler.**

   The nine other sections in this chapter offer a great place to start. For other ideas, turn to Chapter 5 on staying healthy and in shape and Chapter 6 on maintaining the right mindset.

2. **Identify which of these commitments or changes are the most challenging for you to do.**

   Write down the habits you need to change in order to follow the commitments you listed in Step 1.

3. **Change your old habits and develop new ones that will allow you to create a new lifestyle and find success.**

   Use these tips to help you do so:

   • **Set short- and long-term goals.** Write out attainable goals so that you can see when behaviors (even small ones) change. Be patient and realize that breaking a bad habit can be tough.

   • **Define and eliminate the triggers.** Most habits have triggers that lead to them. In order to stop the habit, you may also need to eliminate whatever triggers the negative habit.

   • **Get support.** Pick someone to hold you accountable. Share your bad habits with a close friend, family member, or coach so he can help you change them. The strong bond of a family or team is often enough, but you can also ask others to help you stay aware of your challenges and goals.

   • **Accept plateaus and minor setbacks but don't give up.** Depending on the difficulty of your habit, you may have a temporary holding point where things don't seem to be changing. Accept temporary setbacks as they come, but get right back on track because positive enthusiasm is key to breaking bad habits.

Chapter 17

Ten (Plus One) Wrestling Camps You Should Consider Attending

In This Chapter

▶ Introducing some great wrestling coaches and the camps they run

▶ Knowing where to find helpful camp and clinic information

*I*f you want to become a better wrestler, you should consider attending local or even national camps or clinics. Camps and clinics are a great way to get excellent coaching in a short period of time. Some camps last an entire week, while others last just one day or weekend. With all the camps available in the United States and Canada, you can easily become overwhelmed as you try to choose the right one for you. To help you narrow down your choices, I've picked ten (plus one) of the best camps and clinics out there. I recommend them because their instructors are top notch and the skills they teach can help every wrestler improve his game. In this chapter, I provide a brief overview of each camp and its head wrestling coach. I also provide a website for each camp where you can go for more information.

Ken Chertow Wrestling Camps

After winning two state titles in high school and winning junior nationals in both freestyle and Greco-Roman wrestling, Ken Chertow went on to become a three-time NCAA All-American wrestler at Penn State University and a member of the 1988 U.S. Olympic wrestling team. He then coached at both Penn State University and Ohio State University, where he helped develop numerous conference and national champions.

Coach Chertow offers weekend camps all year long and hosts a number of summer camps for girls and boys of all age groups. The types of camps he offers include technique camps, kid's camps, gold medal camps, peak performance camps, and weekend warrior camps. Although central Pennsylvania is his home base, he holds camps in 24 different states. Regardless of where you live, what your ability level is, or whether you're looking for a winter, spring, summer, or fall camp, you can likely find one of his camps just around the corner. Go to kenchertow.com for more information.

J Robinson Intensive Wrestling Camps

Coach Robinson has spent most of his coaching career as the head coach of the University of Minnesota wrestling program. He has earned numerous coach of the year awards and has led his wrestlers to several national championships. Coach Robinson was a member of the 1972 U.S. Olympic team and has been an assistant coach with the Olympic squad four times in his career.

At his camps, University of Minnesota wrestlers and other all-star regional staff serve as his supporting staff. No matter where you attend Robinson's camps, you and your fellow campers learn technique, as well as Robinson's core values of dedication, discipline, and work ethic. The three types of Robinson camps you can attend are

- **Intensive camps:** These camps are 14 to 28 days in length and are held in Iowa, Pennsylvania, Minnesota, and Oregon.
- **Technique camps:** These camps are five days in length and are perfect for the 8- to 18-year-old wrestler because the focus is on small groups and carefully paced instruction.
- **Takedown camps:** These camps are run at the same time as the technique camps and cover wrestling strategies from the neutral position.

Check out jrobinsoncamps.com for more details.

Iowa Sports Camps with Tom Brands

The University of Iowa is home to one of the best wrestling programs in the country. Since 1974, Iowa has won 23 NCAA team titles, 15 of which were won by legendary coach Dan Gable. Tom Brands is the current head coach; he has won three national titles as a coach, three as a wrestler at Iowa, and a gold medal at the 1996 Olympics.

The University of Iowa and Tom Brands offer a wide variety of camps to fit all stages (ages 10 to 18) and ambitions. The camps provide a variety of learning atmospheres from individualized instruction to lectures by Coach Gable and other camp coaches. All the camps are offered as traditional summer camps in the months of June and July. Here's a list of the different summer camps offered at the University of Iowa:

- ✔ **Takedown and escapes camp:** This camp is a four-day camp for kids 10 to 18. It focuses on wrestling from the bottom position and the neutral position.

- ✔ **Intensive training camp:** This 11-day camp is for the ultimate competitor from age 10 through 18. Through drilling, conditioning, and live wrestling, kids learn the three most critical aspects of wrestling: technique, conditioning, and strength. This camp pushes wrestlers beyond their comfort zone and takes their performance to an entirely new level.

- ✔ **Father and son camp (no age limit):** This three-day weekend camp is an opportunity for fathers and sons to come together and learn wrestling at an introductory level. Along with the fundamentals of wrestling, this camp emphasizes the importance of building meaningful relationships.

- ✔ **Technique camp:** This five-day camp for ages 10 through 18 teaches detailed technique to maximize wrestling ability and scoring potential.

- ✔ **Team competition camp:** This four-day camp for ages 10 through 18 focuses on repetitive drilling of techniques, dual meets, team building, and personal individualized instruction. During competition, wrestlers are taught how to mentally and physically prepare to compete at the highest level.

- ✔ **Elite wrestling camp:** This five-day camp is designed for highly motivated wrestlers with high skill levels who have placed in their high school state tournament. Wrestlers must register with a partner of equal size and ability. There's one coach for every two campers.

For more information, go to www.iowasportscamps.com/sports/ wrestling.

World Class Wrestling Institute Camps with Carl Adams

Carl Adams directs the World Class Wrestling Institute, which has been going strong for more than 30 years. Coach Adams was a four-time national champion wrestler before he spent 22 seasons as the head wrestling coach at

Boston University. All of his camps are held at Boston University. Although most of them take place in the summer months of June and July, the institute also hosts the Carl Adams Wrestling Club in October and November and a one-day World Class Wresting Clinic in November. The staff of the World Class Wrestling Institute includes nationally known coaches, recent athletes, and current athletes, who guarantee that each camper will be well cared for and well supervised.

The institute offers 5-day camps, 7-day camps, 12-day camps, and 19-day camps, all of which serve a wide variety of campers by providing age- and experience-appropriate instruction. The camps include a unique evaluation process to make sure every camp meets the needs of each individual camper. Plus, each camp is offered in both a primary format and an intensive format to accommodate the most elite wrestlers, as well as beginning, intermediate, and advanced wrestlers. Here's a brief overview of the two camp formats:

- The *primary format* (a five-day camp) is for wrestlers who want to improve their wrestling skills but may not have the conditioning to do extra running, weight training, or an abundance of live wrestling. Wrestlers learn how to do takedowns, rides and pins, escapes and reversals, and leg-wrestling techniques.

- The *intensive format* (five days or more) is for more advanced wrestlers who already have a good wrestling background (two or three years) and want to excel. Wrestlers learn how to do advanced moves from the top and bottom positions, including combinations that will give them the edge they need to be successful.

To find out more about these camps, check out www.carladams.com.

Ohio State Wrestling Camps with Tom Ryan

As the head wrestling coach at Ohio State University, Tom Ryan earned the national coach of the year award in 2009 and has coached more than 16 NCAA All-American wrestlers, three of whom have earned individual national championships. As a wrestler at Iowa under Dan Gable, he was named an All-American wrestler two times.

Coach Ryan and his supporting staff offer traditional summer wrestling camps on the Ohio State campus in June and July. The specific camps offered serve specific age groups and ability levels. In addition to a father and son camp and a commuter camp for locals, Coach Ryan and Ohio State offer the following training camps:

- ✔ **Champion builder training camp:** This camp is for kids in grades 7 through 12 and includes hard drilling routines, technique-specific sessions, and live wrestling.

- ✔ **Team duals training camp:** This team-centered camp is for kids in grades 8 through 12. It focuses on strategies for different match and dual meet situations to mentally and physically prepare a team for competition.

- ✔ **Turn and pin mat wrestling camp:** This camp is for kids in grades 7 through 12. It focuses on mat wrestling techniques, such as rides and escapes.

- ✔ **Technique camp:** This camp is for kids in grades 7 through 12 of all experience levels. It focuses on teaching wrestling skills in the neutral, top, and bottom positions.

- ✔ **Takedown camp:** This camp is for kids in grades 7 through 12. It focuses on takedown techniques from the neutral position.

- ✔ **Heavyweight camp:** This camp is for kids in grades 7 through 12 who weigh more than 180 pounds.

For more details, check out www.ohiostatebuckeyes.com/camps/mwrestl-camp2.html.

Azevedo-Hitchcock Wrestling Camps

Originally founded by legendary California coach Vaughn Hitchcock, the Azevedo-Hitchcock Wrestling Camps are held in the summer months in the Olympic Village of the 1960 winter Olympic Games. Their main purpose is to motivate the novice wrestler and challenge the more advanced wrestler. John Azevedo, the head wrestling coach at Cal Poly San Luis Obispo in California, now runs these camps.

The Azevedo-Hitchcock camps teach the basic fundamentals of wrestling with an emphasis on folkstyle; each wrestler receives at least six hours of championship-level instruction daily. The camps also include lecture sessions on weight training, goal setting, weight management, and mental preparation. For more information, go to www.wrestlingcamps.org.

University of Michigan Wrestling Camps with Joe McFarland

Joe McFarland, a four-time NCAA All-American (166-24-4) at Michigan and Michigan head coach since 1999, leads the Michigan Wrestling Camps. He was a silver medalist at the 1986 World Championships and a gold-medal winner in the 1988 World Cup Championship.

All the Michigan Wrestling Camps take place on campus at the University of Michigan in Ann Arbor, Michigan, with the exception of one camp that takes place at a high school near Cleveland, Ohio, to serve the northeast Ohio commuter region. These camps have been around for more than 30 years and are offered in a traditional summer camp format during June and July.

Specific camps serve specific age groups and ability levels. In addition to commuter camps for kids in the local area, the different Michigan Wrestling Camps include the following:

- **Competition camp:** This five-day camp is for kids in grades 9 through 12. It offers each camper four dual meets and ten hours of basic instruction daily.

- **Technique camp:** This five-day camp is for kids in grades 7 through 12. At registration, each wrestler chooses one of six different concentration areas to focus on throughout the camp. The options are leg wrestling, leg takedowns, general takedowns, riding and pinning combinations, escapes and reversals, and countermoves.

- **Heavyweight camp:** This five-day camp is for kids in grades 7 through 12. It focuses on wrestlers in the higher weight categories by addressing their specific needs and techniques.

- **Advanced training camp:** This five-day camp is for kids in grades 9 through 12. It combines technical instruction, drill sessions, combative wrestling, and strength training. This camp is designed for serious, experienced wrestlers; it helps them prepare physically and mentally to win the big match.

For the lowdown on these camps, go to www.michiganwrestlingcamps. org/index.html.

John Fritz's Keystone Wrestling Camps

The Keystone Wrestling Camps, which take place at York College in southeastern Pennsylvania (and a few days in Colorado each July), get their name from Pennsylvania's nickname, the Keystone State. They're directed by four-time NCAA national champion and Olympic Champion Coach Cael Sanderson, who also happens to be the head coach at Penn State. The camp gets its name from ex-Penn State wrestling coach John Fritz, who still owns the camp. Kerry McCoy, head coach at the University of Maryland, and Sanshiro Abe, head coach at Pittsburgh Central Catholic, assist Coach Sanderson with running the camps. Coach McCoy won two NCAA national championships and is a two-time Olympian. Coach Sanshiro is a four-time NCAA All-American and former Olympian.

Held as traditional summer camps in June and July, the Keystone Wrestling Camps boast a world champion–caliber staff, and their main goal is to allow each wrestler to benefit from personal instruction, various drills, live wrestling, conditioning, strength training, and mental toughness training. Each camp offered stresses the concepts of technique, competition, and training.

Specific camps serve specific age groups and ability levels. Here are the main camps offered:

- **Technique and competition camp:** This four-day camp is for kids in grades 6 through 12. It focuses on competition and technique development through a unique drill system.

- **Junior/novice camp:** This four-day camp is for young beginning wrestlers between the ages of 8 and 12. It stresses a fun positive experience to encourage kids to continue wrestling.

- **Advanced junior camp:** This four-day camp is for experienced beginners between the ages of 8 and 12. Its goal is to prepare them for junior high and high school success by giving them a solid foundation of fundamental skills and advanced techniques.

- **Middle school team camp:** This camp is for kids in grades 6 through 11. It emphasizes competition and training as a team.

For additional details about these camps, check out `keystone wrestlingcamp.com`.

The Granby School of Wrestling Camps

Coach Billy Martin is possibly the greatest high school coach in Virginia wrestling history. His team, Granby High School, won 21 state wrestling titles in his 22 years as coach, and he invented the timeless *Granby* roll series (see Chapter 10 for details on how to do these moves). Today, Billy's son Steve Martin (the head wrestling coach at Old Dominion University in Virginia) is the Granby School of Wrestling Camp director. The camp staff includes Coach Steve Martin, members of his college coaching staff, and other well-qualified instructors.

The Granby School offers day camps, technique camps, overnight camps, and team camps each year in June and July. The overnight camps are held at Hampden-Sydney College in Virginia and in various other locations, including Georgia and Missouri. The camp also travels to other sites that want to host Granby clinics and is currently scheduled in Alabama, California, Connecticut, Idaho, South Carolina, Ohio, and Texas. Attendees at these camps learn the basics of the Granby series, including takedown techniques, wrestling techniques from the bottom position, and techniques from the top position. In addition, the Granby School offers the Fargo Training Camp in Fargo, North Dakota, to help wrestlers prepare for the Cadet and Junior Freestyle/Greco-Roman National Championships in that city.

For more details about these camps, go to granbyschool.com.

Oklahoma State Wrestling Camps with John Smith

As the head wrestling coach at Oklahoma State, John Smith has won five national championships, two national NCAA coach of the year awards, and more than 300 matches. As a wrestler, Coach Smith won six consecutive world championships from 1987 to 1992, including two Olympic gold medals, and compiled a 159-12-2 record in high school and college.

The Oklahoma State Wrestling Camps are held at Oklahoma State University in Stillwater, Oklahoma, as traditional resident summer camps in June and July. Wrestlers of various ages and skill levels can attend the camps. The coaches divide the wrestlers into small groups so they can get personal attention with an extra focus on high-percentage takedown techniques, leg attack set-ups, and finishes.

In general, the camps focus on teaching rides, breakdowns, and turns from the top position and the stand-up technique from the bottom position. However, each camp also serves a specific age group and ability level. Here's a brief description of the three main Oklahoma State camps:

- **Technique camp:** This five-day camp focuses on technique development, as well as the easiest ways to get a takedown, to score off the bottom position, and to ride from the top position.

- **Team camp:** This five-day camp focuses on team competition and often attracts as many as 40 teams from more than 20 different states.

- **Intensified training camp:** This 11-day camp is for the serious wrestler; it features two weeks of four workouts per day, including running and weight training.

For more information on any of these camps, go to www.osuwrestling camps.com.

Wabash College Wrestling Camps with Brian Anderson

The wrestling camps at Wabash College, one of the winningest programs in NCAA Division III wrestling under head coach Brian Anderson, are designed for wrestlers of all skill levels who want to improve to a championship level. They provide an opportunity to learn and perfect wrestling skills that are conducive to winning matches. The camps feature sound technique, instruction, and dual meet competition.

Wabash wrestling camps feature not only their very own coaching staff but also the nation's top wrestling names, including Dan Gable, John Smith, Tom and Terry Brands, Rulon Gardner, Brandon Slay, Kevin Jackson, Ben Askren, Bruce Daumgardner, Kenny Monday, Joe Williams, Sammie Henson, and even me.

Each summer Wabash offers the following camps:

- **Intensive/competition camp:** This camp provides intense one-on-one training, technique from world-class clinicians, and participation in live duals. This camp is for the serious wrestler who's looking to take his game up a notch during the summer.

- **Team/technique camp:** This camp provides individuals and teams the opportunity to learn technique from some of the best and most accomplished wrestlers in the country and compete in as many as 12 very competitive dual matches throughout the week.

✔ **Youth commuter camp:** This camp provides the youth wrestler the opportunity to learn not only the fundamental skills of wrestling but also the same cutting-edge technique that the older campers work on. The youth campers have the chance to work with world-class clinicians and get their pictures and autographs.

For more details, go to www.wrestlingindiana.com.

Index

Apple & Mac

iPad 2 For Dummies,
3rd Edition
978-1-118-17679-5

iPhone 4S For Dummies,
5th Edition
978-1-118-03671-6

iPod touch For Dummies,
3rd Edition
978-1-118-12960-9

Mac OS X Lion
For Dummies
978-1-118-02205-4

Blogging & Social Media

CityVille For Dummies
978-1-118-08337-6

Facebook For Dummies,
4th Edition
978-1-118-09562-1

Mom Blogging
For Dummies
978-1-118-03843-7

Twitter For Dummies,
2nd Edition
978-0-470-76879-2

WordPress For Dummies,
4th Edition
978-1-118-07342-1

Business

Cash Flow For Dummies
978-1-118-01850-7

Investing For Dummies,
6th Edition
978-0-470-90545-6

Job Searching with Social
Media For Dummies
978-0-470-93072-4

QuickBooks 2012
For Dummies
978-1-118-09120-3

Resumes For Dummies,
6th Edition
978-0-470-87361-8

Starting an Etsy Business
For Dummies
978-0-470-93067-0

Cooking & Entertaining

Cooking Basics
For Dummies, 4th Edition
978-0-470-91388-8

Wine For Dummies,
4th Edition
978-0-470-04579-4

Diet & Nutrition

Kettlebells For Dummies
978-0-470-59929-7

Nutrition For Dummies,
5th Edition
978-0-470-93231-5

Restaurant Calorie Counter
For Dummies,
2nd Edition
978-0-470-64405-8

Digital Photography

Digital SLR Cameras &
Photography For Dummies,
4th Edition
978-1-118-14489-3

Digital SLR Settings
& Shortcuts
For Dummies
978-0-470-91763-3

Photoshop Elements 10
For Dummies
978-1-118-10742-3

Gardening

Gardening Basics
For Dummies
978-0-470-03749-2

Vegetable Gardening
For Dummies,
2nd Edition
978-0-470-49870-5

Green/Sustainable

Raising Chickens
For Dummies
978-0-470-46544-8

Green Cleaning
For Dummies
978-0-470-39106-8

Health

Diabetes For Dummies,
3rd Edition
978-0-470-27086-8

Food Allergies
For Dummies
978-0-470-09584-3

Living Gluten-Free
For Dummies,
2nd Edition
978-0-470-58589-4

Hobbies

Beekeeping
For Dummies,
2nd Edition
978-0-470-43065-1

Chess For Dummies,
3rd Edition
978-1-118-01695-4

Drawing For Dummies,
2nd Edition
978-0-470-61842-4

eBay For Dummies,
7th Edition
978-1-118-09806-6

Knitting For Dummies,
2nd Edition
978-0-470-28747-7

Language &
Foreign Language

English Grammar
For Dummies,
2nd Edition
978-0-470-54664-2

French For Dummies,
2nd Edition
978-1-118-00464-7

German For Dummies,
2nd Edition
978-0-470-90101-4

Spanish Essentials
For Dummies
978-0-470-63751-7

Spanish For Dummies,
2nd Edition
978-0-470-87855-2

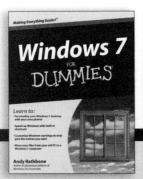

Math & Science

Algebra I For Dummies, 2nd Edition
978-0-470-55964-2

Biology For Dummies, 2nd Edition
978-0-470-59875-7

Chemistry For Dummies, 2nd Edition
978-1-1180-0730-3

Geometry For Dummies, 2nd Edition
978-0-470-08946-0

Pre-Algebra Essentials For Dummies
978-0-470-61838-7

Microsoft Office

Excel 2010 For Dummies
978-0-470-48953-6

Office 2010 All-in-One For Dummies
978-0-470-49748-7

Office 2011 for Mac For Dummies
978-0-470-87869-9

Word 2010 For Dummies
978-0-470-48772-3

Music

Guitar For Dummies, 2nd Edition
978-0-7645-9904-0

Clarinet For Dummies
978-0-470-58477-4

iPod & iTunes For Dummies, 9th Edition
978-1-118-13060-5

Pets

Cats For Dummies, 2nd Edition
978-0-7645-5275-5

Dogs All-in One For Dummies
978-0470-52978-2

Saltwater Aquariums For Dummies
978-0-470-06805-2

Religion & Inspiration

The Bible For Dummies
978-0-7645-5296-0

Catholicism For Dummies, 2nd Edition
978-1-118-07778-8

Spirituality For Dummies, 2nd Edition
978-0-470-19142-2

Self-Help & Relationships

Happiness For Dummies
978-0-470-28171-0

Overcoming Anxiety For Dummies, 2nd Edition
978-0-470-57441-6

Seniors

Crosswords For Seniors For Dummies
978-0-470-49157-7

iPad 2 For Seniors For Dummies, 3rd Edition
978-1-118-17678-8

Laptops & Tablets For Seniors For Dummies, 2nd Edition
978-1-118-09596-6

Smartphones & Tablets

BlackBerry For Dummies, 5th Edition
978-1-118-10035-6

Droid X2 For Dummies
978-1-118-14864-8

HTC ThunderBolt For Dummies
978-1-118-07601-9

MOTOROLA XOOM For Dummies
978-1-118-08835-7

Sports

Basketball For Dummies, 3rd Edition
978-1-118-07374-2

Football For Dummies, 2nd Edition
978-1-118-01261-1

Golf For Dummies, 4th Edition
978-0-470-88279-5

Test Prep

ACT For Dummies, 5th Edition
978-1-118-01259-8

ASVAB For Dummies, 3rd Edition
978-0-470-63760-9

The GRE Test For Dummies, 7th Edition
978-0-470-00919-2

Police Officer Exam For Dummies
978-0-470-88724-0

Series 7 Exam For Dummies
978-0-470-09932-2

Web Development

HTML, CSS, & XHTML For Dummies, 7th Edition
978-0-470-91659-9

Drupal For Dummies, 2nd Edition
978-1-118-08348-2

Windows 7

Windows 7 For Dummies
978-0-470-49743-2

Windows 7 For Dummies, Book + DVD Bundle
978-0-470-52398-8

Windows 7 All-in-One For Dummies
978-0-470-48763-1